GANGSTER CAPITALISM

GANGSTER CAPITALISM

THE UNITED STATES AND THE
GLOBAL RISE OF ORGANIZED CRIME

MICHAEL WOODIWISS

CARROLL & GRAF PUBLISHERS
New York

Carroll & Graf Publishers
An imprint of Avalon Publishing Group, Inc.
245 W. 17th Street
New York
NY 10011–5300
www.carrollandgraf.com

AVALON

First published in the UK by Constable,
an imprint of Constable & Robinson Ltd, 2005

First Carroll & Graf edition 2005

ISBN-13: 978-0-78671-671-5
ISBN-10: 0-7867-1671-1

Printed and bound in the EU

Contents

Acknowledgements   ix

Foreword   1

PART 1 The United States and Gangster Capitalism   17
   Introduction   19

1 Cradle to Crematorium, Womb to Cadaver Lab   23
2 Barons, Crusaders and the Land of Criminal Opportunity
    1880–1920   40
3 The Racket-ridden Twenties and the Origins of the
    Great Depression   47
4 The New Deal and Organized Crime   57
5 States of Denial and Mafia Distractions   68
6 Capital Corruption   90
7 Zero Tolerance and the Rise of the Gangs   107

**PART 2 The United States and Setting the Global Agenda on
Organized Crime**   115

8   The Broken Promise of Roosevelt's Global Freedoms   117
9   Nixon and the New World Economic Disorder   129
10 The War on Drugs and the Rise of International
     Drug Traffic   136
11 Dumbing the International Response to Drugs and
     Organized Crime   149

PART 3 A World of Criminal Opportunity, 1965–   161
   Introduction   163

12 Suharto and the Looting of Indonesia   169
13 Marcos Takes the Philippines   172
14 Mobutu and Debt in Africa   175
15 Bankers and International Crime   179
16 Evasion, Flight and Fraud in McWorld   185

17 Toxic Capitalism 190
18 Smuggling, Violence and Corruption in the International
   Arms Bazaar 198
19 The Traffic in Exploitable People 202
20 SAPs, Slums and the New Slavery 207

Epilogue – The Alternatives 211

Notes 219

Select Bibliography 249

Index 251

To Laurie and Sophia

Acknowledgements

This work had its inception during a seminar series on transnational organized crime run by Adam Edwards and Peter Gill and sponsored by the Economic and Social Research Council (ESRC). Adam and Peter put together several of the best academic researchers from Europe and North America in the area of organized crime with a roughly equal number of practitioners representing various British and international policing and revenue agencies. Papers from the series were later published in a collection edited by Adam and Peter entitled *Transnational Organized Crime: Perspectives on Global Security*, published by Routledge in 2003.

Gangster Capitalism follows on from my earlier books – *Crime, Crusades and Corruption* and *Organized Crime and American Power* – and thus it owes a debt to all those who contributed inspiration and insight to these books, in particular to Frank Pearce and my brother Anthony Woodiwiss.

With the help of a grant from the Nuffield Foundation and support from my own institution, the University of the West of England, I was able to go on two research trips to the United States, visiting archives and libraries and interviewing people in New York, Washington, DC, Houston and Princeton. In New York I was able to interview people associated with the United Nations Centre on Transnational Corporations and gain a deeper understanding of the work of this organization and the reasons for its abolition in the early 1990s and to visit the library of the Drug Policy Alliance, which had particularly useful holdings. In Washington I found a great deal of useful and often exciting material on the construction of organized crime and drug control strategy by the Nixon administration in the Nixon Presidential Materials section of the National Archives. I also found the websites of the *New York Times* and the *Los Angeles Times* particularly useful while tracking contemporary developments.

At Constable and Robinson thanks must go to Helen Kemp for her care and attention and to my editor Dan Hind who brought great commitment and considerable insight to this project from the beginning to the end.

Any mistakes and misinterpretations in *Gangster Capitalism* are, of course, my own responsibility.

I would also like to thank Niki Langham, Margaret Farrow, Anna and Dave Finlay, Daphne, Roger and Paul Derrett, Dave and Assimina Smith, Larry Bull, Lizzie Chambers, Solomon Hughes, Simon and Shona Kitson, Mark and Debs Jamieson, and, as always, my mother Audrey Lawrence, my brothers and sisters, my wife Alison and my children, Laurie and Sophia.

Foreword

Organized criminal activity harms Americans from the womb to beyond the tomb. Fertility-clinic fraud, involving corrupt doctors and administrators, cheats couples desperate to have children out of much of their savings. Internet fraud allows major computer firms to cheat school systems and therefore school children out of millions of dollars. Corporate violation of health and safety laws, consumer- and environmental-protection laws kills thousands prematurely each year. Corporate fraud in the mutual fund business and the insurance business, in particular, as well as the tidal wave of corporate fraud, in general, jeopardizes the funds that many Americans have been putting away to educate their children or sustain a reasonable standard of life in their retirement. Rip-offs and abuse in private nursing homes prove that there is often no respite for many Americans facing death. Funeral fraud shows that wholesale larceny and abuse goes on after death. Finally, recent gruesome revelations concerning a booming illegal trade in the remains of humans shows that organized criminal activity affects Americans even beyond the tomb. Yet the nation with these organized-crime problems and many more besides sets the agenda on international organized-crime control. The United States tells other nations and international organizations, notably the United Nations, how to control organized crime at the same time as so much of its business activity can be defined as simple racketeering.

Pushed by the United States, lamely supported by the European Union and Japan, the United Nations has responded to a rapidly deteriorating global crime situation in an uninformed way that is already proving to be inadequate and in some respects self-defeating. On 29 September 2003, the United Nations Convention against Transnational Organized Crime came into force. By ratifying the convention, states accept an understanding of organized crime promoted by the United States and thereby

commit themselves to adopting a series of organized-crime-control measures pioneered in the United States. These include the criminalization of
participation in an organized criminal group, money laundering, corruption and obstruction of justice, and tactics such as those involving the use
of asset forfeiture and covert tactics including the use of undercover
policing operations and witness protection programmes. According to a
top UN official, 'With the entry into force of the Convention, the
international community will have demonstrated the political will to
counter the world-wide challenge of organized crime by adopting a
corresponding global response.'[1] The key assumption behind the Convention is that US organized-crime-control methods have a proven record of
success and therefore need to be adopted by every other nation in the
world for organized crime to be effectively combated internationally. The
US has not, however, come close to combating organized crime successfully within its own borders and has in fact pursued policies that have
exacerbated the problem both at home and abroad. *Gangster Capitalism*
examines the historic reality of organized crime in the United States as
well as the American impact on organized crime internationally.

The American understanding of organized crime, now accepted uncrit-
ically by governments and many mainstream analysts, essentially equates
the problem with the existence of super-gangster organizations. The usual
suspects amongst these are the American and Sicilian Mafias, the Russian
Mafia, the Chinese Triads and the Colombian drug 'cartels', and they are
often described as 'multinational corporations of crime'. These groups,
according to experts associated with the United Nations, effectively
constitute organized crime since it 'consists of tightly knit, highly organized networks of operatives that pursue common goals and objectives,
within a hierarchical power structure that spans across countries and
regions to cover the entire world'.[2] As *Gangster Capitalism* shows, this
is a deeply inadequate analysis that helps conceal the structural reasons
behind the reality of organized crime in the world today.

There are, of course, criminal networks prepared to use murder, intimidation, deception or bribery to achieve their ends, and some of these have
been able to extend their activities far beyond their own neighbourhoods.
But these groups have proliferated in recent decades partly as a result of
misguided government policies at both national and international levels.
These policies make anti-organized-crime measures by national governments, on their own or in co-operation with others, at best irrelevant, at
worst counter-productive. Gangster groups have certainly grown in number in the United States and other countries in recent years but even the
largest networks, such as the Italian Mafia, have not become corporations
of crime. To compare them to corporations, as governments and most

commentators still do, is far short of the mark. Unlike corporations, criminal networks do not have access to a formal apparatus guaranteeing the security of property rights and employment contracts and this ensures that their growth is always going to be limited and prone to disruption. Treachery, chaos and a lack of bureaucracy characterize the lives of most gangsters, not risk-free profit-making.[3]

John Gotti of New York's Gambino Crime Family, the most famous American mafiosi of recent times, for example, was not the 'most powerful criminal in America' as his first biographers suggested, nor the main beneficiary of the Mafia's $60 billion business, as *Time* magazine and other publications made out.[4] He was more accurately described as 'a cheap thug and not a particularly bright one' by Ronald Goldstock, head of New York Organized Crime Task Force. Hugely overstated assertions about the American Mafia made by most publications and television documentaries on the subject of organized crime should be untenable now we know how gangsters speak and operate, thanks to wire-tap and eavesdropping taped evidence. Recordings of Gotti make the point. Speaking about one of his crew who was actually loyal to him, he accused him of being an informer, saying, 'Pete, now he was a "rat" motherfucker. This fucking "rat" brother was, the brother-in-law was a "rat" motherfucker. A backdoor motherfucker . . . This fucking bastard.' Speaking to his closest crew member, Sammy 'the Bull' Gravano, who would later testify against him, he said, 'These rats. Everybody in the city's got rats next to them, Sammy, but not us.' As for Gotti's alleged billion-dollar earnings, the $60 billion figure is speculative nonsense like most estimates of criminal income. Journalists are rarely subject to the demands of fact-checking where the subject of organized crime is con-cerned. Any amount of lurid nonsense can be recycled without any professional danger as long as they operate in the context established by governments. He and his crew did make a lot of money exploiting New York's corrupt and mismanaged municipal government but, as Gotti himself admitted, much of it went to pay off his defence lawyers and thus returned to the upperworld. 'Gambino Crime Family,' he spluttered at one point when talking about their fees, 'this is the Shargel, Cutler and whattaya call it Crime Family? You wanna go steal? You and your fuckin' mother.' 'They wind up with the money,' added Gravano.[5]

Rather than putting bosses like these at the centre of organized-crime analysis, *Gangster Capitalism* focuses on the responsibility of the upperworld of government officials, professional and business interests for the problem of organized crime in the world today. Gangsters have only ever been continuously replaceable players in a much bigger game. In the US, many more people are damaged by the organized criminal activity of professionals such as doctors and corporate officials than they are by gangsters. Professional and corporate fraud has affected the health and financial security of millions of Americans, while gangster rip-offs affect few. To take another comparison, the reckless and deceptive practices of executives in the tobacco and asbestos industries alone have caused the premature deaths of millions of innocent citizens, while the kill-rate of gangsters is relatively small.

The common assumption that organized crime threatens respectable capitalist society does not square with America's historical record. Organized crime accompanied and often actually aided the development of respectable capitalism. The very founding fathers of American industrial and commercial dynasties used gangster methods to control the markets in which they operated. Although the phrase 'organized crime' was not commonly used until the 1920s, it fitted their business methods perfectly since it implies a willingness to collude with others and commit crimes to gain money and power. The founders of America's industrial and commercial dynasties showed little hesitation in bribing, stealing, cheating and using violence to further their business interests. Some employed private armies or at least groups of thugs to wreck strikes and unions. 'I can hire half the working class to kill the other half,' the railroad operative Jay Gould was said to have claimed as he put down a strike in 1886.[6] Competition from other businessmen was forcibly, often violently discouraged. As for corruption, bribery was seen as such a normal way of expediting business that bags full of greenbacks would be made available to politicians and judges in order to influence legislation or judicial rulings. It was well known that votes in the federal and state legislatures could be bought and sold like meat in a market and that money was frequently used to oil the wheels of justice. 'I think the time is well spent,' said Collis P. Huntington, founder of the Southern Pacific Railroad, 'when it is a man's duty to go up and bribe the judge.'[7]

A type of capitalism evolved that was more subtle but just as ruthless and destructive as that of robber barons like Gould, Huntington and the two best-known examples, Andrew Carnegie and John D. Rockefeller. Business leaders built up large bureaucratic structures and prepared the way for the decline of their own style of proprietary power. Although decisions and responsibilities were still concentrated at the top of corporate hierarchies, the complicated and fragmented new bureaucratic arrangements had the effect of making accountability for illegal or harmful activities far more difficult. At the same time, the new impersonal corporations proved to be just as likely to put profit ahead of the health and safety of workers, communities and consumers as their founders. Corruption of the American political and judicial process ensured that the property rights of these new corporations overrode the human rights of workers, communities and consumers.

Business leaders did more with their money than corrupt legislators and judges. By the beginning of the twentieth century many had supported the tide of moral reform that effectively shifted attention away from the power and behaviour of corporations towards aspects of the personal behaviour of the masses considered to be unhealthy and undesirable in this still very puritan nation. Thus business fortunes were used to fund campaigns that sought to eradicate alcohol, gambling, commercialized sex and the use of certain kinds of drugs such as heroin and cocaine.

The best financed moral reform organization was the Anti-Saloon League. By 1919 about 14,000 American businessmen had contributed funds, including sizeable and regular support from John D. Rockefeller Jr, son of the founder of Standard Oil and one of America's richest men. After the Ludlow massacre, during which strike-breakers associated with the Rockefeller-owned Colorado Fuel and Iron Company set a fire that killed eleven children and two women, Rockefeller felt the need to contribute more funds to Colorado's drive to prohibit liquor. After one $10,000 contribution he was assured that Prohibition was crucial in maintaining 'the peace and order of the state against anarchy and red revolution'. And when the national Prohibition Amendment was first submitted to the states a League representative wrote him these thanks: 'In light of what your money made possible . . . we trust that you will feel repaid for your investment.'[8]

Thanks to the support of business as well as the ceaseless campaigning of moral reformers America became a land where goods and services considered undesirable by some were prohibited to all by law. They were still available, however, but at a higher price because of their outlaw status. The entrepreneurial possibilities for even those at the lower levels of society were obvious.

By the 1920s many Americans knew or at least suspected that much of their society was corrupt. Politicians, judges, lawyers, bankers and business concerns collected many millions of dollars from frauds, bribes and various forms of extortion, while business for gangsters, thieves, fraudsters, pimps, gamblers, bootleggers and industrial racketeers also boomed. Organized crime had become the norm rather than the exception in many of America's political, business, police and legal systems. American capitalism was gangster capitalism but few cared so long as the nation seemed to be prospering.

Given an abundance of newspaper reports, even people in Europe and further afield were well aware that America was a land of gangster capitalism. They read about gang wars in New York and Chicago, the obvious freedom Al Capone and his type had to run rackets, and the regular corruption scandals going to the very top levels of government. There was no disputing the conclusion of the *Manchester Guardian* in 1928, 'all the machinery of law exists in America, but the thing does not work properly.'[9]

The English newspaper was commenting after revelations after the murder of the classic gangster middleman, Arnold Rothstein, had brought home the depth of the problem of organized crime in the US. Rothstein, New York's 'Big Bankroll' of crime, had been among the first to spot the potential profitability of gambling, alcohol and drug prohibitions either by direct involvement in or by sponsorship of businesses that supplied these goods and services. He even bankrolled the operations of Jack 'Legs' Diamond, who preferred hijacking the contraband of bootleggers rather than troubling with the complex operations required to import, transport and distribute illegal liquor. Connections with gangs of thugs enabled Rothstein to provide strong-arm services in industrial disputes, particu-larly in New York's garment industry. At one time employers had the services of Legs Diamond and his men as strike-breakers, while the unions countered with the services of Jacob 'Little Augie' Orgen to protect pickets and beat up 'scabs'. Both sets of gangsters received their payment from Rothstein.

Rothstein had legitimate and profitable covers for all his illegal activ-ities. Apart from restaurants and nightclubs, he owned real estate, an export–import firm and a bailbond firm that provided bail of $14 million in liquor prosecutions alone before 1924. And he had several of the best lawyers to handle the legalistic aspects of his transactions. By the 1920s he had built up unrivalled political connections and this gave him leverage in the city's criminal justice system. He could therefore provide not only capital but protection for numerous illegal enterprises: cases could be 'fixed' and prison sentences shortened. This is the reason why on the police records of the famous gangster names of the future, Frank Costello, 'Lucky' Luciano, Benjamin 'Bugsy' Siegel, there are so many cases marked 'dismissed'. When they stepped in front of the magistrate, prose-cutors found that they had 'insufficient evidence', witnesses failed to show up or police officers admitted that they had overstepped themselves.[10]

Rothstein succeeded for a time in New York because, like other successful businessmen, he knew the price of every man, from politicians to thugs, and their value in a given context. Like any successful business-man of the time, he grew rich by pocketing the difference. People wanted to know Rothstein. Politicians wanted money to fight elections, theatre and film producers wanted money to make plays and films, manufacturers wanted strong-arm services to fight unions, and criminals wanted money to fight court cases or set up new rackets. He was exploiting a business system that had few restraints and a moral crusade that had little prospect of success. The fact that Gotti, other career criminals and a multitude of drug traffickers were still able to prosper nearly a century after Rothstein suggests that the *Manchester Guardian*'s comment in the 1920s is still applicable today. The machinery of law in America still does not work properly.

Organized crime even made a significant contribution to America's traumatic economic collapse at the end of the 1920s. The seemingly unlimited opportunities for fraud and racketeering in Wall Street and the nation's ramshackle banking system helped bring a formerly very productive economic machine to a shuddering stop. In 1932 Americans faced the choice between Republican Herbert Hoover and Democrat Franklin Roosevelt for president. The first was shackled by a commitment to the economic orthodoxy that the market would eventually right itself without any undue interference from government, the second offered Americans an alternative to the brutalities and corruption of what is known as the free market. The voters chose Roosevelt and his New Deal administration and made America less friendly to career criminals and business criminals than at any time before or since. The New Deal restructured the capitalist system in ways that reduced opportunities for business and banking crooks. It made the Federal Bureau of Investigation into a formidable foe for bank robbers who had been crossing state lines almost with impunity and for kidnappers who had been operating much too easily. Roosevelt's Democratic party also eased the passage of the repeal of Prohibition and thus helped make bootlegging liquor an obsolete profession. Opportunities for organized criminal activity still existed in Roosevelt's America of course, some were even newly created, such as fraud involving agricultural subsidies, but for a short time government action was effective against organized crime.

The United States has lost the wisdom on organized crime it briefly possessed during the time of Franklin Roosevelt. The nation turned away from New Deal liberalism after the Second World War and, during the Cold War, became obsessed with defeating communism at the expense of dealing intelligently with the kind of structural problems that allowed organized crime in both legal and illegal markets to flourish. Corporations, for example, were allowed to 'capture' regulatory agencies either by directly bribing government officials or, more discreetly, by holding out the prospect of lucrative employment opportunities once a period of government service had been completed. Officials would often therefore turn discreetly away when fraudulent and often dangerous activity called for a tougher approach. As for illegal markets, only bootlegging became an obsolete profession during the 1930s. Gambling operators and drug traffickers continued to prosper by exploiting other aspects of America's programme of moral reform, protected more often than prosecuted by the authorities.

The fact that organized crime involved wrong-headed laws and structural deficiencies was disguised by the invention of a foreign conspiracy explanation for organized crime. By the 1970s government officials, newspapers and the producers of fiction managed to bypass serious research on the problem and instead chose to give the impression that organized crime was synonymous with a centralized, hierarchical criminal conspiracy called the Mafia. Attention was shifted away from corporate criminality and the government's failure to enforce its morality laws and towards an entertaining distraction that was most successfully exploited by Mario Puzo and Francis Ford Coppola in *The Godfather* books and films.

From the time of President Richard Nixon, there was a slide back towards the brutalities and corruption of allegedly free markets. Nixon prepared the way for the massive movement towards privatization and deregulation that would follow from the 1980s, and not just through his actions and rhetoric as president. Even his disgrace over Watergate did not stop America's profound and to date unstoppable shift to the right. The iceberg of abuse uncovered during the Watergate investigations confirmed the distrust that many Americans already had of American institutions and American leaders. The historian Bruce Schulman has perceptively concluded that the 'principal effect of Watergate was to discredit government itself. Watergate added fuel to a widespread cynicism about . . . government itself as an instrument of the collective good.'[11] Many Americans would agree with Nixon's most charismatic successor, Ronald Reagan, that government was now the problem, not the solution.

Reagan promised to take the government off the backs of the people but instead took it mainly off the backs of the upper levels of the business community. The permissiveness to business of Reagan's and all succeeding administrations led to the non-enforcement of environmental-protection laws, for example, and made America a haven for corporate polluters. This permissiveness also led to the widespread corporate use of what was euphemistically known as 'creative accounting'. Frauds on an epic scale were aided and abetted by the very accounting firms that were supposed to check corporate fraud. Company accounts should be an accurate reflection of their true financial situation and thus a fair guide to potential investors. Instead, accountants used false valuations, false descriptions of profits and manipulation of inter-company loans and transactions as veils to deceive the investing public on a scale that would not be revealed until the Enron, WorldCom and other scandals of the new millennium, when American corporate culture in general was shown to be thoroughly corrupt.[12] Deregulation and inadequate enforcement by the appropriate authorities meant that the system of checks and balances established by the New Deal had broken down. The system that had partly kept the lid on organized corporate crime was destroyed by endless claims made by well-financed and well-connected lobbyists that the market knows best.

At the same time as deregulation of business activity was helping to make the United States a more hospitable place for corporate criminals, another policy introduced during the Nixon years was also having socially destructive results. Nixon's war on drugs manipulated the fears of American parents about the inability of their children to resist temptation and produced a greatly expanded drug law-enforcement effort. This effort has not prevented Americans who want drugs from buying drugs and has been accompanied by violence and corruption that far exceeds anything experienced during the bootleg wars of the 1920s.

The motives for drug trafficking-related violence have generally stayed the same as those that accompanied alcohol prohibition: protecting territory or goods from rivals, discouraging informants or stealing money or drugs from other traffickers. Police estimated that over 100 of Detroit's 690 homicides in 1971 were related to the heroin trade. In New York in 1981 there were 393 drug-related slayings, including 160 in which drug dealers were killed during robberies. From the mid-1970s the homicide rate in South Florida jumped more than 400 per cent in a few years, mainly because of violence associated with the drug traffic. In 1981 the Dade County medical examiner had to rent a refrigerated hamburger van to cope with the increase in corpses, and by then Miami had become one of the world's most dangerous cities. In recent years there has been another upsurge in drug trafficking-related violence.[13]

Violence was most visible in the inner cities where gangs proliferated and competed for territory and drug-distribution networks. According to a nationwide survey, in 1961 there were 23 cities with known street gangs. By 1971 there were 50, and this increased to 78 in 1980. By the early 1990s, nearly 200 US cities had street gangs, mostly composed of African-American, Hispanic and Asian ghetto dwellers.[14]

The motive for drug-enforcement corruption is usually simple greed. Many officers continue to be more involved in the drug trade itself than in the suppression of the drug trade, as the case involving Los Angeles police officer Ruben Palomares indicates. Palomares joined the LAPD in 1993 and because he looked young he was assigned to a juvenile narcotics unit to investigate drug use in high schools. Youthful under-cover policemen and women had in fact been infiltrating high schools for several years before Palomares. In some cases they had exploited their sexuality and attractiveness to entice the slower and more gullible students to get hold of drugs and thus provide an easy source of arrests. Next Palomares was transferred to the famously corrupt Ramparts Division where he joined with a number of other officers to take part in armed robberies across Southern California staged to look like police raids. Palomares has admitted to the theft of hundreds and thousands of dollars' worth of drugs, cash, guns, jewellery and other items between 1998 and 2002. Some of his network's robberies involved violence, with beatings, shootings and, on one occasion, intimidation involving burning a man and putting a gun into his mouth. Not surprisingly, given this type of revelation, the LAPD has been considered by many street-gang members as just another gang.[15]

Drug law-enforcement officers like Palomares and his crew are only the latest manifestation of one of the main problems with American drug-prohibition policies. Soon after the first federal anti-drug law was passed in 1914, the problem of corruption surfaced as the first of many thousands of drug-enforcement officers was found to be on the take. Regular scandals peppered the following 90 years, and one important federal drug-enforcement agency, the Federal Bureau of Narcotics, even had to be abolished in 1968 when it was clear that too many of its officers had been operating their own criminal enterprises.[16]

Essentially America's anti-crime policy since Nixon has been based largely on mass imprisonment for poorer criminals in general and those involved in a growing drug trade in particular. Predictably, however, overcrowding the prisons and locking up hundreds of thousands of young men with career criminals succeeded only in creating many more, much more ruthless drug-trafficking networks than had been disrupted. Drug-related organized-crime problems in America have been getting worse, yet the United States, again since the Nixon era, has been telling the rest of the world to follow its lead on drug control.

Nixon was the first American president to make a concerted effort to internationalize the war on drugs, with undesirable consequences for many countries and catastrophic consequences for those like Colombia and Afghanistan, already wracked by conflict and brutal but weak governments. From the 1970s on, efforts to bully or bribe other countries into acceptance of an American-based global drug-control regime were intensified at the expense of serious consideration of alternative models of drug control, such as the once distinctive and successful British approach.

Like the United States, Britain has had drug-control policies since the early part of the twentieth century. These were not based on absolute prohibition, however, and no special effort was expended against habits which, although sometimes personally destructive, did not threaten the rest of society. Individual doctors cared for individual addicts, using professional judgement rather than state-imposed moral ideals, and this meant they could prescribe heroin and other drugs legally. People who did not have the willpower to give up their habits had the opportunity for normal and productive lives under medical supervision. The system was imperfect but crucially it did help to keep the black market in drugs small and not very profitable in contrast to the vast clandestine commerce in the United States. Smuggling heroin into Britain was simply not worth the risks for its relatively small profit potential. Most foreign experts not connected to the US drug-enforcement community envied British policies. Partly as a result of American pressure, things began to change.

From 1968 only a limited number of doctors, usually psychiatrists in treatment clinics, were allowed to prescribe heroin for addicts. They were to be licensed, not by the government ministry responsible for the provision of health care, but by the ministry responsible for law enforcement: the Home Office. The conditions were created for a much larger black market as the clinics prescribed much less heroin than the general practitioners from whom they took over. There was a large, organized, illicit traffic in heroin for the first time in Britain as smuggling and distribution networks realized the profit potential that a myopic government policy had given them. Britain now had its own drug 'barons' and 'Mr Bigs' and its own police officers deeply involved in the drug trade. Over the following three and a half decades a succession of British governments made increasingly expensive investments in trying to suppress the drug traffic, while heroin addiction and cocaine use spread from the cities to the remotest of villages. A report from the European Union's drug monitoring centre putting Britain at the top of the continent's cocaine and cannabis league table was published in November 2004.[17] The main solution offered by the politicians was intensified and more aggressive drug-law enforcement and, again on the American model, more intrusive practices and stiffer penalties for drug offenders. More police were transferred to anti-drug duties, squads were reorganized, intelligence centres were set up, 'hot-lines' were established for informers, and new prisons were promised. All were strategies tried and found wanting in the United States because with the profits to be made, manufacturers, smugglers and distributors found ways to circumvent each new initiative. The strategies, moreover, took resources away from the only approach that can reduce the demand for dangerous drugs.

Treatment and education, of course, should be available, but more important, is making policy that attacks the causes of social problems, not the symptoms. But British governments, along with all those who were forced or persuaded to accept the American-based global drug-control regime, watched helplessly as counter-productive consequences followed, among which were more opportunities for successful organized crime and corruption.[18]

The current bankruptcy of the British response is best illustrated by the planned creation of the Serious and Organized Crime Agency (SOCA) as a kind of British FBI. The assumption behind SOCA and accompanying new American-style organized-crime-control powers to be given to prose-cutors and police is that these powers work, that they control organized crime. The reality could hardly be further from the truth.

Every nation has criminals but very few nations can create conditions that facilitate or even foster serious criminality internationally. Unfortunately, the United States, admittedly supported by most of the developed world, became one of these few and, as we shall see, has changed the nature and extent of organized crime in both legal and criminal markets throughout our now 'borderless' world.

The United States is by far the most powerful of all the states pulling the strings that move the limbs of international organizations that attempt to control legal markets, as Susan Strange rightly reminds us in her analysis of global finance.[19] The United States was the only country with a decisive power either to deregulate the international financial system and make it more conducive to organized criminal activities or to set rules that would govern financial transactions in the major international capital and money markets. Again, from the time of Nixon, it chose the first option. Globalization has been mismanaged in many other ways that have multiplied criminal opportunities and increased the destructive capacity of organized crime.

An international system has emerged of legal agreements that guaran-tee the global rights of capital, often at the expense of human rights. They also leave regulatory voids that lie not only beyond states but also beyond the interstate system.[20] A new breed of often murderous kleptocrats and sophisticated international business criminals emerged to exploit these regulatory voids to plunder. Suharto in Indonesia, Marcos in the Philippines, Mobutu in the Congo led the way by accumulating billions of dollars, essentially by robbing their peoples with the com-plicity of American and other western banks and financial institutions. In the 1980s the Bank of Credit and Commerce International (BCCI) helped not only kleptocrats escape with the profits of crime but also arms traffickers, drug traffickers and even terrorists. Since its exposure as a criminal bank in 1991, evidence has shown that the BCCI's banking practices were not unusual but instead merely reflected a more pervasive culture of corporate criminality.

Leading global financial institutions, notably the International Monetary Fund (IMF) and the World Bank, have done little to combat opportunities for serious organized criminality. In fact these institutions have served mainly to legitimize an international system open to widespread abuse. The IMF, for example, continued to lend and encourage other institutions to lend to Marcos, Suharto and Mobutu long after their pillage was common knowledge. And the World Bank's failure to notice or respond to BCCI's criminality over a long period of time may have been related to the large number of high-level personnel connections between the two institutions.[21]

More generally, as long as corporate and financial criminality is seen as being secondary to Mafia-type organized crime and as long as political criminality throughout the world is defended in terms of *realpolitik*, the global political economy is endlessly vulnerable to criminal activity. While the global media focused on the criminality of Gotti in America, Totò Riina in Italy, Pablo Escobar in Colombia and their equivalents throughout the world during the 1980s and 1990s, far too little attention was paid to the witting, systematic role of foreign banks in the kleptocrats' ascents, and the specific role of the global haven banking system, which fostered the accumulation of massive, public, foreign debts side by side with the accumulation of massive, illicit, foreign private assets.[22]

The culture of corporate criminality is not of course restricted to American corporations, as BCCI and the Parmalat collapse and scandal in Italy in January 2004 show. Parmalat, like many other big companies, had interests in offshore havens, mainly to avoid or perhaps evade paying tax. The low reporting requirements in many of these havens allow them to mask the transactions, profits and even the ownership structure of their offshore subsidiaries. An environment has emerged that encourages secrecy, and for those inclined to cook the books this has obviously been too tempting an opportunity to resist. In the case of Parmalat, large-scale fraud was clearly involved in the company's bankruptcy and the threat to the livelihood of its 36,000 staff in 30 countries.[23]

Kleptocrat plunder and corporate fraud has contributed to making the world we live in less equal, with millions mired in poverty and many of these desperate to flee towards a better life. Every day of the year thousands of people from poor countries are desperate enough to fill the pockets of people traffickers in the hope of finding work in rich countries.

They make this decision largely because life in their own countries has become intolerable. Many had been pushed from the land in rural areas by economic adjustment programmes imposed on their governments by international loan agencies, such as the IMF and the World Bank. They then had to fight for their survival in the rapidly increasing and expanding slums around the 'mega-cities' of the developing world, where the infrastructure to support decent communities is almost non-existent and where young people are more likely to join predatory gangs than to find meaningful work.[24] It is not surprising that those who can afford it pay traffickers for the privilege of risking death in transit or capture by home government border agents followed by a forced return to the woeful conditions in the country of their origins. If they succeed in getting into North America or European countries where there is a demand for their cheap labour, they risk exploitation and often their health and safety. In 1996, for example, it was revealed that more than a hundred illegal immigrants from Asia and South America were forced to live and work like slaves in sweatshops surrounded by barbed wire and razor wire near Los Angeles.[25]

Drug traffickers, arms traffickers, corporate fraudsters, kleptocrats, people traffickers, sweatshop operators and a host of other networked criminals have all profited by changes that accompanied globalization. They have been allowed to do so because national and international organized-crime-control policies are woefully inadequate and the rights of people to be protected from crime have been subordinated to the rights of property. The situation now is best described as a global fix. This type of fix is not synonymous with bribery and corruption but it does, of course, involve both of these. The fix in this case involves world-wide networks of alliances, commitments and obligations, all mutually reinforcing, of such a nature as to move much of the world towards a condition of almost complete paralysis of law enforcement and observance. Crucial to this paralysis are the patterns of understanding that define the limits of debate about criminality and the meaning of terms like 'organized crime'. Precisely those things that need to be addressed become either inaccessible to thought or else are understood to be 'inevitable' – that is, beyond politics, unfortunate facts of human nature. So, for example, IMF and World Bank policies are considered almost exclusively as belonging to the realm of economics and therefore cannot be connected in anything like a meaningful way with the discussion of organized crime. This despite the fact that their interventions in the developing world have often led to orgies of theft, violence and institutional madness.

Back in the 1930s Franklin Roosevelt's New Deal administration gave Americans more than an alternative to German and Italian fascism, Stalinist communism and Japanese militarism. Equally importantly he gave them an alternative to the brutalities and corruption of unregulated capitalism. In fact, as we shall see in Chapter 4, while campaigning for the presidency in 1932, Roosevelt made it very clear that the so-called American free market was free in name only and that business interests often operated in ways designed to control their markets at a great cost to both workers and consumers. As president, Roosevelt taught Americans a lesson that people world-wide need to be reminded of today. The American economy had been in a mess and the dominant political and economic orthodoxy had said there was essentially nothing to be done except restore business confidence and wait for prosperity to return. Unregulated capitalism must rule and there was a strong implication that people were powerless to improve their own lives. Responding to this interest-serving attitude while campaigning for president, Roosevelt charged that, 'Our . . . leaders tell us economic laws – sacred, inviolable, unchangeable – cause panics which no one could prevent. But while they prate of economic laws, men and women are starving. We must lay hold of the fact that economic laws are not made by nature. They are made by human beings.'[26]

At an international level, globalization is often said to be a force of nature, driven by technology and by the power of big business, and people are told that there is no more chance of taming it than there is of taming the weather. However, the policies that govern globalization or, to be more accurate, the policies that fail to govern globalization, were also made by human beings and can be changed by human beings. If they are not, opportunities for criminal activity globally will continue to increase. The price of this will be felt mainly by the millions who live below subsistence levels in undeveloped nations but also by the working and middle classes in developed nations who have seen their incomes decline or stagnate and their plans for a comfortable retirement threatened. There are alternatives to gangster capitalism but they are not at present on the agendas of nation states and international organizations. It is up to us to identify the causes of gangsterism and organized crime at the global level and to impose the necessary remedies.

PART 1

The United States
and Gangster Capitalism

The spirit of graft and lawlessness is the American spirit.

Lincoln Steffens, *The Shame of the Cities*, 1902

It is by the goodness of God that in our country we have those three unspeakably precious things: freedom of speech, freedom of conscience, and the prudence never to practice either of them.

Mark Twain, *Following the Equator*, 1897

Introduction

Although it has been convenient for the US government to blame the Mafia and other supercriminal organizations for America's intractable organized-crime problems, its own failure to control legal and illegal markets is at the heart of the problem.

American academics and commentators began the serious study of organized crime at the beginning of the twentieth century when minds were still open to the subject.[1] The phrase was used, according to context, in two main ways. Often its meaning was literal: writers would simply and accurately refer to systematic criminal activity such as dealing in stolen property, fraud, illegal gambling, trafficking in drugs and liquor, or extortion as organized crime. At other times the phrase was used to describe a fluid set of criminal relationships that might include police officers, politicians, respectable business interests, professionals such as lawyers and accountants, as well as gangsters. The present-day association of organized crime almost exclusively with frozen images such as foreign 'godfathers' and 'crime cartels' had not yet dulled the public perception of the problem. In fact, the only mention of criminal 'godfathers' in the academic literature referred to lawyers. The lawyer, according to G.L. Hostetter and T.Q. Beesley in an article written for the *Political Quarterly* in 1933, 'constituted the most important cog in the machinery of crime . . . He is the godfather of every criminal gang worthy of mention in America. He devises the clever legal instruments that constitute the charters of rackets.'[2]

It was also widely understood that organized crime thrived in American legal markets because of an ideological rigidity that favoured the development of a poorly policed business system that left the door wide open to fraud, extortion and other types of organized criminality. In a 1907 book endorsed by President Teddy Roosevelt, for example, the sociologist Edward A. Ross argued that lawless and destructive business practices had created a need for a redefinition of ideas about crime. The typical new criminal of industrial society was, for Ross, one who prospered by destructive 'practices which have not yet come under the ban of public opinion'.

Criminals from the poorer classes, he argued, had few opportunities to damage society. Big business 'criminaloids', on the other hand, were 'beasts of prey' who could 'pick a thousand pockets, poison a thousand sick, pollute a thousand minds, or imperil a thousand lives'. Modern crime was based on betrayal rather than aggression, and monstrous treacheries existed on all levels of modern life: 'Adulterators, peculators, boodlers, grafters, violating the trust others have placed in them.'[3]

By pointing out that many of the actions of businessmen were more destructive than more familiar forms of crime, Ross was attempting to broaden the definition of crime. Big business 'criminaloids' robbed and killed on a much grander scale than ever witnessed before, but 'so long as morality stands stock-still in the old tracks, they escape both punishment and ignominy. The man who picks pockets with a railway rebate, murders with an adulterant instead of a bludgeon, burglarizes with a "rake-off" instead of a jimmy . . . does not feel on his brow the brand of a malefactor . . . Like a stupid, flushed giant at bay, the public heeds the little overt offender more than the big covert offender.'[4]

America's moral authoritarianism was just as rigid as the nation's pro-business ideology and many commentators pointed out as a result that organized crime thrived in American illegal markets. America's 'high level of lawlessness is maintained by the fact that Americans desire to do so many things which they also desire to prohibit', as Walter Lippmann made clear in his famous 'Underworld as Servant' argument in 1931. 'To the amazement of the older nations of the earth,' he continued, 'we have . . . enacted new legal prohibitions against the oldest vices of man. We have achieved a body of statutory law which testifies unreservedly to our aspiration for an absolutely blameless . . . life on earth.' Lippmann pointed out that the main gainer from this situation was the American underworld. It flourished because it offered 'something in return to the respectable members of society'. While ordinary criminals were wholly predatory, the 'underworld has a different status': 'Its activities are in some degree countenanced by the respectable; from among them it draws its revenues; among them it finds many of its patrons; by them it is in various ways protected.'[5]

Ross, Lippmann and many others clearly understood that the key to understanding organized crime is opportunity. The chance to make large illegal profits with minimal risks encourages organized crime. It follows that groups or individuals that have partially or completely escaped effective regulation and control will tend to be engaged in organized criminal activity. Financiers, corporate leaders, and those lower down the corporate hierarchies – politicians, police officers – all will tend towards criminality if the risks are small, and they were small in an America where property was clearly king. America had become a land of criminal opportunity by the 1920s as Chapters 2 and 3 demonstrate. Endemic business fraud also contributed mightily to the onset of the Great Depression of the 1930s, the gravest economic crisis the United States has ever faced. The pinnacle of America's moral reformers' achievements, the prohibition of alcohol, had also 'left a trail of graft and slime', to quote a popular poem of the time.[6] As Donald C. Stone, a historically conscious expert in public administration, put it in 1934, 'With the centralization of business enterprise, with the dawn of big finance, and with the tremendously increased variety of business and social activities, rapacious manipulation and self-seeking avarice more easily victimize the rank-and-file of the citizens . . . The variety of rackets is endless,' he continued, 'they thrive in small towns as well as large, wherever men try to get something for nothing.' He also illustrated a problem that has frustrated those studying organized crime ever since: 'the difficulty if not impossibility of drawing the line between legitimate practice and genuine rackets'.[7]

Chapter 4 argues that the era of Franklin Roosevelt's New Deal was the one period in American history when policy was made that reduced opportunities for organized criminality at every level of society. The problem of organized crime was briefly understood as requiring more than extra police effort to arrest and convict wrongdoers. The repeal of alcohol prohibition was a rare admission in America that moral ideals are no match for human ingenuity and human nature. The restructuring of capitalism during the New Deal was the equally rare admission that capitalism needs protection from capitalists. 'Government by organized money', Roosevelt declared in a 1936 campaign speech, was just as dangerous as 'government by organized mob'.[8]

Roosevelt died on 12 April 1945, just months before the end of the Second World War. By that time the New Deal era of reform had ended and government activity had become far more deferential to the demands of big business and far less likely to seek to limit the damage of corporate, organized crime. By the 1950s corporate officials and Wall Street financiers were seen as socially responsible rather than as the greedy and corrupt capitalists who had almost led America into economic ruin a generation before. Many of the checks and balances introduced by the New Deal did remain in place for decades and to an extent kept the lid on organized, corporate crime. They were slowly watered down, however, and eventually even removed. As the checks were weakened, corporate, organized criminality became more institutionalized and destructive.

At the same time the problem of organized crime was redefined in ways that got corrupt business interests, graft-seeking police and politicians, and other professionals off the hook. These were now seen as deviant aberrations in the otherwise flawless American economic system. The system itself was usually described as one based on free enterprise, ironically at a time when enterprise in America was becoming less free. As corporate ownership became more concentrated, corporate dominance over the rest of society became less questioned.

Organized crime had to be seen as something external to America in the Cold War era and the idea of the Mafia dominating organized crime took root. The Mafia was said to be a major threat not just to America but to the rest of the world. 'The Mafia', according to New York journalist Ed Reid, was 'history's greatest threat to morality' and 'the principal fount of all crime in the world, controlling vice, gambling, the smuggling and sale of dope, and other sources of evil'.[9] This limited focus also implied there could be no compromise contemplated in waging war against the activities that were thought to be the lifeline of organized crime and in the control of the Mafia. Calls to legalize gambling or medicalize the problem of drug addiction were shouted down, if they were heard at all, condemned as capitulation to a foreign enemy.

As Chapter 5 shows, the Mafia conspiracy theory allowed politicians such as Richard Nixon to claim that the only way to combat organized crime was repression. Nixon supported a series of measures in the 1970 Organized Crime Control Act that form the basis of not just American efforts against organized crime but now increasingly international efforts. The result was acceptance of the type of organized-crime-control regimes internationally that clearly did not come close to controlling such crime in the United States. Many important out-and-out gangsters and others involved in organized crime have been arrested and convicted but other factors have undermined any positive benefits to be derived from the removal of these from society. In fact, since the 1970s, as Chapters 6 and 7 document, the moves to deregulate large areas of American business activity and intensify the war on drugs have opened up vast new areas of both corporate and gangster criminal activity. The scandals at Enron and other corporations testify to this, as does the proliferation of increasingly more violent street gangs and prison gangs. Despite mountains of evidence indicating the failure of American organized-crime-control efforts, the minds of government leaders across the world remain closed on the subject.

Meanwhile, as governments hide behind interest-serving definitions of organized crime and claim that tougher policing is the only answer, organized crime in all its many and varied forms continues to damage and destroy far too many lives.

1

Cradle to Crematorium, Womb to Cadaver Lab

Organized Crime and the American Life Cycle

It is frequently proclaimed that the United States has controlled or at least drastically curbed organized crime. American success has been trumpeted in newspapers, magazines and television documentaries. The message was crystallized in the titles of three recent books: *The Good Guys: How We Turned the FBI Round and Finally Broke the Mob*, *Gangbusters: The Destruction of America's Last Great Mafia Dynasty* and *Mob Nemesis: How the FBI Crippled Organized Crime*.[1] The clear implication of this assumption is that the way to control organized crime is by using the methods that the US government has pioneered. The most serious problem with this assumption is that the United States has not come close to controlling its organized crime as the following survey demonstrates.

Thanks to recent technological advances in medicine our survey of organized crime and the American life cycle can begin pre-conception with fertility fraud. In the late 1980s Dr Cecil Jacobson pioneered this form of profitable deception on couples desperate to have babies in a particularly repellent way. He led the couples to believe that he operated a donor programme that selected sperm from carefully screened men, but then used his own sperm, fathering as many as 75 children in the process. As part of his pitch to anxious would-be patients, he told them he was 'the baby-maker' and, with even more conscious irony, 'God doesn't give you babies . . . I do.' Another part of his particularly cruel form of solo racketeering involved lying to some women that they had become pregnant before informing them they had miscarried after he had charged for his fees. In March 1992 he was convicted on 52 felony counts of fraud and perjury.[2]

A related case of fertility fraud was uncovered in 1995 when the first incident of egg and embryo theft was revealed. Three whistle-blowers informed California state officials and the media that doctors at a fertility clinic operated by the University of California, Irvine, were taking eggs from some women and implanting them into others without donor consent. These ethical lapses were compounded by alleged large-scale fraud. An audit concluded that three of the clinic's doctors had cheated patients, insurance companies and the university out of hundreds of thousands of dollars. A study of the case suggested that fertility-fraud cases are likely to increase in the future now that hundreds of fertility clinics have opened in the United States in a field that is less regulated than 'animal-breeding'.[3]

Many studies make it clear that these two examples of fertility fraud are by no means aberrations in a health-care system organized around the profit system. In particular, many medical professionals have abused the Medicare and Medicaid programmes since they began in the 1960s. These are largely federally funded programmes set up to improve health care for the poor and the old respectively. Medicare now purchases health and long-term care services for over 50 million low-income Americans.[4] A study by Paul Jesilow, Henry Pontell and Gilbert Geis found fraud to be endemic from prenatal care for expectant mothers through to unnecessary procedures, which included surgery in cases that would have been more safely treated with a course of drugs. They reported on studies that found that the rate of surgery performed on those less well-off and therefore reliant on government support was twice that of the general population.[5] In August 2003 the Tenet Healthcare Corporation agreed to pay $54 million to settle government claims that doctors at one of its hospitals in Northern California conducted unnecessary heart procedures and operations on hundreds of patients.[6] Surgery can, of course, be dangerous and contributes to an estimate of more than 12,000 deaths each year as a result of unnecessary procedures.[7] Accordingly, Neil Getnick, an anti-fraud specialist lawyer, described the Tenet case as 'not just a health care fraud that takes dollars out of the system' but one that was 'rank patient abuse' and 'as bad as it gets'.[8]

In June 2004 federal investigators revealed a particularly shameless insurance racket involving Southern Californian surgery centres. The clinics employed recruiters to offer healthy people, usually immigrants, cash, vacations and even cosmetic surgery to undergo needless and overpriced medical procedures, from routine examinations to major surgery. Some of these 'rent-a-patients' were left with serious medical complications. The clinics collected their money from insurance claims and shared their gain with doctors and recruiters.[9]

It is difficult, however, to feel too sorry for insurance companies, because criminal activity in their industry appears to be rife. On 14 October 2004 New York's Attorney General Eliot Spitzer charged that the world's largest insurance broker, Marsh and McLennan, conspired to cheat business clients out of hundreds and millions of dollars. Marsh and McLennan have, according to Spitzer, 'participated in a massive bid-rigging scheme that has cost the American consumer – in auto insurance, life insurance, health insurance, every insurance market – untold sums of money. And they have, meanwhile, been blaming everybody else for the rise in insurance premiums.'[10] In January 2005 Robert Stearns, a senior vice-president of Marsh, pleaded guilty to a felony related to fraud and bid-rigging in Spitzer's investigation of industry practices. Stearns admitted that he had been instructing insurance companies to submit non-competitive bids to obtain business contracts and that he conveyed those bids to Marsh clients under false pretences.[11]

America's expensive private-health system has also provided countless opportunities for confidence tricksters. The Vanguarde Asset Group, for example, sold insurance in states despite not being licensed to do so. Its operators chose a name that resembled an established investment group and created marketing literature designed to give the appearance of legitimacy. It then signed up scores of customers who, if they needed treatment, could incur costs of thousands of dollars in medical bills before realizing that their insurer was fraudulent. One case in 2001 involved a patient having brain surgery as a result of a stroke. When he died two years later he left his widow $250,000 in unpaid medical bills. For the fraudsters that ran Vanguarde there was little deterrence, because in many states it is only a misdemeanour to market or sell unauthorized insurance. This problem is likely to get worse as more people struggle to find affordable medical insurance. Mila Kofman, a researcher at Georgetown University's Health Policy Institute, has argued that regulators could not solve the problem unless health insurance becomes affordable, 'It won't go away until you get rid of the demand for it.'[12]

Those sold bogus health insurance can at least check the credentials of their insurers. Patients in New York mental institutions had no such check on criminal activity. In 2002 an investigation by the *New York Times* found that homes for the mentally ill had become little more than 'psychiatric flophouses': 'Deaths under questionable circumstances went uninvestigated, minimum-wage aides supervised residents while haphazardly distributing large amounts of psychotropic drugs, and medical fraud was common.'[13] In the 1970s New York State had closed its large regimented and oppressive mental hospitals, and patients were provided with federal social security assistance and relocated in nursing homes, single-room occupancy hotels or in private proprietary homes for adults that sprang up like mushrooms in the wake of the government reforms.[14] The rhetoric behind the changes claimed to be about giving the mentally ill a chance of a better life integrated into the wider community. The reality was one of abuse, neglect and exploitation. Clifford Levy consulted state inspection reports and interviewed workers and residents to report on Seaport, one of these homes, for the *New York Times*. The home had been called 'The New Warehouse for the Insane' in a 1997 study by the Office of Mental Health and failed to improve in the years that followed. Instead, Levy writes,

> During a typical visit to the home, residents can be seen sitting for hours in the crowded smoking room, rocking back and forth, speaking only to themselves . . . Current and former workers said two residents openly deal crack from their rooms, contributing to the drug abuse, loan-sharking, prostitution and violence that have gripped the home for years. In this predatory atmosphere, the frail quickly learn that the safest place is behind the closed doors of their rooms. Others find different ways to get by . . .
>
> For years, workers said, a security guard subdued psychotic residents by beating them. Other employees are convicted drug dealers, prison records show. Several former workers said the home sometimes continued to collect the monthly disability benefits of residents after they died, or gave their Social Security numbers to illegal immigrants the homes hired.[15]

Levy documented other ways in which the loosely regulated system could be exploited for illegal profit. In the early 1990s Beryl Zyskind ran a home until he was found to be stealing money from residents, including $120,000 in Veterans Benefit Administration benefits from a Vietnam War veteran. After his conviction, the state allowed his brother-in-law Sherman Taub to take over the running of the 125-bed home. Taub was soon charged with engaging in an elaborate scheme to siphon millions of dollars from the home through improper mortgage transactions and other manoeuvres.[16] In July 2004 he pleaded guilty to the crime of grand larceny in the first degree and agreed to pay $1.65 million in restitution.[17]

Doctors as well as the operators of the homes took advantage. Shaul Debbi, for example, regularly billed Medicare and Medicaid from 1998 through 2001 for eye surgery, examinations and other procedures, often on patients who had not complained about vision problems. Debbi had not come under scrutiny from the State Health Department, which regulates the homes, despite reports of his medical misconduct from at least one home.[18] Other doctors found other imaginary complaints to bill the government for.

Fraud by doctors and mental home operators in America is, however, dwarfed by fraud by drug manufacturers, as indicated by a study prepared for the Taxpayers Against Fraud Education Fund. The study found that between 2001 and the report's publication in November 2003, six giant pharmaceutical manufacturers, including Pfizer, GlaxoSmithKline and AstraZeneca settled seven cases with the Department of Justice involving allegations of pricing fraud against Medicare and Medicaid for a total of $1.6 billion. Thus the loss from this one kind of fraud alone far exceeded the yearly total loss from all bank robberies nationwide (approximately $70 million in 2001).[19] Among the practices detailed by the study were 'marketing the spread' and 'lick and stick'. Medicare and the majority of state Medicaid programmes pay for the drugs they cover on the basis of what is called 'average wholesale price' (AWP), as that price is reported by manufacturers to commercial price-listing services. 'Marketing the spread' involves manufacturers reporting AWPs for purposes of government reimbursements at very high levels and then discounting steeply from those prices. The manufacturer is thus able in effect to use government programme funds to reward health-care providers that purchase and dispense its products. In 'lick and stick' techniques manufacturers give steep discounts on brand-name drugs to large customers, often managed care plans, and then place labels on the packages of drugs shipped to the customers identifying the drugs as those of the customer, not of the manufacturer. The purpose of this labelling is to exclude the discounted price at which the drug was sold to the customer from the prices that the manufacturer is required to report to the Medicare programme for calculating the rebate owed on the drug.

Both 'marketing the spread' and 'lick and stick' techniques involve concealing deep discounts to privileged customers and this results in higher net prices to Medicare programmes and a greater financial burden on the clinics and hospitals that serve the poor in America.[20]

In the United States drugs have become so expensive that a profitable trade in counterfeit drugs has resulted. In July 2004, for example, the US Food and Drug Administration warned the public about counterfeit versions of the drug Zocor (simvastatin), a cholesterol-lowering drug, that Americans had been importing from Mexico. The counterfeit versions had no active ingredient and were thus of no use to the patients who bought them. Counterfeiters are also becoming better at placing their fakes into the massive US distribution system, where billions of packages flow from manufacturers to distributors to pharmacists to patients. In some states it is very easy for a distributor to get a licence, and no national regulation exists to trace the path any particular drug takes from manufacturer to pharmacy. The potential profits are said to be as great as heroin and cocaine trafficking with far less risk.[21]

The ongoing fraud scandals at HealthSouth are on an even higher level than those of the drug manufacturers and counterfeiters. HealthSouth is the largest provider in the United States of outpatient surgery, diagnostic imaging and rehabilitation services, operating more than 1,700 medical facilities, mainly in the United States but with some in Australia, Britain and Puerto Rico, employing more than 51,000 people. In 2003 fifteen former executives of the company, including all five of its chief financial officers since the mid-1980s, pleaded guilty to taking part in accounting tricks that misled investors and lenders. According to prosecutors, these top executives would meet regularly to inflate HealthSouth's publicly recorded earnings and falsify reports of HealthSouth's financial condition. These meetings were conspiratorially called 'family' meetings and fraudulent postings to fill the 'hole' between real and desired earnings were called the 'dirt'. In January 2004 HealthSouth officials said that an audit was expected to reveal that the total amount involved in this fraud amounted to up to $4.6 billion. As a result of the scandal HealthSouth has laid off thousands of its workers and its stocks have plummeted in value, greatly damaging its employee pension plan, which held approximately 3.3 million shares of company stock.[22]

Although opportunities for fraud in the American education system are fewer than in health, they exist, and are taken. The fraud involved in a $2.25-billion federal programme that helps schools and libraries connect to the Internet, for example, is on a grand scale. The Universal Service Fund had once existed to help rural areas get phone services at affordable prices, but expanded from 1996 in an effort to increase the web skills of millions of Americans. The fund, known as the E-Rate or Universal Service Fund (USF), comes from charges to phone companies who in turn add an extra fee to the bills of virtually every American who uses a phone. Most of the fund's largess goes to the IBM corporation, which received payments of more than $352 million in 2001, with other giant telecom and technology companies, such as NEC and SBC Communications, sharing out the rest. In December 2002, fund administrators began denying or delaying applications involving IBM. This was because either the schools and libraries or IBM had not followed proper competitive bidding procedures and thus had not complied with rules that usually act as the first line of defence against fraud and financial mismanagement in such government programmes. A Federal Communications report to

Congress noted that other wrongdoing uncovered so far within the programme ranges from simple paperwork and reporting errors to false billing and other fraud potentially involving hundreds of millions of dollars.[23] The report concluded that oversight of the massive fund was woefully inadequate. It stated that, 'Until such time as resources and funding are available to provide adequate oversight for the USF program, we are unable to give the Chairman, Congress and the public any level of assurance that the program is protected from fraud, waste and abuse.'[24]

Responsibility for the high levels of fraud and waste associated with the USF programme is divided amongst three groups, according to a *USA Today* report. These are over-eager public officials who fail to impose safeguards on the schemes, school administrators who want the federal money but have little background in setting up high-tech systems and, finally, the big companies who 'prey on wide-eyed school officials in hopes of feeding at the trough of taxpayers' money'.[25]

★

Despite the violent proclivities of young street gangsters, which will be surveyed in Chapter 7, pre-teenage American children are far more likely to be victims of serious crime than to be perpetrators. The US Department of Justice estimates that between 100,000 and 3 million children are currently involved in prostitution and child pornography.[26]

Child abuse is of course an ancient evil but technological advances have commercialized it to an unprecedented degree and opened up opportunities for entrepreneurs. Thomas Reedy, a computer consultant, became the most notable of these after he was convicted in August 2001 for running an Internet child porn ring. Reedy had the technical skills to supply a demand by allowing secure access to porn sites while protecting the identity of the user. After paying a monthly subscription fee via a post office box address or the Internet, customers from around the world could visit such graphic child pornography sites as 'City of Innocents' and 'Lolita Hardcore'. Reedy protected the identity of his Texas 'gateway' by building up a sophisticated network of sites and data stores, so that the material being accessed was sited around the world, principally in Russia and Indonesia, making it more difficult for investigators to locate the centre of the operation. At its peak, 'Landslide', as Reedy's paedophile operation was called, had around 250,000 subscribers and turned over $1.4 million a month. Investigators brought down the operation by cracking the code that scrambled subscribers' credit card numbers, finding their identities and then linking them to Reedy. In December 2000 he was found guilty of 89 charges including sexual exploitation of minors and distribution of child pornography. The following August he was sentenced to 180 months for each of the charges with the sentences running concurrently, amounting to a total of 1,335 years! Although Reedy's conviction represented a significant triumph for the US Postal Inspection Service and the Department of Justice, the disturbing aspect of the affair is that Reedy's Internet skills were not exceptional and it took a complex and time-consuming international effort to bring about his capture.[27] 'Fly by night' operators therefore continue to supply the gap in the market and children are still real and potential victims.

★

Adult, working Americans are far more likely to die young as a result of organized, corporate crime than any other form of criminal activity. As many criminologists have documented, corporate fraud is not restricted to direct extraction of money. Industrial corporations have been consistently deceptive in dealing with dangerous substances such as PCBs, beryllium, cotton dust, coal dust, Kepone, mercury, cadmium, lead, chlorine, arsenic and, most deadly of all, asbestos.[28]

Asbestos is a fibrous material that has been produced and used by American industry since the beginning of the twentieth century, primarily as a heat insulator and a fire retardant. The car industry put asbestos into brake linings and gaskets, construction companies used it for insulation and roofing materials and the mineral became a component in thousands of products. The first indication that asbestos was a major health risk came in 1906, but by the 1930s there had been many more. By that time industry executives, notably those in the giant Johns-Manville corporation, and insurance companies were well aware of the product's risks but failed to inform unions and workers and in many cases actually suppressed evidence. On top of that the industry actually funded and controlled research to conceal the dangers, lied to the workers and the public, fought against adequate safety standards, and obstructed or corrupted enforcement efforts. By the mid-1960s, Johns-Manville and other corporations could no longer rely on managing information, and conceded the dangers of asbestos by attaching health warnings to its products, but by that time the commercial use of asbestos was at its height.[29]

The Environmental Protection Agency (EPA) attempted a ban on the manufacture and sale of around 84 per cent of asbestos products in the United States in 1989, but manufacturers used the courts to overturn the ban. The 5th Circuit Court of Appeals in New Orleans reflected the anti-regulatory consensus of the period and ruled in favour of the asbestos companies. The court blamed the EPA for 'its failure to give adequate weight to statutory language requiring it to promulgate the least burdensome, reasonable regulation required to protect the environment adequately'. The argument that the ban would have potentially damaging economic consequences won over the EPA's well-supported case that asbestos is a potential carcinogen at all levels of exposure. The administration of President George Bush Sr would not allow the EPA to appeal the case and the asbestos companies were allowed to market their products with minimal government regulation. As Michael Bowker concluded in his study of the continuing dangers of asbestos in America, the asbestos lobby 'included some of the wealthiest and most powerful companies in the world', listing 11 corporations, including Raybestos-Manhattan, National Gypsum and Union Carbide: 'Few politicians dared take on the asbestos Goliath.'[30]

The result of corporate deception and political weakness is an immense death toll from asbestos-related diseases. A study by the Environmental Working Group, an advocacy group that researches health issues, has estimated that 100,000 Americans will die in the decade following 2004 from diseases caused by exposure to asbestos 20 to 40 years ago when commercial use was at its height.[31] The current response of the asbestos industry is to join an increasingly powerful chorus of business interests calling for tort reform to reduce class-action lawsuits and cut the amount of damages to victims of corporate fraud. The administration of George W. Bush is likely to be receptive to such calls.

★

Consumers as well as workers are at risk from corporate fraud. Although it is not illegal to sell unsafe products, it is illegal to make deceptive statements to increase sales or avoid expensive lawsuits.[32] There is a long list of products that have caused death and injury to Americans. Amongst the better known cases are the burn deaths of 180 people resulting from the poorly designed gas tank on Ford Pintos that caught fire with little impact, and the 38 deaths due to toxic shock syndrome attributed to the use of Procter and Gamble's Rely tampons. Evidence in both cases suggests that corporate officials knew very well that the use of their products could be lethal.[33]

Americans also run risks with adulterated food products, dangerous prescription or over-the-counter drugs and breast implants, but the cigarette is the single product responsible for most deaths. Tobacco industry executives had been well aware since the early 1960s and from their own research that cigarettes contained cancer-causing elements but it was decades before they were forced by court action to admit their product endangered health.[34] In 1995 the American Medical Association (AMA) charged that the industry had deceived the public by concealing decades of research on the harmful effects of smoking and that the tobacco industry 'has used its money to distort the truth, influence politicians and intimidate any who would expose its secrets'. Many once secret documents support the AMA's charges such as memos, for example, showing that corporate officials have a long history of intending to destroy incriminating evidence. One case in the 1970s involved the cigarette manufacturer Philip Morris secretly commissioning a German research laboratory to do biological studies that might have yielded unwanted results. In a handwritten note, the company's director of research described a clandestine channel for checking on the progress of research, stating that 'if important letters or documents have to be sent, please send them to home, where I will act on them and destroy'.[35] In the 1980s, Philip Morris went even further by using the threat of economic reprisals to intimidate a drug firm marketing a product designed to help smokers give up. When Merrell Dow put Nicorette gum on the market, Philip Morris cancelled chemical purchases from Merrell Dow's parent company, Dow Chemical. Dow responded by downplaying its advertising campaign for the gum so that the appeal was limited to a narrow band of smokers. Dow assured Philip Morris that it was not in the anti-smoking business and the chemical orders were resumed.[36]

From the beginning of 1990 through 1994, more than 2 million American deaths were attributed to smoking, according to the US Centers for Disease Control.[37] Subsequent figures suggest smoking continues to kill more than 400,000 Americans a year.[38] The tobacco industry, as Stephen Rosoff and his colleagues argue in *Profit Without Honor* (2003), symbolizes the 'postponed violence' of white-collar crime: 'Although it is less obvious, less immediate, and less directly traceable to its perpetrators than the violence associated with street crime, it is no less devastating to its victims.'[39]

As Eric Schlosser graphically demonstrated in *Fast Food Nation* (2002), both workers and consumers are endangered by changes in the meat industry. After years of union struggle, workers in the meat-packing industry had achieved decent wages and conditions, until the 1960s and the beginnings of 'disassembly line' production that eliminated the need for skilled workers: 'Each worker stood in one spot along the line, performing the same simple task over and over again, making the same knife cut thousands of times during an eight-hour shift.' These new processes were pioneered by Iowa Beef Packers (IBP) who also began to locate their slaughterhouses in rural areas 'close to the feedlots – and far away from the urban strongholds of the nation's labour unions'. As other corporate meat-packing concerns followed suit a once well-paid, relatively safe job became a low-paid and high-injury job often taken by desperate illegal immigrants.[40] Schlosser lists the names of job assignments at a modern slaughterhouse to convey some of the brutality inherent in the work: Knocker, Sticker, Shackley, Rumper, First Legger, Knuckle Dropper, Navel Boner, Splitter Top/Bottom Butt, Feed Kill Chain. 'Meatpacking', he continues,

> is now the most dangerous job in the United States. The injury rate in a slaughterhouse is about three times higher than the rate in a typical American factory. Every year more than one-quarter of the meatpacking workers in this country – roughly forty thousand men and women – suffer an injury or a work-related illness that requires medical attention beyond first aid. There is strong evidence that these numbers, compiled by the Bureau of Labor Statistics, understate the number of meatpacking injuries that occur. Thousands of additional injuries and illnesses most likely go unrecorded.[41]

Unrecorded and, of course, uncompensated. The power of the corporations and the weakness of government regulatory agencies means that most criminal activity in the slaughterhouses goes unpunished.

Such regulatory neglect is unfortunately not restricted to the meat industry. From 1982 to 2002, the federal Occupational Safety and Health Administration (OSHA) investigated 1,242 cases of workplace death that were potential crimes. Workers decapitated on assembly lines, shredded in machinery, burned, electrocuted or even buried alive. These deaths were not accidents, according to David Barstow of the *New York Times*, they 'happened because a boss removed a safety device to speed up production, or because a company ignored explicit safety warnings, or because a worker was denied proper protective gear'. Yet in 93 per cent of the 1,242 cases OSHA did not seek prosecution. In addition, having been spared prosecution on one occasion, at least 70 of the employers involved continued to violate safety laws, and only a few of these recidivists were prosecuted. The newspapers' reporters found that OSHA, instead of representing the interests of workers at risk from unsafe practices or those of the bereaved family, has increasingly helped employers, particularly corporate employers, avoid the threat of prosecution altogether. Current and former OSHA officials told reporters of 'a bureaucracy that fails to reward, and sometimes penalizes, those who push too hard for prosecution, where aggressive enforcement is suffocated by endless layers of review, where victims' families are frozen out but companies adeptly work the rules in their favor'.[42]

Consumers have of course benefited from cheaper meat but inadequate regulation puts many of them at risk. Government inspectors monitoring the Shapiro Packing meat plant, for example, found faeces on carcasses moving down the processing line on more than 50 days in the first half of 2001. Faeces are a host for bacteria that can be fatal to consumers and Shapiro meat ended up in schools, supermarkets and fast-food restaurants across the country. Despite these and other safety violations, the Department of Agriculture's response to this repeat offender was slow and weak.[43] Schlosser also documents some of the health costs involved in mass food production:

> Every day in the United States, roughly 200,000 people are sickened by a foodborne disease, 900 are hospitalized, and fourteen die. According to the Centre for Disease Control and Prevention (CDC), more than a quarter of the American population suffers a bout of food poisoning each year. Most of the cases are never reported to authorities or properly diagnosed . . . And there is strong evidence not only the incidence of food-related illnesses has risen in the past few decades, but also that the lasting health consequences of such illnesses are far more serious than was previously believed. The acute phase of the food poisoning – the initial few days of diarrhoea and gastrointestinal upset – in many cases may simply be the most obvious manifestation of an infectious disease. Recent studies have found that many foodborne pathogens can precipitate long-term ailments, such as heart disease, inflammatory bowel disease, neurological problems, autoimmune disease and kidney damage.

Medical researchers have found important links between modern food processing and the spread of dangerous diseases, but regulatory efforts to address the problem are blocked by the agribusiness lobby and its Republican party allies. 'Today', Schlosser concludes, 'the US government can demand the nationwide recall of defective softball bats, sneakers, stuffed animals, and foam-rubber toy cows. But it cannot order a meatpacking company to remove contaminated, potentially lethal ground beef from fast food kitchens and supermarket shelves.'[44]

Price-fixing is another form of corporate fraud that gives the lie to the common assumption that American business is a system of free enterprise that works in the interests of consumers. Price-fixing conspiracies are a 'way of life', according to 58 per cent of the presidents of the nation's largest industrial firms.[45] In recent years, courts or government agencies have found these conspiracies operating in many industries, including:

steel, lead smelting, glass, oil drilling, natural gas, trash hauling, road building, electrical contracting, commercial explosives, disability insurance, urology services, athletic shoes, residential doors, scouring pads, plastic dinnerware, toys, video games, motion pictures, infant formula, soft drinks, white bread and Passover matzo.[46]

One of the best-documented cases of price-fixing in recent years involved Archer Daniels Midland (ADM), a major agribusiness concern that called itself 'the Supermarket to the World'. It had grown dramatically from the late 1960s, thanks largely to the energetic efforts by its chairman Dwayne Andreas in cultivating political leaders from both major parties with large campaign contributions and getting their support in return. ADM's main business was processing grains and other farm staples into oils, flours and fibres and its products could be found in everything from baby food to detergents, but in 1989 it took a new direction by entering the field of biotechnology, feeding dextrose from corn to tiny microbes. The microbes, or 'bugs' as they were called, converted the sugar into an amino acid called lysine, which could be used in animal feed to bulk up chickens and pigs, making it the ideal product to sell to giant food companies like Tyson and ConAgra.[47]

After an intensive FBI investigation, built largely around the co-operation of ADM executive Mark Whitacre, the company was found to be heavily involved in international price-fixing arrangements involving citric acid as well as lysine and required to pay a then record $100 million fine in 1996. Whitacre was willing to 'wear a wire' so that meetings could be taped and helped arrange secret video surveillance and so we have a record of the routine nature of much corporate criminal activity. Amongst the revelations was the common assumption of corporate officials that competitors should be 'friends' against the common 'enemy' – customers. The extra pennies and dimes paid by these customers at supermarkets throughout the world amounted to millions of dollars of extra profits for ADM and its co-conspirators.[48] As a complication to the story, Whitacre himself was convicted of criminal activity, stealing around $9 million from a company that already paid him handsomely.

ADM's $100 million fine was little more than a slap on the wrist for a company that held over $2 billion in cash at the time and its stock actually rose following the settlement.[49] The ADM case did, however, reveal large-scale corporate greed and an almost complete contempt for law. Not for the last time it confirmed the accuracy of Adam Smith's observation made more than two centuries earlier in *The Wealth of Nations*, 'people of the same trade seldom meet together, even for merriment and diversion, but the conversation ends in a conspiracy against the public, or in some contrivance to raise prices.'[50]

★

Beginning in the 1970s, Americans began to take far greater risks with their savings, and the ongoing mutual fund scandal shows that opportunities for fraud have increased as the large pool of invested money has grown. Mutual funds were thought to be a secure investment and were favoured by people for retirement plans or their children's college funds. Now around 95 million Americans, representing about half the households in the country, invest in mutual funds, but these investments have often been unsafe.[51] As Frank Partnoy details in *Infectious Greed* (2004), actively managed mutual funds have often been the riskiest because they give fund managers incentives to take excessive risks: 'Investors who buy funds based on past performance are taking on more risk than they think – in many cases, those funds have performed well historically because they invested in companies that had hidden risks or were involved in fraudulent accounting schemes.' He cites a case involving Enron, now a byword for corporate corruption, and Alliance Capital Management, the gigantic mutual fund. Alliance allowed one of its portfolio managers to make a huge bet on Enron, buying shares at prices ranging from $9 to $80. Alliance became Enron's largest shareholder by 2001, with 43 million shares, worth several billion dollars, until Enron's frauds became public knowledge. Even with such a vast investment, top managers at Alliance failed to dig beneath the hyped-up surface of Enron. When Alliance did sell its shares they were worth 28 cents per share, a fraction of their former value, and Alliance investors paid the price. By contrast, Alliance paid the portfolio manager who made the original gamble on Enron $2 million in 2001![52]

In 2003 New York State Attorney General Eliot Spitzer launched a campaign against mutual fund industry abuse by focusing on two methods of improper trading: 'late trading' and 'market timing'. Late trading involves buying mutual fund shares at the 4 p.m. price after the market closes. This, as Spitzer pointed out, was like 'allowing betting on a horse race after the horses had crossed the finish line' and was clearly illegal. Market timing exploits the lag between the pricing of a mutual fund share and its net asset value by buying and then selling the fund once it has been repriced. Each of these trading practices cuts the value of shares held by long-term investors. On 3 September 2003, Canary Capital Partners, a large hedge fund, agreed to settle with Spitzer's office for $40 million based on charges that it engaged in such illegal trading practices and since then revelations about the practices of other hedge funds and mutual funds have continued.[53] The integrity of the fund industry is now in tatters and the college and retirement plans of many hard-working Americans severely jeopardized by fraud.

★

Even Americans facing death have no respite from corporate fraud. Private nursing homes, like those for the mentally ill mentioned earlier, mushroomed as federal Medicare and Medicaid funds became available. More than 2 million Americans now live out their final days in nursing homes that are run for profit and staffed by low-paid workers. A continuing stream of horror stories shows that abuse is common. Some of the worst nursing home abuses have been reported in North Carolina, as Stephen Rosoff and his colleagues detail in *Profit Without Honor* (2003). Home operators in that state made substantial contributions to state and local politicians, 'and have profited in return by slack regulation and a ineffectual sanctioning system of paltry fines'. One of the cases they detail involved an 89-year-old patient whose hands, face and vagina swelled abnormally for a period of at least 16 days. No doctor was called even as her condition got worse. 'One morning, a nurse found her with "frothy mucous" around her mouth and "puffy breathing", but did not even check her vital signs or assess her condition. The patient died 25 minutes later.'[54]

As with most areas associated with America's health care system, nursing homes provide opportunities for fraud. There are many examples of companies systematically overcharging Medicare for services such as therapy. One case involved a company billing Medicare for $8,415, of which a $4,598 fee was charged just for processing the claim![55]

Those readers who have watched the television series *Six Feet Under* will not be surprised to find that this survey of organized, criminal activity and the American life cycle will be almost completed by a description of recent cases of funeral fraud. A particularly gruesome example of this was revealed in February 2002 when law enforcement officers discovered at least 120 rotting corpses in sheds and on the ground near the Tri-Crematory in Noble, Georgia. Vernon Keenan, assistant director of the state Bureau of Investigation, said, 'There were bodies stacked like cordwood, just discarded and thrown in a pile.' The crematorium operator, Ray Brent Marsh, was arrested and faced 787 state felony charges mainly involving theft by deception. In January 2005 Marsh was sentenced to 12 years in prison for dumping 334 bodies. Marsh was simply taking people's money and then failing to do the cremation.[56]

The amounts Marsh made pale by comparison with the profits of the four corporate funeral-industry giants who control the market and set the prices of most American funeral parlours. The country's largest funeral service provider, Service Corporation International (SCI), had by 1995 gained control of over 1,494 funeral homes, 275 cemeteries and 102 crematoriums. In addition they acquired conveniently situated florist shops and death-product manufacturers, in 'calculated demographic buying binges – they go where the dying is', using the words of the *Consumer Digest*. SCI and its fellow industry giants also lobby hard to influence the legislation that governs this minimally regulated industry. Abuses are, not surprisingly, common, and SCI was itself faced with a class-action lawsuit based on the mishandling of bodies and the desecration of graves at two of its cemeteries. In March 2004 a Florida judge indicated preliminary approval of a $100 million settlement of the case.[57]

A description of the lucrative trade in body parts is a grimly appropriate end to this life-cycle survey. According to John Broder, writing in the *New York Times*, those who seek body parts for profit constantly approach others involved in handling corpses, including licensed funeral directors and morgue workers, and many are tempted. He cites numerous cases involving mistreatment of the dead. One of these involved Michael Francis Brown, the owner of a crematorium in Riverside Country, California, who was convicted in 2003 of embezzlement and the mutilation of corpses. He received 20 years in prison for illegally removing and selling heads, knees, spines and other parts from bodies he was supposed to cremate and making more than $400,000 in the process. Subsequently, Broder cites a scandal at the cadaver laboratory of the University of California, Los Angeles (UCLA). In March 2004, the university suspended its Willed Body Program and university police arrested the programme's director and a man accused of trafficking in as many as 800 cadavers in a six-year body-parts-for-profit scheme. The business was well organized, according to Vidal Herrera, a morgue professional interviewed by the newspaper. 'It's no secret,' Herrera said. 'Everybody knows who to call – the buyers, the sellers, the disarticulators, the schools, the crematoriums. It's a lucrative business.' He described the business as a world of 'thugs, hacksaws and back-alley body pickups'. Tissue, organs and bone can be illegally procured from university programmes like UCLA's, hospital and county morgues that perform autopsies, and crematoriums and funeral homes. Middlemen serve the needs of the medical companies and medical societies who want raw material for their doctors and researchers. Some of the growing demand for body parts is provided legally as the remains of more Americans are signed over by their relatives to disarticulators for medical study to cut down on the high costs of burial. But when legitimate ways cannot be found, Herrera said, middlemen 'come calling'. A man with a van is dispatched to a crematorium to pick up boxes of arms and legs and heads. Later, he continued, 'someone is handed an urn of ashes. Who's going to know?'[58]

None of the cases referred to in this chapter involved a member of the Mafia or any of the other supercriminal organizations that constitute organized crime according to government sources. Governments that focus their organized-crime control efforts on the Mafia or the 'Mob' or any other nebulous abstraction are merely fooling themselves and their citizens by implying that organized crime can be isolated and dealt with simply by giving more power and resources to law-enforcement agencies. By contrast, the implication of this life-cycle survey is that organized crime is too embedded in the American economy for such a simple solution to work. Genuine organized-crime control would require much more fundamental reforms and an admission that the American record on such crime control is shameful rather than admirable.

2

Barons, Crusaders and the Land of Criminal Opportunity, 1880–1920

In 1934, during the depths of the greatest economic crisis of the twentieth century, the writer Matthew Josephson helped explain to Americans how they had got into such a desperate situation. In *Robber Barons* (1962), Josephson wrote authoritatively about the rise of such giants of capital as John D. Rockefeller in oil, Andrew Carnegie in steel and J.P. Morgan in banking. These magnates had originally grown wealthy in the final decades of the nineteenth century, conquering large parts of US industry and finance during the post-Civil War era, an era described by Josephson as 'a paradise of freebooting capitalists, untrammelled and untaxed'.[1] The booty amassed by these industrial and commercial titans did not lie idle. It helped propel the stock market boom of the 1920s, making the families and corporations of America's economic founding fathers richer while the masses of American workers and farmers saw their wages and incomes stagnate or decline. Josephson described the ruthless, brutal, corrupt and very successful means by which the original robber-baron fortunes were amassed.

Various forms of organized fraud and theft were commonplace. One notable example involved the combining of various New York street railways into the Metropolitan Street Railway Company by William C. Whitney and Thomas F. Ryan in the early twentieth century. This merger, according to another historian of business crime, Gustavus Myers, was 'accompanied by a monstrous infusion of watered stock'. Hundreds of millions of dollars of worthless stock were sold to the public while Whitney and Ryan became multi-millionaires. A contemporary noted that the 'Metropolitan managers have engaged in a deliberate scheme of stealing trust funds, their own stockholders' money. Their crimes comprise conspiracy, intimidation, bribery, corrupt court practices, subordination of perjury, false reporting, the payment of unearned dividends year after year, the persistent theft of stockholders' money, carried on over a long period by a System constituting the basest kind of robbery.'[2]

Although this scandal attracted the attention of New York's financial press in 1907 and 1908, the intimidation, bribery and destruction of evidence was successful and Ryan kept his loot, conveniently put most of the blame for the whole affair on Whitney, who had died early in 1908, and went on to enhance his reputation in a world where money was worshipped no matter its origins.

American industrialists at the beginning of the twentieth century were far more careless about human life than most gangsters. Government statistics indicated that industrial accidents killed 35,000 workers each year and maimed 500,000 others. The overall accident rate in American coal mines in the period between 1900 and 1906 was almost four times that of France and twice that of Prussia.[3] As one historian has concluded, 'Speed-ups, monotonous tasks, and exposure to chemical toxins, metallic, and organic dusts, and unprotected machinery made the American workplace among the most dangerous in the world.'[4]

The workers most at risk were recently arrived immigrants. Over 3,000 (nearly 25 per cent) of recent immigrants employed at the Carnegie Steel Works in Pittsburgh alone were killed or injured each year between 1907 and 1910. Employers were doubtless aware that language problems would make it far more difficult for the victims' families to press for compensation. The accident rate for non-English-speaking workers in many industries was frequently twice that of the rest of the workforce. In 1911 Arno Dosch illuminated this situation in an article for *Everybody's Magazine* entitled, 'Just Wops'. He included the following comment from a manager's assistant of a construction company about a recently excavated railroad cut after noting that the newspapers had reported no casualties: 'There wasn't anyone killed except just wops.' When asked to elaborate on what wops were, the assistant replied, 'Dagos, niggers, and Hungarians – the fellows that did the work. They don't know anything, and they don't count.'[5]

Legal restraints were at most inconveniences to major business concerns before the Great Depression, to be ignored or circumvented. Daniel Drew, one of the most notorious of the early railroad barons, was reported to have observed: 'The law is like a cobweb: it's made for flies and the smaller kinds of insects, so to speak, but lets the big bumblebees break through ... When technicalities of the law stood in my way, I have always been able to brush them aside easy as anything.'[6] His rival and contemporary Cornelius Vanderbilt made the same point more concisely, 'Law. What do I care about the law. Ain't I got the power?'[7] Others similarly ignored laws and regulations that impeded the accumulation of profits.

Robber barons, their representatives and those seeking to emulate their success shared certain Social Darwinist assumptions that dominated American thinking during this period and served to excuse crimes committed by those in positions of power. At the end of the nineteenth century, the English philosopher Herbert Spencer and his American equivalent William Graham Sumner reshaped the Darwinian concept of the 'survival of the fittest'. They found ways to apply it to all aspects of human society, not just to the animal and plant kingdoms. Social Darwinism conveniently rationalized the success of the few even if it involved violence and theft and the failures of the many. From this perspective, success was the result of being superior. The rich are rich because they deserve to be and the poor deserve their fate because they are biological and social failures and therefore unable to succeed in the competitive struggle. Aspects of this philosophy not only permeated American business circles during this period but also American academia, journalism and politics, and it has remained influential ever since.

Using arguments based on Social Darwinism, social reforms such as welfare to the poor were opposed because they rewarded the unfit and penalized those considered fit through the necessary taxation. Poverty, according to Spencer, was nature's way of 'excreting ... unhealthy, imbecile, slow, vacillating, faithless members of society'.[8] Welfare reforms, Sumner argued, would interfere with the normal workings of society, halting progress and perhaps even contributing to a regression to an earlier evolutionary stage. In fact, according to this way of thinking, the government should interfere with the economy and society as little as possible. *Laissez-faire* was justified because individual self-interest was said to be socially beneficial, putting more people to work and keeping the cost of goods low. Social Darwinism gave business interests forceful and consistent arguments to maintain their free hand in the market. They promised that in enriching themselves they 'would build up the country' or as Andrew Carnegie put it, 'Millionaires are the bees that make the most honey and contribute most to the hive even after they have gorged themselves full.'[9]

Social Darwinism was challenged of course, most significantly by the progressive reformers of the first two decades of the twentieth century. These mainly middle-class citizens were appalled by evidence of the brutality and corruption of big business presented in popular investigative or 'muckraking' journals such as *McClure's*. They responded with calls to check capitalism, emphasizing government as a benevolent influence balancing the claims of selfish, private, business interests with the wider public interest. Despite some minor reform, however, the walls of *laissez-faire* and selfish, private interest were still intact by the end of the First

World War and they were fortified when Warren Harding became the first of three conservative Republican presidents to be elected in the 1920s. Business influence on these administrations was clear from their policies, based as they were on cutting taxes on the wealthy, impeding the growth of trade unions and only regulating business activity when it suited the interests of big business. There were few checks and balances on the world of business in America until the 1930s and criminals from all walks of life would take their chances.

★

Although contemptuous about laws that attempted to restrain their activities, however, these founders of American big business and their successors did care about order. They wanted their workers and consumers to be well disciplined. In particular, they cared about moral order and added their weight to many of the campaigns to make America a more moral and abstinent society during this period.

The United States experienced its most significant moral crusade in the first two decades of the twentieth century. As millions of migrants and immigrants struggled to make new lives for themselves in the cities, many native-born Americans saw a threat to the dominance of Protestant values. These reacted by forming or joining anti-vice, anti-alcohol societies, and lobbying intensely in state capitals and city halls for laws to eradicate gambling, prostitution and drug-taking throughout the entire country.

Working-class morality and abstinence made dollar-sense in many ways to the business interests that provided much of the financial backing and political pull in the campaigns that put morality on the statute books. Drinking, gambling, prostitution and drug-taking diverted wages from the purchase of manufactured goods; if wages were not spent on wasteful activities there would be less demand for wage rises. Alcohol hit work efficiency at a time when most managers were searching for ways to get more productivity out of their workers. Business interests also used their alliance with prohibitionists and America's preoccupation with vice and crime to divert the reform element from attacks on corporate corruption and other economic evils. Finally, businessmen believed that the way saloons had become the focus of working-class political and economic activity was simply not in their interests. It was unacceptable to them that labour unions were using the saloons to recruit and organize workers.[10]

The success of the campaigns to prohibit alcohol and drugs can only partly be explained by the undoubted harm that these substances can do to individuals. Although the campaigns did detail many of the sad and sometimes tragic consequences of alcoholism and drug addiction, they would not have succeeded without the mobilization of a particularly virulent racism across the country. Mass immigration and migration of non-white groups from the late nineteenth century onwards led to an ignorant backlash from America's white majority, stirred by moralistic politicians and organizations. Chinese, African-Americans and Mexicans, in particular, were vilified and perceived as having habits that threatened the American mainstream. Opium consumption was associated with Chinese immigrants, cocaine with blacks and, from the 1920s, marijuana with Mexicans. In 1910, for example, the *Report on the International Opium Commission* claimed that cocaine made rapists of black males and that blacks achieved immense strength and cunning under its influence. Dr Hamilton Wright, the man most responsible for this report and for much of the national and international anti-drug effort that followed, came to the conclusion that 'this new vice, the cocaine vice, the most serious to be dealt with, has proved to be the creator of criminals and unusual forms of violence, and it has been a potent incentive in driving the humbler negroes all over the country to abnormal crimes.'[11]

The development of American drug-control policies was also shaped by a persistent and dogmatic moralism that survives and influences to the present day. Drugs were thought of as products of the devil, breaking down a person's self-control and leading to consequences on the rest of society that could only be imagined. The moralists who campaigned for anti-drug laws in the late nineteenth century felt that promising damnation for the users of certain kinds of drugs was inadequate given the perceived severity of the problem. For them, drug use, drug production and trafficking were scourges or cancers that had to be extirpated from society.[12] As with gambling, commercialized sex and liquor, the thought of regulating drug use was as unthinkable as regulating violence or robbery. By the early twentieth century America's moral leaders could smell legislative victory and got the laws they wanted to prohibit drugs and make the personal behaviour of millions of Americans a problem that the police were supposed to handle.

The anti-drug laws failed to prevent large numbers of Americans from consuming the newly illegal drugs. Addicts were forced to pay more for their habits and many were prepared to commit crimes to get the needed funds. Their suppliers capitalized on the fact that the laws inflated the value of cocaine and heroin substantially. The main impact of these laws internationally gave a similar boost to criminal activity. The laws made crops that were easy and cheap to grow and substances that were easy and cheap to produce far more profitable. In the New York of the 1920s, as the historian Alan Block narrates, the demand from users and addicts fed a fragmented and sprawling industry in cocaine: 'Cocaine was imported, wholesaled, franchised, and retailed . . . It was traded in movies, theaters, restaurants, cafes, cabarets, pool parlors, saloons, parks, and on innumerable street corners.'[13]

Moralists were wrong to equate drugs with murder or robbery in terms of the criminal sanction. Drug deals involve cash transactions between willing parties; the best evidence is lacking – no injured or robbed citizen complains to the police and serves as a witness. The police therefore had to learn to develop cases through informers and covert methods, before making arrests, seizing evidence and interrogation. Until a case reached the courts, the police controlled the situation totally since they alone decided whether an offence had been committed and whether they had a legal case against the suspect. This situation increased the possibility of corruption and decreased the possibility of ever controlling this corruption. In 1917 the first American police officer was convicted for taking a large bribe to protect a drug trafficking operation.[14] Countless more operations were successfully protected and completed, and at no time since has the anti-drug crusade not been fatally compromised by corruption.

American leaders were never able to accept the reality of drug prohibition. Anti-drug laws made the undesirable problem of dangerous drug use into a tragedy of immense proportions. Instead of changing their approach to drugs, they looked abroad for scapegoat explanations. This allowed them to continue to believe that drug prohibition at home could be achieved by establishing a global drug-prohibition regime. In the 1920s, for example, Richmond P. Hobson, who set up groups with names like the World Narcotics Defense Association to influence press and political opinion, claimed that North America was surrounded by other dangerous continents. According the Hobson, 'South America sent in cocaine; Europe contributed drugs like heroin and morphine; Asia was the source of crude opium and Africa produced hashish.' These poisoned the US by supplying the demonic substances. Asia, in particular, he claimed, was just as responsible for 'the scourge of narcotic drug addiction' as it had been for 'the invasions and plagues of history'.[15] Hobson's ignorant xenophobia was not exceptional in the America of the 1920s and foreigners were thus blamed for the supply of drugs. The fact that the demand came from the richest nation on earth was conveniently passed over.

Global drug prohibition, Hobson argued, was the only answer to this 'malignant racial cancer' which threatened the whole of white civilization. In 1930 Hobson applied unsuccessfully to be the US government's chief anti-drug enforcement officer as Commissioner of the Federal Bureau of Narcotics (FBN). Harry J. Anslinger, the man who got the job, however, shared many of his opinions, racist assumptions and ambitions for a toughened-up national and global response to drugs. Since 1961, as we shall see in Chapter 9, the international response has been to build on the prohibitionist framework designed and implemented by the likes of Wright, Hobson and Anslinger.

Paradoxically, therefore, there was one area of American business life where *laissez-faire* was not thought to be appropriate: the business in 'sin'. Local, state and federal governments were expected to eliminate, not just control, the supply of alcohol and certain kinds of drugs, the selling of sex, and the provision of opportunities to gamble. Owing to the years of moral campaigning, tens of thousands of laws attempted to prohibit these activities. The intention was to end all behaviour that a Protestant culture defined as sinful and non-productive; the result was a vast area of American business opportunity that those prepared to break the law could exploit.

Thus, with a business system wide open to abuse and hundreds of unenforceable morality laws, the stage was set for the 1920s to be a classic period of gangster capitalism. By the end of the decade few intelligent Americans would have disagreed with the verdict of Chicago's most famous gangster, Al Capone, talking to Genevieve Forbes of the *Chicago Tribune*, 'Lady, nobody's really on the legit when it comes down to cases.'[16] Capone himself, if it wasn't for his inability to stay out of prison, was a fair representation of American capitalism in the 1920s.

3

The Racket-ridden Twenties and the Origins of the Great Depression

The number and variety of rackets in the United States during the 1920s and early 1930s was vast. Many Americans knew or at least suspected that politicians, judges, lawyers, bankers and business concerns collected many millions of dollars from frauds, bribes and various forms of extortion. At the same time, business for professional career criminals was also booming. Organized crime was the norm rather than the exception in the American political, business, police and judicial systems. American capitalism was crooked and few seemed to care so long as the nation prospered.

Members of President Warren Harding's administration led the way in the early 1920s, as the Teapot Dome and other related scandals showed. Albert B. Fall, Harding's Secretary of the Interior, forced through the transfer of naval oil reserves from the Navy Department to his own department so that he could lease these reserves, one of which was in Teapot Dome, Wyoming, to private companies. He then took large bribes from oil companies to put millions of dollars' worth of business his friends' way.[1] Equally corrupt deals were found to be common in the Veterans Administration and, in the Department of Justice, bootleggers routinely bought immunity from prosecution.

Corruption in most industries tended to be pervasive but discreet. Corruption in the power industry, however, was too blatant to be ignored. By the end of the decade, aided by the policies and practices of these administrations, a small number of private power companies dominated the gas and electricity industry and made vast profits at the expense of American consumers. They then got their accountants to hide these profits by artificially increasing the value of their investments. These 'write-ups' were a form of the 'stock-watering' already mentioned in connection with the New York street-railway frauds. In the case of the power companies they concealed actual earnings on investment that could be as high as 40 per cent, or even 600 per cent in a few cases. A government commission estimated the value of this inflation at just under a billion dollars, while the power companies were feeding newspapers stories about the superiority of private ownership and the expense and 'socialistic' dangers of municipal, state or federal forms of power supply. If the public had been aware of the stock-watering, they would have been able to demand a reduction in their rates from the public commission or the courts.[2]

Adequate regulation that would have ensured that the power monopolies provided a good, affordable and honest service did not exist. The Federal government had a hands-off approach, leaving any regulation there was to the individual states. State regulators were easily 'captured' by those they regulated. President Herbert Hoover's attitude towards utilities regulation was epitomized by the appointment of James W. Good, the former legal representative of the Alabama Power Company, as head of the Federal Power Commission. Soon afterwards, Good sacked staff members whose zeal had irritated the utilities. Trusting corporate officials to be honest and responsible was thought to be enough.[3]

While corruption in the power industry was based mainly on cronyism, corporate power in other industries had a harder edge. Many companies routinely employed gangsters to damage competitors or break strikes or unions. Brutality and murder had long been a part of newspaper circulation disputes in Chicago, for example. During the 1920s more than two dozen newspaper dealers lost their lives and many hundreds more were injured for selling the wrong newspaper by gangsters representing the interests of either William Randolph Hearst or the McCormick family-owned *Tribune*.[4] Stan Nettleton, who worked for the Hearst *Herald-Examiner*, reflected the almost institutionalized nature of this violence when relating his first day as a circulator:

> The boss was talking to two men as I came in and the boss motioned me to sit down as he went on talking. After a few minutes the boss said to the men, 'Take the kid out and teach him to be a circulator.' We went downstairs to a car by the loading platform and drove out Madison Avenue nearly to Cicero. I was sitting next to the driver in the front seat and the driver says to me, 'Tell the man to bring us a paper.' I called over to the newsstand operator and says, 'Hey, bring us a paper.' When I asked for the paper the newsstand operator walked over and handed me a *Tribune*. When he did that, the man sitting in back of me reached out and hit him over the head with a club, knocking him to his knees. When the man got up, the man who had hit him said, 'Look you bastard, when somebody asks for a paper, you bring him a Hearst paper.' Well, that completed my formal education as a circulator.[5]

Not surprisingly, given the use of such tactics and other illegal activities, newspapers were reluctant to expose the crimes of other corporations.

Violence against unions or even those who supported them was just as pervasive. Standard Oil, for example, paid Pete DeVito half a million dollars in 1929 to break strikes. He did this using thugs to shoot and stab union members, and only came to public attention when he was arrested for failing to pay income tax on his Standard Oil money.[6]

The most prominent American businessman to employ gangsters in the battle against unions was the car manufacturer Henry Ford. His company used both the stick and the carrot to keep unions out. It usually paid better to work for Ford, but the stick was often literally the stick wielded by thugs and gangsters, or fists, or lengths of rubber hoses and, sometimes, guns. As late as 1940 the National Labor Relations Board described Ford methods as 'organized gangsterism'.[7] For decades the Ford Motor Company had been ensuring uninterrupted assembly lines and ever increasing productivity by keeping its Detroit workforce powerless and unorganized.

More costly in terms of lives lost was the widespread corporate violation of laws and practices meant to ensure the safety of their workforce. There are many examples but this form of corporate violence was most vividly illustrated by the death of nearly 500 workers at Gauley Bridge, West Virginia.

In 1929 the New Kanawha Power Company – a Union Carbide subsidiary – chose the Rhinehart-Dennis Construction Company as the subcontractor to build a tunnel near Gauley Bridge. Rhinehart-Dennis recruited a mainly black and unskilled workforce for the task who were desperate for work during the Depression and began the construction of the tunnel in 1930. The workers were forced to work immediately after rock with a heavy silica content was blasted and could not see beyond a few feet even with strong lighting. Although New Kanawha Power warned its engineers to use masks when entering the tunnel, there were no such precautions for the workers.

Most major newspapers ignored or downplayed the tragedy that resulted, but the socialist *People's Press* captured its brutality and injustice:

Their only gravestones cornstalks waving in the wind, their shrouds the overalls in which they died, 169 tunnel workers killed at Gauley Bridge were tossed into trenches in this field at Summerville, W. Va., to rot. As they keeled over in the death tunnel, one at a time or several in a day, choked to death by silicosis, they were hauled 40 miles to Summerville and dumped into the grave the same day. No identification, no coffins. The company paid the undertaker $50 a piece to bury them. A wife who came tearfully to claim the remains of her loved one was quietly driven away. There was no way in which his body could be found. They were all victims

of America's worst industrial disaster. The government officials, newspapers and others conspired to keep this story from the public knowing that
soon the witnesses would all be dead. The 26 foremen are already dead. In
Gauley Bridge, Town of the Living Dead, men once strong and hearty
waste away while loved ones grimly await their death.[8]

An estimate of the project's final human cost put it at 476 dead and 1,500
disabled. Senator Rush Dew Holt of West Virginia called it, 'The most
barbaric example of industrial construction that ever happened in this
world. That company well knew what it was going to do to these men.
The company openly said that if they killed off those men there were
plenty of other men to be had.'[9]

Some survivors took Rhinehart-Dennis and New Kanawha to court for
negligence but the cases were sabotaged by public and private corruption
in West Virginia. The chief of West Virginia's Mines Department testified that he had observed no dust in the tunnel in 1930 or 1931, although
he had written letters to the company in 1931 urging them to do something about the dust condition. One of the jurors was found to be riding
home every night in a company car and there were many more rumours
of jury tampering. Eventually, 167 of the suits were settled out of court
for $130,000, with one-half going to the workers' attorneys. One of the
workers' law firms was later found to have accepted a $20,000 side-
payment from the companies. No punitive action was ever taken against
Rhinehart-Dennis or New Kanawha Power.[10] New Kanawha Power dis-
solved as soon as the tunnel was completed in 1934, but Union Carbide
continued to increase in size and strength, nationally and internationally
until it became one of the world's leading multinationals with 130
subsidiaries in around 40 countries, approximately 500 production sites,
and 120,000 employees. Union Carbide produced everything from industrial gases and fertilizers, to a host of plastic goods including plastic bags
for 80 per cent of American shoppers.[11] In December 1984, as we shall
see in Chapter 17, the company was involved in an episode in Bhopal,
India, that was far more destructive than Gauley Bridge.

Organized crime in the America of the 1920s and 1930s was just as
prevalent in small businesses as in the giant concerns that dominated
markets like oil, gas, electricity, newspapers and car manufacturing.
Florists, butchers, bakers, barbers, coal merchants, ice cream sellers,
window cleaners, drivers, funeral parlours, shirt makers and taxi cab
operators were amongst the scores of small businesses in New York,
Chicago and other towns and cities hit by organized extortion of one form
or another.[12] The term 'racketeering' was coined to describe these
schemes and had become, according to commentators in the *Political*

Quarterly, 'an established philosophy of business, criminal in its ethics, and subversive in its economic and political programme'.[13]

Contemporaries were also aware that instead of enforcing the law, many police forces were running their own rackets. James Thurlow Adams, for example, reporting on an investigation into police corruption for the *New York Times*, noted the following ways in which police officers and court bondsmen used their power as a tool for racketeering:

> Nearly all of the cases which come into the Magistrates' Courts emanate from arrests made by the Police Department. The outcome of these proceedings is largely in the control of the arresting officers, upon whose testimony the case must stand and fall. Experience shows that many police officers have not been blind to the opportunities for extortion which this power puts into their hands. In some cases they would make arrests and immediately offer to sell immunity without requiring the prisoner even to go to the Police Station.

In other cases, as Adams goes on to describe, police co-operated with bondsmen to 'mulct' the defendant of all money possible: 'The procedure was the same whether the person arrested was guilty or whether the arrest was a pure frame-up.'[14]

★

Crime in legal markets like oil, gas, electricity and the host of small businesses mentioned was matched by the crime in those illegal markets that had been created by America's moral crusade.

As a result of the 18th Amendment, known as the Prohibition amendment, and the Volstead Act, trading in beer and spirits was illegal in the United States from 16 January 1920 until 5 December 1933. None the less, Americans who chose to drink carried on drinking. As many commentators pointed out, prohibition made the problems associated with alcohol far worse, creating or worsening a situation of widespread and systematic lawlessness in the country's cities and states.[15] An unenforceable law, corruption and an endless supply of willing customers gave unprecedented opportunities for a new breed of gangsters, many of whom were graduates from street gangs, to emerge as businessmen capable of running quite complex operations. Supplying middle- and upper-class demand for imported spirits, for example, required contracting for the liquor in sometimes distant countries, getting it past the Coast Guard and the Customs, landing it on the docks, loading it on to trucks, carting it to warehouses and delivering it to the retail outlets. And every large-scale smuggling or bootlegging operation needed to pay for gunmen to deter hijackers or to discourage or fight off violent competition at the retail level.

Such competition for markets and territory was fierce, expensive and, at least in the nation's two largest cities, New York and Chicago, relentless. Newspapers made the most of the lurid details. Rival gangsters were simply shot or machine-gunned on the streets. Other methods were more imaginative. Some were 'taken for rides', persuaded or forced into cars and then their brains blown out from behind. Others, notably those involved in Chicago's St Valentine's Day Massacre, were lined up and shot by firing squads. Many were just left dead where they fell but others were disposed of more discreetly, being packed in cement, tied up in sacks or pinioned with wire and then dropped into lakes or rivers. In all, thousands lost their lives because both the liquor trade and the gun trade were unregulated. The murder of a minor bootlegger became so ordinary that newspapers scarcely took notice. Police conducted cursory investigations and no one worried that they never got convictions. Being a gang boss was no protection as the deaths of many demonstrated. Maxie Eisen, a Chicago racketeer, captured the essence of the situation when he was reported as saying, 'We're a bunch of saps killing each other and giving the cops a laugh.'[16]

In 1929 the new president, Herbert Hoover, responding to the bad image these gang wars were giving the country and recognizing the widespread nullification of the 18th Amendment, announced the creation of the National Commission on Law Observance and Enforcement, to be headed by former Attorney General, George Wickersham. After a two-year investigation the Wickersham Commission's reports made it clear that Prohibition had failed to deliver the hard-working and moral population that was promised by its supporters.

The evidence was overwhelming that the dry law had a rotting effect on American society in general and, in particular, on American law enforcement and criminal justice. 'Fixing' cases had become even more of an American institution during Prohibition. There were thousands of arrests but when protected bootleggers stepped in front of judges, district attorneys suddenly found that they had 'insufficient evidence', witnesses failed to turn up, or police officers admitted that they had overstepped themselves in the performance of their duties. The blatant fixing of cases had caused Assistant Attorney General Mabel Willebrandt to complain that she spent more time prosecuting prosecutors than the people they should have prosecuted.[17] Judges were also more prone to the pressures of corruption and anyway were forced to dispense an assembly-line justice to relieve the congestion of the courts.

The Commission's evidence suggested that economic realities would always undermine prohibitionist ideals and that Prohibition had worsened a situation of widespread and systematic lawlessness in America. Its reports gave even more force to the arguments of those who wished to repeal Prohibition by the onset of the Great Depression. More and more Americans were convinced that Prohibition deprived people of legitimate employment, deprived government of revenue, contributed to the continuing economic problems and only succeeded in enriching a few murderous and corrupt individuals. Even the notably pro-American politician Winston Churchill was moved to point out the absurdity of America's dry law to a reporter on a visit in 1929, 'We realize over £100 million a year from our liquor taxes, an amount I understand that you give to your bootleggers.'[18]

In the 1920s most Americans realized that the prohibition of alcohol greatly exacerbated the high crime rate of the decade. In more recent times, a more thorough and imaginative propaganda campaign and the claims of experts who often have a financial stake in the war on drugs have ensured that few Americans understand that the same applies for drugs. What marks out the war on drugs from Prohibition is the replacement of old ideas of moral reform linked to evangelical Christianity with a new drama of all-out warfare between the forces of law and order and the forces of evil represented as mainly foreign enemies producing, smuggling and distributing drugs. Cops and drug dealers have become the new cowboys and Indians.

★

Bootleggers and racketeers like Al Capone, Arnold Rothstein and Dutch Schultz were not the only criminals to attract significant media attention during the 1920s and early 1930s. In fact, after the incarceration of Capone on tax-evasion charges in 1931, the nation was much more interested in the deeds of kidnappers and bank robbers.

In these early Depression years, few Americans were talked or written about more than Bonnie Parker and Clyde Barrow, George 'Baby Face' Nelson, Charles 'Pretty Boy' Floyd and John Dillinger: outlaws, mainly operating in the American South and West, who robbed banks and, for a short while, got away with it. Their methods were similar. They tended to be well armed, often with sub-machine guns, and were willing to take part in shoot-outs with the authorities. They made their escape at speed in cars and, if necessary, crossed state lines where the jurisdiction of their pursuers usually ended.

Even more dramatic than bank robbing was kidnapping, however, where the victim took centre stage. Most dramatic of all was the abduction of the baby son of Charles Lindbergh from his New Jersey home on 1 March 1932. He was only one of nearly 300 kidnap victims that year but his father's place in the hearts of Americans made this crime touch a particularly sensitive nerve. In 1927 Charles Lindbergh had been the first man in history to fly the Atlantic non-stop and single-handed. News of this feat was greeted with unprecedented mass excitement and the adulation lasted long after the 1,800 tons of ticker tape had been swept off the streets of New York. His picture still hung in countless school-rooms and homes when his baby was snatched.

For weeks the kidnapping dominated the news, with Lindbergh and his wife offering immunity to the kidnappers in a signed statement, giving out the hopeful but pathetic details of the baby's diet, and asking two racketeers named Spitale and Bitz to serve as intermediaries with the kidnappers. All to no avail, as the baby's half-buried body was found in a thicket on 12 May, about six weeks after the kidnapping.[19]

This was seen as more than a crime against the individual. According to the *New York Herald Tribune* the kidnapping was 'a challenge to the whole order of the nation . . . The truth must be faced that the army of desperate criminals which has been recruited in the last decade is winning its battle against society.'[20] Hyperbole, of course, but the crime did certainly add to the demoralization of an already demoralized nation.

Federal law enforcement had only the conviction of Capone to impress during the administration of President Herbert Hoover. Meanwhile rack-eteering remained rife, and the series of successful bank robberies con-tinued. But the Lindbergh baby kidnapping above all brought the fear of crime into every American home. The *Saturday Evening Post* was not the only publication to demand a decision on 'who is the Big Shot in the United States – the criminal or the Government?'[21] The president responded to such questions limply and in one more area failed to catch the mood of an increasingly disenchanted nation.

Fraud, corruption and racketeering went so deep as to make an important contribution to the greatest single crisis the United States faced during the twentieth century – the Great Depression.

First, the nation's ramshackle banking structure was as poorly regu-lated as the power industry and, not surprisingly, was just as susceptible to fraud and insider abuse. Much of the vast wealth of cash and credit generated by the American industrial machine was simply stolen rather than usefully invested or spent to improve the lives of those whose work had made it all possible.[22] More than fifty-five hundred banks closed during the 1920s, mainly because insiders looted the banks they were pledged to protect with the complicity and sometimes the co-operation of lawyers and government regulators. The insiders, when they were not involved in simple embezzlement, attempted to use depositors' money in often unsafe and speculative schemes to make more money, and when their schemes failed so did their banks. According to Raymond B. Vickers' study, more than 90 per cent of the bank failures in Florida during the 1920s involved abuse or fraud by insiders. The accepted version of the Florida banking crisis absolved bankers and officials for responsibility for the crash by claiming that a precipitate drop in real estate values created a regional recession that caused an unprecedented number of bank failures. Vickers consulted government records that had been kept secret for 63 years to expose the accepted version as interest-serving fiction.[23]

Fraud was also an important factor in the spectacular bursting of the stock market bubble in October 1929 that wiped out a great proportion of the savings of millions of Americans. Investigations later showed how Wall Street operators conspired with company insiders to manipulate the prices of stocks on the Exchange. The huge profits they made were made mainly at the expense of small investors and played a part in fostering the speculative mania of the 'roaring twenties'. Powerful bankers had also fooled the unwary into buying stocks and bonds through high-pressure salesmanship and had made millions trading in the securities of their own banks at the expense of their own stockholders.[24] Politicians from both major parties took an active part in such frauds, justifying the title of a 1930 book by Emanuel H. Levine, *Gimme: or How Politicians Get Rich*. 'The fact was', as John Kenneth Galbraith put it in his history of *The Great Crash*, 'that American enterprise in the twenties had opened its hospitable arms to an exceptional number of promoters, grafters, swindlers, imposters and frauds. This, in the long history of such activities, was a kind of flood tide of corporate larceny'.[25]

Despite the denials of many economists, corporate fraud and corruption should therefore be accepted as factors contributing to the onset of the Great Depression. America's uneven distribution of income was a more fundamental cause, but that of course was related to some of the crimes we have discussed. According to studies, the top 0.1 per cent of America's families in 1929 had an aggregate income equal to that of the bottom 42 per cent. Seventy-one per cent of American families, in what was the most prosperous year that the country or even the world had ever known, had incomes under $2,500 and the trend was well set to continue. Some of America's 1920s wealth was leaking through to the less well-off but the rich were getting richer at a much more rapid rate than the poor were becoming less poor. This growing gap between rich and poor was caused largely because the productivity and therefore the profitability of American industry were increasing at a far faster rate than wages. A strong union movement would have increased labour's share of the pie but government and employer hostility blocked this happening. Americans were amazingly productive during these years but too few of them could consume at a level sufficient to sustain a healthy economy – mass-production societies require mass consumption at home and abroad to maintain prosperity. As Robert McElvaine explains, uneven distribution of wealth and income was only one amongst many roots of the Great Depression, but 'it was the taproot. It led to both underconsumption and oversaving, and it helped fuel stock speculation.'[26] Shops and factories closed, breadlines in poor parts of cities lengthened, and settlements of shacks constructed from packing boxes and other rubbish sprung up around the outskirts of cities and were given the ironic name of 'Hoovervilles' after their president. More Americans began to wonder why so many of them were going hungry and cold in the midst of plenty.

The explanations, reassurance and help Americans were getting from President Hoover were clearly inadequate. He continually played down the depth and seriousness of the Depression. He believed that the country's problems were more psychological than economic and claimed that a return of confidence in American business would be shortly followed by economic recovery. He supported a public works programme to find work for some Americans but his intervention in the economy fought shy of structural reform since he believed that the capitalist system was essentially sound. 'The only trouble with capitalism', he confided to a friend, 'is capitalists, they're too damn greedy.'[27]

Hoover's failings concerned many of the nation's business elite. They felt that many citizens would lose faith in the American business system itself and might perhaps turn to socialism, communism or fascism as a result. The possibility that the Depression would lead to a wider breakdown in law and order amongst the poor and recently dispossessed also served to concentrate their minds. Fifteen million men were out of work, thousands of 'panhandlers' or beggars walked the streets, and riots broke out in several cities. In some cities businessmen formed committees to take control 'should railroad and telephone lines be cut and surrounding highways blocked'.[28] New York hotels found that 'wealthy guests who usually leased suites for the winter were holing up in their country homes'.[29] Some even had machine guns mounted on their roofs. In this context of fear and insecurity, along with a widespread cross-class acknowledgement that the Depression was showing American capitalism to be flawed, perhaps fatally, structural reform became a requirement rather than an option for many of the powerful as well as the powerless in America. Americans needed a type of capitalism that worked, not the gangster capitalism they had. They needed a saviour, not just a president, when they voted at the end of 1932.

4

The New Deal and Organized Crime

Unfinished Business, 1933–45

Franklin Delano Roosevelt's campaign for president in 1932 made it clear that his intention was both to rescue and to clean up capitalism at home. He had partially succeeded in the first of these aims by the end of his second term and the great boost the Second World War gave to the American economy completed the rescue. Although the effort to clean up capitalism would stall, some important steps were taken. New Deal reform did make America less vulnerable to the brutalities and chicanery of a *laissez-faire* system and in this and in other ways made the country a less hospitable place for career criminals, racketeers and corporate criminals. During this period the US government addressed the problem of organized crime in a wider sense than the sense in which it is understood today and thus it did more than simply lock up bad guys. There were, as we shall see, limits to the New Deal's effectiveness against organized crime in America, but this period of reform was the only time in American history when the opportunities for organized crime diminished.

In Roosevelt's 1932 presidential campaign, he constantly attacked the inadequacy of Hoover's response to the Depression and by extension the *laissez-faire* philosophy it represented. Hoover's limited measures, he told Americans in an April radio address, might be desirable but they were inadequate: 'A real economic cure', he emphasized, 'must go to the killing of the bacteria in the system rather than to the treatment of the external symptoms.'[1]

The best American minds had been concentrated by America's economic plight. Every thoughtful commentator knew that the Depression had shown that something was fundamentally wrong with American capitalism and that the cure would involve much more than the orthodox dependence on the market righting itself. There was Adolph Berle, for example, a law professor who co-wrote one of the most significant analyses of modern capitalism in *The Modern Corporation and Private Property* in 1932 and who later joined Roosevelt's famous 'brains trust' of advisers. Berle believed that corporate power needed to be checked and made more accountable to the state, funnelled into the service of 'the paramount interests of the community'. A community he defined as a collection of all those affected by the workings of corporate organizations, not just capital but also labour, consumers and government. There needed to be new forms, in other words, of public control over corporate power.[2]

Others wrote in more scathing terms of the problems of capitalism exacerbated by *laissez-faire*, including the many opportunities to organize and profit from crime. Contemporary commentators such as Charles Beard, Walter Lippmann and Murray Gurfein made the clear suggestion that organized crime was one of the unfortunate products of unfettered capitalism. It followed from their analyses that more rigorous business regulation was necessary to lessen the opportunities for successful organized crime in legal markets. In 1931 Charles Beard, the leading historian of the time, wrote an article on the widely disseminated myth that America's greatness was based on 'rugged individualism': 'The cold truth is that the individualist creed of everybody for himself and the devil take the hindmost is principally responsible for the distress in which Western civilization finds itself – with investment racketeering at one end and labor racketeering at the other . . . It has become a danger to society.'[3]

The same year Lippmann, one of the most influential newspaper columnists, recommended that Americans should at least enquire 'whether certain forms of racketeering are not the result under adverse conditions of the devotion of legislatures, courts, and public opinion to the philosophy of laissez faire'.[4] Gurfein, a respected New York lawyer, wrote a definitional essay on 'racketeering' that can be seen as remarkably prescient given the wave of corporate scandals that followed the Enron collapse in 2002. He listed the following characteristics of the American business system as key to the problem of organized crime: 'the pegged market in stocks, the manipulation of subsidiary companies, the reckless puffing of securities, the taking by corporate management of inordinately large bonuses, the rather widespread evasion of taxes, the easy connivance of politicians in grabs'. These 'illustrated the temper of the times' and furnished 'a key to the parasitical racketeer', he continued. 'The racketeer as a type', he summed up, 'is a natural evolutionary product of strict laissez faire.'[5]

Roosevelt himself made specific points about the connections between organized crime and capitalism but, of course, had to be circumspect in his language. In a speech in April 1932, this time to an audience in Portland, Oregon, he launched a strong attack on the power companies and the absence of government control over their fraudulent practices. 'Electricity', he argued 'is no longer a luxury. It is a definite necessity. It lights our homes, our places of work and our streets. It turns the wheels of most of our transportation and our factories ... Selfish interests', he continued, had made this crucial resource too expensive for widespread public use, 'private manipulation had outsmarted the slow-moving power of government.' Referring to the complex web of companies and subsidiaries put together to form the business empire of Chicago-based businessman, Samuel Insull as a 'monstrosity', Roosevelt then detailed the ways in which both the public and investors had been cheated out of billions of dollars:

> They did not realize that there had been arbitrary write-ups of assets, inflation of vast capital accounts. They did not realize that excessive prices had been paid for property acquired ... They did not realize that ... subsidiaries had been milked and milked to keep alive the weaker sisters of the great chain. They did not realize that there had been borrowing and lending between the component parts of the whole. They did not realize that all these conditions misstated terrific overcharges for service by these corporations.

Roosevelt blamed the inadequacy of federal and state regulation for allowing these conditions to develop. This allowed, he said, 'many utility companies to get around the common law, to capitalize themselves without regard to actual investment made in property, to pyramid capital through holding companies and, without restraint of law, to sell billions of dollars' worth of securities which the public has been falsely led into believing were properly supervised by the Government itself'. The public, he concluded, 'has been fleeced out of millions of dollars'.

As a solution to the massive fraud and extortion of the power companies, he proposed a far more positive role for government in the regulation of industry in general and the power industry in particular. Power companies had been able to fleece the public because their deals had been mainly conducted behind closed doors, and Roosevelt demanded, amongst his remedies, 'full publicity as to all capital issues of stock, bonds and other securities; liabilities and indebtedness; capital investment; and frequent information as to gross and net earnings'. Let us 'turn on the light', he demanded, echoing a recurring theme amongst those who wished to check the flaws and abuses of unfettered capitalism.[6] 'Publicity', as he put it in a later speech, 'is the enemy of crookedness.'[7]

The need to control capitalism was also the theme of his most famous campaign speech on 22 May. Addressing the students and faculty of Oglethorpe University, he spoke about the gigantic waste of America's industrial advance, 'much of which could have been prevented by greater foresight and by a larger measure of social planning'. Instead of this advance being directed in the national interest, he charged that it was under the control of small groups of special interests. The nation could no longer allow 'our economic life to be controlled by that small group of men whose chief outlook upon the social welfare is tinctured by the fact that they can make huge profits from the lending of money and the marketing of securities . . . We need to correct, by drastic means if necessary, the faults in our economic system from which we now suffer.'[8]

Roosevelt had thus set himself apart from Hoover and his own rivals for the Democratic nomination by finding fault with the structure of American capitalism. He expressed a central belief of liberal thought at the time – that something was wrong with capitalism and government should find a way to repair it.[9]

Roosevelt reiterated the above themes in his speech accepting the Democratic party nomination for president in July and also turned his attention to the only other issue besides the Depression that seriously concerned Americans at the time – Prohibition. We 'must abolish useless offices', he said, referring to the Prohibition Bureau amongst others, and we 'must eliminate unnecessary functions of government'. He then pledged his support for the repeal of the 18th Amendment.[10]

Here Roosevelt was again reflecting the tide of intelligent opinion. Many commentators had made a strong case to the effect that Prohibition and other aspects of America's moral reform programme were at best useless and even counter-productive in their effects. When responding to calls for more police and prisons to be used in the enforcement of Prohibition, for example, Senator Robert Wagner, a powerful political ally of Roosevelt, had asked an unanswerable question, 'Why heap more sacrifice upon the altar of hopelessness?'[11] Roosevelt's support for repeal recognized the strength of such arguments and gave more momentum to the campaign that ended alcohol prohibition on 5 December 1933 when Utah became the final state to ratify the 21st Amendment. Roosevelt was able to announce that Prohibition was at an end, after an existence of nearly 14 years.

The impact was almost immediate. The legalizing of alcohol provided legitimate employment for over a million people in brewing, distilling and related jobs, from bar work to making barrels and pretzels. Federal, state and local tax and licence receipts exceeded a billion dollars yearly by 1940. Two more undoubtedly positive consequences of repeal were that the number of deaths from cheaply made contaminated liquor declined dramatically as did the number of deaths in bootleg gang wars. The prohibition of alcohol was no longer the main financial basis for organized crime in illegal markets. There was no noticeable increase in drunkenness and alcohol-related health problems.[12]

Bootlegging continued to be a flourishing but localized business in the few Southern states that preserved anti-liquor laws. In such states as Mississippi and Oklahoma, the temperance lobby could always rely on the covert support of bootleggers whose business required that the attempt to impose abstinence continued.[13]

In most states, however, gangster bootleggers could not successfully compete once the legal liquor trade was fully established and soon folded up or adapted to the new conditions. Some successfully legitimized smuggling operations to become importers and others of the more thuggish variety were employed by companies to 'persuade' retail outlets to sell particular brands of liquor. Others, such as Abner 'Longy' Zwillman of New Jersey, continued as liquor distributors at the local level. After repeal Zwillman and his partners formed Browne Vintners to distribute liquor in the New York area. In 1940 they sold the company to the giant Seagram corporation for $7.5 million.[14]

Repeal immediately cut off an immense source of illegal income. However, corrupt networks, consisting of gangsters, career criminals, businessmen and public officials, continued to supply the demand for activities that remained prohibited in America, notably gambling, commercialized sex and the use of certain kinds of drugs such as heroin and cocaine.

★

In his speech accepting the Democratic party's nomination for president, Roosevelt announced a crusade to 'restore America to its own people', and pledged 'a new deal for the American people'.[15] When he took office as president in March 1933 he was thus committed to take radical action to restore people's faith in the American system, taking particular aim at the bankers and those in business whose conduct he called 'callous and selfish wrongdoing': 'Practices of the unscrupulous money changers', he charged, 'stand indicted in the court of public opinion.'[16] Roosevelt then began an intense and unprecedented period of legislative and executive activity intended to reform America's corrupted and unproductive system. He explained, in one of his many 'fireside chats' to Americans, the rationale for such a fundamental transformation of American capitalism in September 1934. He told the millions listening on the radio that 'private enterprise in times such as these cannot be left without assistance and without reasonable safeguards lest it destroy not only itself but also our processes of civilization.'[17]

His administration began this task by setting up a key recovery agency, designed to revive industry. The National Recovery Administration (NRA) was an attempt at joint economic planning by government and industry, aiming at stabilizing prices, restricting competition, expanding purchasing power, relieving unemployment and improving working conditions. Although it failed in its primary but probably unachievable aim of economic recovery it did begin processes that significantly reduced gangsterism in American industry.

First, Section 7a of the law which set up the NRA guaranteed the right of collective bargaining, and paved the way for the National Labor Relations Act of 1935. So long as unions did not have the right to bargain collectively on behalf of their members, employers felt it was their right to use any methods, including those practised by gangsters, to suppress them, and in this they were invariably supported by the courts. The new law required more effective enforcement of the right to join trade unions. It created the National Labor Relations Board (NLRB) with the power to bargain on behalf of workers and also to restrain management from employing gangsters to break unions and using other 'unfair labor practices' such as blacklists and company unions. To begin with the NLRB was ineffective but a series of exposures of methods used by industrial corporations to combat unionism in 1936 and 1937 strengthened its hand. These methods included accumulating weapons especially adapted for use in industrial disputes such as sub-machine guns, tear gas, sickening gas, grenades and shells. These weapons were used by the corporations' private police forces against strikers and unionists. Thanks largely to the work of the NLRB, only a few of the die-hard opponents of unionization continued to rely on crude thuggery in anti-union fights.[18]

Legalized price-fixing introduced under the auspices of the NRA also undercut the stabilizing role of the industrial racketeer in such service and small-scale industries as garment manufacturing and trucking, food distribution, laundries and dry-cleaners. In these disordered and cutthroat industries, according to the sociologist Daniel Bell, the racketeer, paradoxically, had played a stabilizing role by regulating competition and fixing prices. 'When the NRA came in and assumed this function', Bell explained, 'the businessman found that what had once been a quasi-economic service was now pure extortion and he began to demand police action.'[19] Business associations, therefore, put increasing pressure on the authorities to act and stamp out this kind of industrial racketeering.

In New York, special prosecutor Thomas E. Dewey was the personification of the authorities' response. He investigated and secured convictions in the poultry and restaurant industries and began an investigation into the bakery, trucking and garment rackets which eventually broke the hold of Lepke Buchalter, Jacob Shapiro and many other gangsters. However, the authorities in New York and elsewhere were much slower to act when it was a case of gangsters infiltrating unions with the compliance or collaboration of employers.[20]

The New Deal did not therefore end mobster involvement in American labour relations but it did mark the beginning of the end for classic industrial racketeers of the Lepke type. The end was slow in coming largely because labour reforms did not attempt to democratize many of the most corrupt unions or to provide any kind of protection for the welfare and pension funds of these corrupt unions. These would be freely looted by criminal hard men for decades to come. Prosecutions for labour racketeering did, however, begin in the 1960s, and there were major successes against such corrupt unions as the Teamsters in the 1970s and 1980s.

Government action at local and federal level during the Roosevelt era ensured not just the conviction of large numbers of gangsters, but also at least some of their political protectors. Foremost amongst the gangsters, at least according to sensationalist press reporting, was Charles 'Lucky' Luciano in New York, who was convicted of organizing a large-scale prostitution racket in 1935. Foremost amongst their political protectors was Jimmy Hines, the corrupt Democratic party political boss of Manhattan's Upper West Side, who was closely associated with the numbers rackets of gangster luminary Dutch Schultz. Both Luciano and Hines were prosecuted and convicted by Thomas E. Dewey. Amidst the law-enforcement 'heat', Schultz met a particularly spectacular gangster death in the Palace Chophouse, New Jersey. The gibberish of his last words included the possibly regretful, 'Mother is the best bet and don't let Satan draw you too fast.'[21]

The agency chosen to represent the New Deal's commitment to making law enforcement more efficient and professional was the Federal Bureau of Investigation (FBI). By 1934 the FBI had been given jurisdiction over a variety of inter-state felonies, such as kidnapping and auto-theft. Its director, J. Edgar Hoover, immediately directed his agents against the bank robbers, who had been avoiding capture by crossing state lines. In rapid succession 'Baby Face' Nelson, 'Pretty Boy' Floyd and John Dillinger were shot down by Mr Hoover's agents. Although some gangsters surrendered and were taken alive, the toughness of the federal response was encapsulated by the much quoted advice to agents by Attorney General Homer S. Cummings, 'Shoot to kill and then count ten.'[22] These gangsters, as we have noted, had been exploiting the limited jurisdiction of local and state police by fleeing across county, city and state lines after robbing banks. By 1936 the FBI could claim with some justification that every kidnapping case in the country, including that of the Lindbergh baby, had been closed.[23] The expectation of a federal presence in these cases undoubtedly encouraged a more committed and professional response by local and state police. Kidnapping became a much more difficult occupation in America from the 1930s onwards.

The Roosevelt administration also used the anti-crime atmosphere of the time to push through much needed gun-control laws. The National Firearms Act authorized the collection of a federal tax on machine guns, silencers, sawed-off shotguns and rifles; the licensing of arms dealers and the registration of weapons and restrictions on the importation of all weapons. The Act, however, was much watered down due to pressure from the National Rifle Association; pistols, automatic hand guns and semiautomatic rifles were removed from coverage and it took no criminal mastermind to saw off a gun barrel![24]

Hoover meanwhile was using his new powers and the keen support of his superiors to build his agency into the most efficient and least corrupt policing agency in the nation. Local and state police forces had shown themselves to be almost universally inefficient and corrupt, and there was thus a need for a federal agency to set standards of professionalism. There was also a need for the FBI to investigate and suppress 'subversive' activities as the nation entered the war against fascism and Hoover was one of the earliest and most prescient opponents of Germany's Nazi regime. However, after the war was won, there was no need for Hoover to define 'Communist subversion' so broadly as to encompass even New Deal-inspired demands for social and economic reform, but he did and joined a dangerously right-wing shift in American thinking.

★

New Deal reforms made America a less hospitable place for gangsters and kidnappers. They also reduced the opportunities for successful organized criminal activity in at least three important sectors of the economy, as the following accounts of changes in the structure of the power, banking and finance sectors demonstrate.

Power companies, using the Press and other media outlets, did what they could to try and block Roosevelt's nomination and election, given his stance against their greed and corruption. They fought every New Deal reform that affected the electricity industry. Despite these efforts the administration successfully established new government agencies, completed four major hydroelectric projects and, in general, managed to make low-cost electricity more available to both rural and urban Americans. To prevent the abuses that Roosevelt referred to in his speech in April 1932, the Federal Public Utility Holding Company Act (PUHCA) was passed in 1935. The intention of this was to break up the huge power trusts or holding companies around the country with their complicated structures that allowed for deceptive practices. As a result of the better regulation that followed PUHCA and 'the light' that was let in on provision of electric power in America, ratepayers saw their bills drop substantially. They were no longer 'fleeced' to the extent they had been.

However, this relatively healthy situation did not long survive the end of the New Deal. By the time of the Eisenhower administrations of the 1950s, much of PUHCA had been watered down, the power companies were again resurgent, and the core of the old abuses remained intact.[25]

The cornerstone of banking reform was the Glass-Steagall Act of 1933, which addressed the regulatory void that had allowed crooked bankers to operate freely in many state systems. Glass-Steagall and other banking laws and regulations significantly added to the power and independence of the Federal Reserve, making it a true central bank capable of exercising effective control over the nation's monetary policy.[26] The new laws restricted the speculative use of bank credits, secured private deposits with a government-run insurance programme which required big banks to contribute to the security of small banks, and forbade commercial banks from engaging in the investment business. Glass-Steagall thus drastically curbed the practices of those 'unscrupulous money changers' that had most riled Roosevelt. The measures helped to sustain stability in the banking industry. This was reflected in a sharp decline in the number of bank failures after reform. Federal regulatory activity thus succeeded in bringing stability to American banking by reducing opportunities for fraud and protecting the savings of ordinary Americans.[27]

The Securities Act of 1933 and the Securities and Exchange Act of 1934 were intended to address another regulatory void, the one that had allowed so much stock market fraud and wild speculation during the years of Republican ascendancy. Wall Street before the 1930s was, as David Kennedy puts it in *Freedom from Fear* (1999), 'a strikingly information-starved environment. Firms were not required to publish regular properly-audited reports and only a handful of investment bankers like J.P. Morgan could make sound financial decisions because they had a monopoly of the necessary information. Opportunities abounded for insider manipulation and wildcat speculation and in the tradition of *laissez-faire* the main check on fraudulent activity was the clearly inadequate *caveat emptor* or "let the buyer beware"'![28] The Roosevelt administration intended to supplement *caveat emptor* with 'let the seller also beware', making those who managed banks, corporations and other agencies handling or using other people's money accountable for this trust. The law, Roosevelt insisted in a message to Congress, must put 'the burden of telling the whole truth on the seller' and called for a law that was designed to prevent fraud by requiring companies to register all new issues of stocks and bonds with the Federal Trade Commission. It required issuing corporations to make 'full and fair' disclosure of all relevant financial information about the new issues and the companies involved in them.[29] In sum, the intention was to let in the light on stock market transactions.

The Securities Act and the Securities Exchange Act set up a five-person Securities and Exchange Commission (SEC) to enforce the new regulations. Roosevelt chose Joseph Kennedy, a Wall Street insider and father of a future president, to be the first head of the Commission because, as he put it, 'you need to set a thief to catch a thief'. The intention was for Kennedy to use his insider knowledge to educate the Commission's staff to police the stock frauds that had helped make his fortune. The SEC's investigative history since its establishment shows that corporate representatives, stock-buyers and -sellers, stockbrokers, investment advisers, accountants, and attorneys are at least as likely to be thieves as those in less respectable jobs. The difference is they have greater opportunities.[30]

In such ways New Deal legislation had transformed and at least partially cleaned up the energy, banking and finance sectors of the American economy. The New Deal policed business in these and other ways, restricting corporate freedoms and powers, while creating new rights and protections for workers. 'We were to use the . . . powers of government', Roosevelt later explained, 'to fight for [constitutional] ideals . . . because the American system visualized protection of the individual against the misuse of private economic power, the New Deal would insist on curbing such power.' Much of American history since that time has been about corporations regaining the special privileges that Roosevelt often railed against.[31] As we shall see, this programme to regain ground lost in the New Deal at home would find a parallel with efforts to globalize freedom for American business and so create staggering opportunities for criminal profit.

★

Although New Deal reform showed what could be done to manage and contain crime and capitalism, the nation was still recognizably the America created by business barons and moral crusaders. Despite the great effort put in by New Deal reformers there were still large areas of American life that allowed or even fostered opportunities for successful, organized, criminal activity. Instead of continuing to make progress in addressing the structural deficiencies of American capitalism, the Second World War and the Cold War shifted the nation's attention away from internal reform and towards national security. As part of this shift, organized crime began to be redefined – it went from being seen as an indication of problems in the management of American capitalism to being seen as a conspiratorial entity which therefore was a threat to national security almost as great as communism.

During and since the Cold War no American government would admit that there were any structural problems with American capitalism. Corporations were more intent than ever that corporate wrongdoing should not be seen as criminal. Government bureaucrats and ambitious politicians began to see that moral crusading would boost their careers. Organized crime had to be viewed as something external to the US business system and to American morality in general. What had been widely understood as being a consequence of unregulated capitalism needed to be redefined. An alien conspiracy had to be produced.

5

States of Denial and
Mafia Distractions

During the 1920s, as we have seen, business dominated almost every aspect of American society. The New Deal challenged that supremacy. The state grew to a degree unprecedented in peacetime and was able to curb business autonomy in ways that included offering support to the labour movement. Organized labour responded by using its new power to protect the rights and welfare of workers more forcefully than ever before. It also attempted to make alliances with the Democratic party that would have refashioned the political economy of modern America. Had these efforts succeeded America would have been committed to full employment, social planning and the expansion of the welfare state that was still in its New Deal embryonic form. Instead, the Democratic party retained its links with big business while putting increasing distance between itself and organized labour. Democrats would prove incapable of defending the key achievements of the New Deal.

After a massive wave of strikes in 1945 and 1946 the frightening prospect for American business of more limits to their power seemed a strong possibility. It prompted a full-scale assault on labour and New Deal liberalism. The historian Elizabeth Fones-Wolf has analysed this assault most comprehensively in *Selling Free Enterprise* (1994). The most visible aspects of this battle for power, she writes, 'took place over major policy issues at the national level, pitting executives of large firms and major business organizations . . . against liberal democrats and union leaders'. At this level business's weapons included such techniques as lobbying, campaign financing and litigation or threats of litigation.

Fones-Wolf's research found that national business leaders and smaller employers at a local level also struggled to reshape the ideas, images and attitudes through which Americans understood their world. They did this specifically by undermining the commitment of workers to unions and of citizens to the type of government that would interfere in the workings of the market. Corporate leaders claimed the right to control America's economic destiny without significant interference from unions or the state while acknowledging their responsibility to make the benefits of industrial capitalism available to all. Organizations such as the National Association of Manufacturers orchestrated multi-million dollar public-relations campaigns that used newspapers, magazines, radio and television to 'reeducate the public in the principles and benefits of the American economic system'. These campaigns successfully projected a vision of America as the perfect society. Perfect because it was 'harmonious, classless, free, productive and, therefore, affluent and successful'.[1]

This assault on liberals and unions was aided considerably by the fear, paranoia and rising anti-communism that characterized the late 1940s and early 1950s. The Cold War at home has aptly been called *The Great Fear* (1978) by David Caute. Legions of informers were organized by J. Edgar Hoover's FBI to report on the movements and activities of communists or alleged communists. The House Committee on Un-American Activities forced thousands of journalists, diplomats, authors, trade unionists and scientists to testify against themselves or their colleagues. If they exercised their 5th Amendment rights and refused to answer questions, this was interpreted as an admission of guilt and many lost their jobs as a result. Individual states and cities emulated the federal government and instituted loyalty programmes and demanded loyalty oaths from employees. Local interrogation bodies and private vigilante groups also hounded suspected communists.

The famous Hollywood blacklist, which saw many actors, writers and directors barred from the American film industry for holding 'un-American' views, was only one of many. Hundreds of academics and journalists lost their jobs for 'un-American' thinking. In most cases, however, American intellectuals, journalists and film-makers wanted to keep their jobs. Academics retreated to the specialist journals to publish; frequently caution and qualification obscured critical analysis. Journalists stayed with safe subjects and tended to find fault with deviant individuals rather than with government or business institutions. Film-makers stayed with patriotic or harmlessly entertaining themes, many anxious not to break rules listed by Ayn Rand of the Motion Picture Alliance for the Preservation of American Ideals: 'Don't Smear the Free Enterprise System. Don't Deify the "Common Man." Don't Glorify Failure. Don't Smear Industrialists. Don't Smear Success.'

Given this and more subtle pressures on writers and directors, few 1950s films featured bankers and businessmen as villains, crooks, chisellers or exploiters. This contrasted with many of the key films of the 1940s, such as *It's a Wonderful Life* (1946) with James Stewart taking on the ruthless banker Henry F. Potter. No film like *This Gun for Hire*

(1942), which portrayed the hired killer more sympathetically than his corrupt, treacherous capitalist employer, nor *Force of Evil* (1948), which equated New York numbers racketeering with capitalism, could have been made under Hollywood's new rules.[2] In fact, the film of the most notable play of the time, *Death of a Salesman* (1951), was reworked by Hollywood scriptwriters to remove its strong critique of capitalism. The cartoon version of *Animal Farm* (1954) was also significantly different from George Orwell's original. The book ended with a description that made the rottenness of capitalism and communism indistinguishable: 'The creatures outside looked from pig to man, and from man to pig, and from pig to man, again; but already it was impossible to say which was which.' In the film's ending there are no human farmers and the sight of the pigs prompts the other watching animals to mount a successful counter-revolution by storming the farmhouse. Viewers thus got the message that the movie's discreet sponsors, the Central Intelligence Agency, wanted them to get. Only communism could be seen as corrupt.[3]

Politically, New Deal liberalism gave way to the 'compensatory' state liberalism of Harry Truman, John F. Kennedy and Lyndon Johnson. While public policy during Roosevelt's first two administrations involved efforts to restructure capitalist institutions, confront big-business power and redistribute wealth, post-war liberal public policy was mainly committed to sustaining economic growth using fiscal tools and compensating those left out of the general prosperity with welfare protections. Johnson's Great Society reform package of the 1960s was a dramatic attempt to eliminate poverty in America but it stopped short of attempts to reorganize and modify the market place. It gave the American business community little cause for concern since it left alone the organization of work and the patterns of investment. Johnson's 'war on poverty' was therefore a 'very timid call to arms', according to historian Ira Katznelson.[4]

The pro-business, anti-labour, anti-New Deal agenda was equally present in other media such as radio, television and the press. From the late 1940s on it was far less likely that the powerful in society would be portrayed as criminally deviant. Although it was acceptable to show that some businessmen were criminals, they were presented as being exceptional individuals in a fundamentally sound business system.

The threat of litigation forced the criminologist Edwin Sutherland to drop such corporate names as General Motors, Sears Roebuck and Westinghouse from his book *White Collar Crime* (1949), in which he had meticulously documented cases of bribery, fraud, embezzlement, antitrust violations, false advertising and theft of trade secrets. Sutherland had found that the criminality of the corporations was organized crime. It was persistent, extensive, usually unpunished, most often deliberate, and it involved the connivance of government officials or legislators. Not being able to name the corporate criminals involved significantly reduced the impact of the book. Only from the 1970s did a few criminologists choose to resist the easy option by stepping outside the prevailing pro-business consensus and exposing pervasive organized crime in business.[5] Their task was made increasingly more difficult by the virtual absence of funding in the United States available for research into corporate crime.[6] This contrasts with the vast amounts that have been spent in recent decades on gang and drug research tending to produce results that either contribute nothing of value or support a pre-existing 'must try harder to get the bad guys' agenda.

From the 1950s history was rewritten in ways that presented late nineteenth-century 'robber baron' industrialists and financiers as 'captains of industry' or 'industrial statesmen' who guided the nation to its prominent position amongst other nations. Past abuses were dismissed as relatively minor transgressions along the way to greatness, respectability and responsibility.

In the meantime, taking the spotlight off organized business crime did not diminish its destructive impact. Lewis Brown, for example, who was president of Johns-Manville, the world's leading asbestos producer, was also the founder of the American Enterprise Institute, which existed to spread the belief that big business represented all that was right in America and should be freed of all government restrictions and regulations. In 1949, one of Johns-Manville's doctors sent a memo to headquarters regarding seven asbestos mill employees whose x-rays showed early signs of asbestosis. The doctor's memo advised company executives not to share this information with the workers concerned and therefore let them work on in an environment that was killing them.[7] This doctor's concern for the profitability of the company rather than the survival of the workers led Brown to promote him to be a medical director of Johns-Manville. It was an act representative of a type of corporate policy that led to the disease and death of hundreds and thousands of workers. In the absence of effective regulation, corporations were bound to drift in this direction. Their legal structure meant that as long as there were no risks to the survival of the organization or the life and liberty of executives, murderous indifference to workers and consumers would increase.

Such deceptions gave Americans the false impression that the business and government institutions of the United States were fundamentally faultless. Problems were either minimalized, or externalized as the result of foreign conspiracies. The Mafia fitted the bill perfectly in the case of organized crime. The real but usually separate activities of Italian-American gangsters in different cities were conflated to provide a catch-all explanation of American organized-crime problems. By the 1960s most commentators could pretend that the American systems of government and business were fundamentally sound but were under threat from a hierarchically organized criminal conspiracy known as the Mafia or Cosa Nostra. The Mafia, according to politicians, law-enforcement officials and the media, now threatened the integrity of local government. The Mafia corrupted police officers and lawyers. The Mafia infiltrated legitimate business. The Mafia, according to a government commission, 'subverted the decency and integrity of a free society'.[8] It was blame-shifting on a colossal scale and it was achieved because of a widespread acceptance of little more than a wild conspiratorial fantasy.

From the late 1940s, thanks to the efforts of business-sponsored crime commissions and patriotic newspaper proprietors, the spotlight that had been on organized-business crimes during the 1930s now shone on illegal gambling, drugs and labour racketeering. These were all repeatedly said to be controlled by the Mafia and its mainly Jewish 'associates'. The involvement of the upperworld in these and other types of systematic criminal activity was consistently downplayed.

The crime writer Gus Russo provides an early example of America's lop-sided approach to organized crime that resulted from the over-concentration on the Mafia. In the early 1950s, he writes, Meyer Dirlove, Joe Siciliano and others were jailed for bulking out ground beef burgers with horsemeat in Chicago's 'horseburger' episode. However, adding horsemeat to ground beef did not sicken or kill any consumer. By contrast, as the US Department of Agriculture revealed, upperworld food-processing plants knowingly sold food contaminated with cockroaches, flies, rodents, mouse droppings, faecal and urine waste, pesticides, mercury and salmonella, resulting in 4,000 deaths per year and millions of cases of non-fatal food poisoning. The food plants were able to get away with this mass poisoning because of the routine bribery of Department of Agriculture inspectors. 'Unlike the horsemeat scammers', Russo adds, 'no food industry executive has ever been imprisoned for the processing crimes.'[9] These types of crimes are a continuing problem, as we saw in Chapter 1.

The Kefauver Committee of 1950–51 was the first senate investigating committee to shine a light on the Mafia's alleged control of organized crime in America and also the first systematically to misrepresent the problem of organized crime in general and illegal gambling and drug trafficking in particular. Its influential *Third Interim Report* gave undeserved substance and respectability to the idea of the Mafia dominating organized crime in America and thus also to the idea that such crime had foreign origins.

Despite a great deal of hopeful effort no evidence was produced at the hearings to support the view of a centralized Sicilian or Italian organization dominating organized crime in the United States. The Kefauver Committee's most significant legacy was to misrepresent the problem of organized crime and commit the federal government to becoming more involved in the policing of gambling and drugs.

The committee's lack of evidence for its Mafia conspiracy theory did not matter since its conclusions had been decided upon before the hearings began. In effect its goal was to reduce the complexities of organized crime to a simple 'Good versus Evil' equation. The committee had accepted the arguments against gambling and drugs, and no serious consideration was given to the possibility of government regulation and control of these activities. The public had to be convinced that prohibitions were the only options and prohibitions had to be made effective. Enforcement had to be seen as the only answer. The committee thus chose to put the weight of its opinion behind a bizarre and unsubstantiated interpretation of America's organized-crime problems. Organized crime was, according to this interpretation, a centralized conspiracy. Alternative ways of regulating and controlling gambling and drugs were out of the question; that would be a capitulation to powerful and alien criminal interests. The only solution, according to the committee and a growing consensus of opinion in the law-enforcement community and amongst opinion makers, was increased federal commitment. This involved the enactment of more laws and the establishment of a federal law-enforcement capacity that was capable of succeeding where local authorities had failed. By some means, according to the new line, people had to be prevented from indulging in activities that filled the coffers of the Mafia.

The Mafia conspiracy theory gave the nation's media managers an easy way to edit a multitude of disparate events into a digestible package that was consistent with American thinking during the Cold War era.[10] Hundreds of books and articles had produced a formula that lazy and ill-informed journalists would regularly turn to when writing about US organized crime. The trick was to describe briefly how a secret criminal brotherhood, developed in feudal Sicily, was transplanted to urban America at the end of the nineteenth century, and then took over organized-crime operations in the entire country. As 'proof' of the supercriminal Mafia all editors required were unrelated anecdotes about Italian-American gangsters, mainly from New York, with the narrative livened up with words like 'godfather', 'tentacles', and most essentially 'omerta', the 'secret and unwritten' code of silence of the Mafia. Ordinary gangsters such as Charles 'Lucky' Luciano, 'Uncle' Frank Costello and Vito

Genovese were credited with almost unlimited power. These were mythical interpretations, magically stringing together disconnected fears, prejudices and hatreds about organized crime and foreigners. The idea of a foreign conspiracy dominating organized crime effectively absolved the United States from any responsibility for its drug and organized-crime problems. The Mafia, according to a hugely popular book published in 1952, 'controls practically all crime in the United States'.[11]

Real events such as the meeting of around 60 mafia gangsters at Apalachin in 1957, the association of the nation's top labour leader Jimmy Hoffa with Italian-American and other gangsters, and the televised testimony of Joseph Valachi in 1963 were interpreted in essentially the same way. They were all said to demonstrate that the Mafia not only existed as a centralized, national organization but also dominated organized crime in America.[12]

After Apalachin, even J. Edgar Hoover of the FBI changed his tune about organized crime. Previously, he had publicly considered such crime to be a problem most associated with local political corruption. He had never denied its existence (as is frequently alleged) but he stressed the role of corrupt local politicians and police in protecting organized criminal enterprises. In fact, this was an accurate assessment of gambling-related organized crime, the type of organized crime that concerned the American media and politicians most during the 1950s and early 1960s. Hoover, quite sensibly, kept his agency away from the corrupting and fruitless tasks of gambling control.

By the 1960s, however, Hoover had joined the chorus of law-enforcement officials and media commentators that was making the terms organized crime and Mafia virtually synonymous. In 1960 he wrote in the *F.B.I. Law Enforcement Bulletin* that the Mafia was a 'lawless legion' that 'infiltrates through every loophole, its booty flowing into underworld coffers whether it be nickel and dimes from a juke box in a bar in the smallest town or from a multi-million-dollar stranglehold on large metropolitian centers obtained through the domination of a few dishonest labor officials'.[13]

In 1993 a bestselling book by Anthony Summers suggested that Hoover was blackmailed into keeping the FBI out of gambling and racketeering cases because of the Mafia's possession of photographs of him having sex with a male colleague.[14] There was undoubtedly a great deal of gossip about Hoover's sexuality during those prurient, homophobic times but Summers' alleged photographic evidence for this has not been produced and the claim was built largely around second-hand rumours. Hoover may have been homosexual or he may have been too interested in power to have any sexual involvement, but there were good reasons for his reluctance to accept the alien conspiracy theory. First, it was wrong. Second, to do so would have required FBI involvement in drug control as well as gambling control, since these were the alleged sources of the Mafia's wealth and power. Hoover could see which way the wind was blowing, however. From 1960 he chose to go along with the consensus of law-enforcement opinion and reduce organized crime to a single conspiratorial entity with unfortunate consequences, as we shall see.

The FBI now became the leading standard bearer against what it called the 'La Cosa Nostra' and Hoover began to repeat the new conventional wisdom about organized crime. This was stated most comprehensively in the 1967 report of President Lyndon Johnson's Commission on Law Enforcement: 'The core of organized crime in the United States consists of 24 groups operating criminal cartels in large cities across the nation. Their membership is exclusively Italian, they are in frequent communication with each other, and their smooth functioning is insured by a national body of overseers.' The Commission's report recommended a complete package of laws to combat the Cosa Nostra's subversion of 'the very decency and integrity that are the most cherished attributes of a free society'.[15]

Before the 1950s very few people would have associated organized crime exclusively with Italian ethnicity. By the late 1960s, thanks to endless claims by journalists and the phenomenal success of Mario Puzo's The Godfather (1969), the thousands of conspiracies that constitute organized crime were reduced to just one – the Mafia. Government officials were more than happy to supply journalists with the 'facts' to support this explanation for the country's organized-crime problem. The knowledge that some Italian-American gangsters had become rich and powerful in their own cities, and had contact with other gangsters in other cities, was distorted into something far more mysterious and menacing.

It is true that Italian-American gangsters have been prominent in US organized crime since the Prohibition years. It is also true that some of these gangsters have reached positions of prominence in some American institutions. New York's Anthony 'Fat Tony' Salerno, for example, and several others were malign influences in the Teamsters Union between the 1950s and 1980s.[16] Finally, it is true that Italian-American gangsters played a role in covert aspects of US foreign policy. The CIA, for example, famously and fruitlessly employed Chicago's Sam Giancana and John Rosselli in their efforts to assassinate Cuba's leader, Fidel Castro.[17] While all this is undeniable, many of the assertions made in the media about the Mafia are fiction. Serious researchers have long ago debunked the common identification of organized crime before the 1970s almost exclusively with Italian-Americans, and the alleged monolithic nature of the Mafia itself.[18] However, as a result of these conspiratorial ideas being repeated endlessly in the media, many people, in every part of the world, not just in America, believe that something called the Mafia ran organized crime in the United States. Most will continue to do so. Mafia mythology was able to take a firm grip on people's imagination, a paranoid conspiracy theory had finally been given almost universal credibility by constant repetition of an image.

The phrase 'organized crime' had thus become a common noun by the 1960s, signifying a hierarchically organized criminal conspiracy with a meaning far removed from its early use. It now threatened the integrity of local government. It corrupted police officers and lawyers. It infiltrated legitimate business. It subverted the decency and integrity of a free society. Organized crime was now seen as a criminal army far away from earlier perspectives that emphasized the involvement and responsibility of 'respectable' society for the pervasive problem of organized-crime activity in the United States. This new conceptualization of 'organized crime' thus got officialdom, business interests and 'respectable society' off the hook.

Since it was now commonly accepted that a foreign conspiracy was corrupting the police, the police had to be given more power to fight this conspiracy. This was despite the fact that, as most serious commentators understood, police corruption was a key part of the problem of organized crime and so increasing police powers was hardly going to solve this problem. Compromise such as reconsideration of the laws governing gambling and drug taking was out of the question. The only answer was increased law-enforcement capacity and more laws to ensure the swift capture of gambling operators and drug traffickers behind whom the Mafia or Cosa Nostra was always supposed to be lurking.[19]

By the 1960s Mafia mythology had provided US bureaucrats and politicians with an easy-to-communicate threat to the nation; concentration on the Mafia and its alleged control of illegal markets diverted attention away from corruption in government and business. This not only saved much embarrassment but also helped to limit people's awareness of the flaws in an approach to organized crime based exclusively on giving the government more power to combat threats to America's morally authoritarian and business-dominated system. By criminalizing popular goods and services, the state created a permanent pool of official corruption and private criminality. Moral sentiment proved to be easy to stir up for electoral purposes but ending the symbiosis of law-enforcement institutions and illegal markets was never seriously considered.

The Mafia never did control or even dominate organized crime in America although Mafia families certainly had a great deal of influence in some areas in some cities. Many historians and criminologists, beginning with Joseph L. Albini in *The American Mafia: Genesis of a Legend* (1971), have demonstrated the almost complete absence of evidence and logic behind most commonly accepted versions of organized-crime history. Albini's aim was to describe the structure of the criminal syndicate as well as how it performed its functions and he supported his argument with evidence gained from those close to or involved in criminal syndicate operations as well as from law-enforcement personnel and archival sources. He refuted the two key assumptions of legislators and government officials involved in the construction of organized-crime-control laws. First, he found that a national cartel of crime did not exist. Second, the structures of criminal syndicates in the United States were not characterized by a consistent bureaucratic format composed of specific ranks. Instead, Albini's research pointed to syndicates as being systems of patron-client relationships varying from syndicate to syndicate. As such, he concluded, 'each syndicate can be understood only within the context of its own development' and 'the types of patron-client relationships that exist within and between syndicates come in a multitude of variations'. Albini insisted that making terms like 'Mafia' and 'Cosa Nostra' synonymous with organized crime obliterated 'the reality of American syndicate crime – the reality that it belongs to America'.[20] In the years following the publication of Albini's work, the wealth of quality research confirming the accuracy of his findings has sadly been buried by the endless repetition of Mafia myths or updated variations.

★

Federal government officials got the power they claimed would enable them to fight the Mafia conspiracy in the Organized Crime Control Act of 1970. Organized-crime-control provisions now included: asset forfeiture; special grand juries; wider witness-immunity provisions for compelling or persuading reluctant witnesses; witness protection measures; extended sentences for persons convicted in organized-crime cases and the use of wire-tapping and eavesdropping evidence in federal cases. With concurrent anti-drug legislation, a far stronger policing presence was established in America.

The Act added superficial substance to the tough law-and-order image Nixon had been trying to cultivate since his narrow presidential election victory in 1968. In many ways it was appropriate that Richard Nixon was the man who presented the paradigm of organized-crime control to the American people. He was dishonest, morally authoritarian, expedient and corruptly indebted to the big business interests that had paid for his campaigns.

In the process of getting the 1970 Act passed, Nixon had articulated the law-enforcement consensus on organized crime. He gave the Mafia conspiracy theory the seal of presidential approval in a message to Congress on 23 April 1969. In it he described the Mafia's influence as 'more secure than ever before', and warned that its operations had 'deeply penetrated broad segments of American life'. 'It is vitally important', he continued, that Americans see this alien organization for what it really is – a totalitarian and closed society, operating within an open and democratic one. It has succeeded so far because an apathetic public is unaware of the threat it poses to American life.'

He claimed that gambling was 'the lifeline of organized crime' and would thus be the focus of the administration's efforts. Gambling, he elaborated, 'provides the bulk of the revenues that eventually go into usurious loans, bribes of police and local officials, "campaign contributions" to politicians, the wholesale narcotics traffic, the infiltration of legitimate business and to pay for the large stables of lawyers and accountants and assorted professional men who are in the hire of organized crime'.

In the same month as he made these claims, Nixon directed a group of presidential advisers to examine the effectiveness of the Executive Branch in combating organized crime. Nixon's advisers focused their study on the effectiveness of the federal anti-organized crime programme in nine mainly north-eastern cities. After reviewing it with more than a hundred federal, state and local state criminal-justice and law-enforcement personnel, they came to the damning conclusion that federal organized-crime control was failing badly. The advisers made many recommendations for improvement but their mandate restricted them to suggestions for structural and administrative changes in the Executive Branch. These they made but added the following comment, which would have seriously undermined the Nixon line on organized crime had it been made public: 'We would be negligent, however, not to emphasize that organized crime flourishes in today's legal and social environment. Even with administrative improvement, organized crime will continue to thrive so long as the community relies primarily on criminal sanctions to discourage gambling and the use of drugs.'[21]

The Nixon administration paid no heed to the report's conclusions and recommendations, making sure that its findings were classified and destroying most copies. It then stepped up the war on first gambling and then drugs.

The Nixon administration's efforts against gambling were the final futile chapter in this part of America's programme of moral reform. By the mid-1970s the increased federal effort against gambling had subsided, with little accomplished despite the enormous expense involved in surveillance and prosecution. Relatively few prison sentences resulted and those that did were short. A former strike force chief later told the *Wall Street Journal* that gambling cases had become something to keep the statistics up: 'We would investigate a couple of low grade bookmakers, call them organized crime figures and go after them.'[22]

By the middle of the 1970s the trend towards decriminalization and legalization of gambling was well established. Pompous lectures about the evils of gambling and deceptive claims for the potential of anti-gambling measures could no longer halt a re-examination of policy by many state and local authorities looking for ways to increase revenue and influenced by an increasingly expansive corporate gambling sector. Casino and other forms of gambling in the United States still have problems with racketeering and fraud but no more so than in other highly profitable sectors of the legitimate economy.

The Nixon administration had meanwhile substituted drugs for gambling as the 'lifeline' of organized crime after a cynically devised escalation of the country's drug control efforts. The intention was first to inflate the drug problem, second to blame crime on drugs and, finally, to give the impression of firm executive action by waging 'war' on drugs.[23]

The main legislative innovation on drugs was to secure the passing of the Comprehensive Drug Abuse Control Act of 1970 – a statute that brought together everything Congress had done in the drug field since opium-smoking curbs in 1887. The law gave the Department of Justice an array of powers over licit and illicit drugs, covering possession, sale and trafficking. Drug offenders faced severe sanctions including life for those engaged in 'continuing criminal enterprise' or any who qualified as a 'dangerous special drug offender'. Treasury funds were to be made available to enforcement agents to hire informants, pay for incriminating information and make purchases of contraband substances. Agents were given the power to seize on sight any property they thought was contraband or forfeitable, and to execute search warrants at any time of the day or night.[24]

Nixon had stated that his intention was to 'tighten the noose around the necks of drug peddlers, and thereby loosen the noose around the necks of drug users'. For this, federal drug-enforcement agencies were given more men and ever larger budget appropriations, and in July 1973 the Drug

Enforcement Administration (DEA) was created by the presidential fiat of Richard Nixon to take over the functions of other federal drug-enforcement and intelligence agencies. By 1975 the new agency had a staff of more than 4,000, about half of whom were investigators, and it possessed, in the words of one commentator, 'every armament and prerogative that could conceivably be conferred on a peacetime domestic agency'.[25]

Nixon's rival in the 1972 presidential election, Senator George McGovern, was successfully identified with a 'soft' attitude to drugs and crime, and in November the President was re-elected by an overwhelming margin. His commitment to fight the 'totalitarian' Mafia and the 'menace' of drugs had achieved its primary purpose and Nixon's tough law-and-order image was maintained. The corrupt realities behind the image were, for a while, still concealed.

As Nixon's Chief Domestic Advisor, John Ehrlichman, later told a Senate committee, the expansion of drug-enforcement capacity and anti-drug rhetoric was mainly a show for the voters. 'I think there is a genuine question of hypocrisy in all of this', he said. 'The people in the Federal Government' were 'kidding the people when they say we have mounted a massive war on narcotics ... They know darned well', he concluded, 'that the massive war that they have mounted on narcotics is only going to be effective at the margins.'[26]

After Nixon, however, hypocrisy remained in the ascendant and American drug-control policy was in a straitjacket. Politicians continued to follow his lead and talked tough on the issue or kept their own counsel if they did feel unease about the repressive direction of federal drug-control policy. Governments continually increased anti-drug spending and attempted to give the appearance that 'something' was being done. Criminals and corrupt public and private professionals continued to prosper as the law of the land continued to accommodate to the law of supply and demand.

Since the 1980s the local and national attack on the twenty-plus Italian-American crime families that undoubtedly existed, and at times co-operated, has been impressive. There is no doubt that many Italian-American gangsters swore blood oaths of allegiance, made inter-state or regional alliances to try and regulate competition, and used murder and intimidation to protect territory, markets and operations. In 1986 a series of trials in New York began that were used by the government to claim victories against the Mafia. The government's efforts were coordinated by Rudolph Giuliani, the US Attorney in

Manhattan who brought Anthony 'Fat Tony' Salerno and Anthony 'Tony Ducks' Corallo to trial on racketeering charges in September. These crime bosses, both in their seventies, could not contest evidence that they were part of a 'commission' of New York Mafia families. It was shown at the trials that they had lucrative stakes in garbage disposal and building trades rackets and that Salerno, in particular, was a significant influence on the Teamsters Union.

But the evidence also showed the limits of 'commission' power. Old men meeting in dingy social clubs could approve new Mafia members and could resolve some of the conflicts amongst their associates but they could not direct or control criminal activity in New York, let alone nationally. All five of the commission members were from New York and it was clear that New York's gangster set-up was very different from the set-up in other parts of the country. They were certainly gangsters but definitely not part of a tightly knit, all-powerful national syndicate.

From the 1980s American prosecutors experienced success after success against mafiosi in every city in which they were known to operate. The most notable of these was the arrest, trial and incarceration of New York mobster, John Gotti.

There is no doubt that federal and local police and prosecutors did well to put Salerno, Corallo and Gotti and hundreds of other American mafiosi behind bars. However, as another aspect of the New York Mafia story shows, had effective regulatory structures existed before the 1990s they would not have achieved any significant power in the city in the first place. Rudolph Giuliani, who as a prosecutor had led many of the successful anti-mafia prosecutions in the 1980s, became Mayor of New York in 1993. He then used his executive power to construct an administrative structure that to date seems to be effective in purging mafiosi from large parts of the city's economy. His initiatives addressed problems that the city's corrupt political infrastructure had left to fester for decades. He used the city's regulatory and licensing powers, for example, to rid the Fulton Fish Market of gangster-dominated unloading companies. In June 1996 he supported the New York City Council's decision to create the Trade Waste Commission (TWC) with the explicit goal of eliminating Mafia-connected waste-hauling companies. The TWC was structured as a regulatory agency with a law-enforcement agenda. Its executive officers, attorneys, monitors and police detectives were recruited for their experience in related investigations and prosecutions. As well as checking for mobster involvement in waste-hauling companies the TWC also sought to strengthen the customers' position by setting maximum rates, regulating contract duration and keeping customers informed of their rights.[27] By the late 1990s customers were paying between 30 and 40 per cent less to have their waste removed. Historically, the gangsters who owned and operated New York waste companies had set their own rates, retained contracts through force and tended not to emphasize customer service.

A survey of New York's organized-crime experience demonstrates a truth that should be obvious, but clearly is not, to many politicians tied to a free-market agenda. Gangster-related organized crime, as well as any other form of organized crime, thrives in poorly regulated societies and can only be reduced through better government regulation. Law enforcement in the city had brought down a multi-ethnic assortment of gangsters since the 1930s without affecting the political and economic conditions that allowed them to flourish in the first place. In certain sectors of the economy, as we have just discussed, regulatory reforms eliminated gangster dominance during the 1990s, but the lack of change elsewhere or sometimes the deregulation of other sectors of the economy meant that gangsters were still in business in the nation's largest city.

The lax approach to regulation in Wall Street and telecommunications opened up new lines of criminal business for gangsters just as the old lines were being closed down. In 1997 the *New York Times* reported that the city's Mafia crime families were shifting their sights towards white-collar crimes. Having lost millions of dollars' worth of revenue as a result of the termination of their waste disposal rackets and their elimination from the Fulton Fish Market, mafiosi turned to securities fraud and various other white-collar scams.[28] By 2000 several mafiosi had been convicted on various charges involving fraud and extortion on Wall Street in association with brokers who often used high-pressure sales tactics and false statements to manipulate stock.[29] Subsequently, in February 2004, federal prosecutors charged several men associated with the Gambino crime family of cheating millions of unsuspecting customers out of more than $200 million over five years by 'piggybacking' false charges on their telephone bills. This scheme of billing fraud is known as 'cramming' and in this case it involved charging callers responding to adverts for free samples of services like psychic phone lines and adult chat lines up to $40 a month on their phone bills for services they never requested or used. It worked, according to *New York Times* reporter William K. Rashbaum, because many telephone-related services are now paid through local phone companies' monthly bills, with the companies passing on the payments to the service providers. The Gambinos allegedly used a company that consolidated billings for service providers, allowing them to collect phoney fees for 'voice-mail services' or for other 'innocent-sounding' items hidden amongst the genuine fees on customers' bills.[30]

Although mafiosi made millions of dollars in securities fraud and 'cram-ming' rackets it is important to stress that their gains were just the pickings of a much bigger feast for criminals of all types and varieties.

★

By the 1980s it was clear that gangsters from every racial and ethnic origin were involved in systematic criminal activity and that making organized crime synonymous with the Mafia was no longer viable. Federal officials began to make an often repeated claim that although the Mafia had once been the dominant force in US organized crime, it was now being challenged by several crime 'cartels' emerging amongst Asian, Latin American and other groups. As Gary W. Potter argues in *Criminal Organizations* (1994), this was an adaptation of the alien conspiracy interpretation rather than an overhaul in official thinking about organized crime. The argument remained the same: forces outside of mainstream American culture threaten otherwise morally sound American institutions. Potter described the new official consensus as the 'Pluralist' revision of the alien conspiracy interpretation.[31]

The American media accepted this new interpretation without question, along with its corollary that the government's successes against the Mafia must be accompanied by an effort to 'stay in front' of the emerging 'cartels'. In sum, as every mainstream commentator agreed, the US government's basic approach to the problem of organized crime was sound but needed a harder line on all fronts: more wiretaps, informants and undercover agents in order to get more convictions, which would require more prisons. And more criminal assets forfeited to help pay for at least some of this.

The dominance of pro-business right-wing thinking from the Nixon era meant that America could not contemplate tighter regulation of legal markets as an answer to organized crime. The resurgence of 'moral majority' authoritarianism equally meant that America could not con-template alternatives to the crime-breeding drug prohibitions.

Those in power chose to ignore the mountain of evidence that showed that corruption and poor policy created the conditions for successful organized crime. They thus denied American people opportunities to reconsider responses to organized crime that could complement or pro-vide alternatives to the one-sided law-enforcement approach to its control. The approach would remain based on long-term investigation, undercover operations, informants, wiretaps and asset forfeiture and would be best described as a 'rat-trap' strategy. Criminal justice becomes like those 1930s experiments where psychologists built labyrinthine traps for rats, to learn whether or how soon they can get out of them. A more holistic approach would have concentrated on reducing the opportunities for rats to multiply in the first place.[32]

By the 1980s, however, Americans saw organized crime as composed of groups of separate and distinct gangsters rather than the more fluid, varied and integrated phenomenon portrayed by commentators before the Cold War put limits on critical thought. There was now no need to consider corruption within the business or criminal-justice systems or unworkable laws as part of the problem of organized crime because the American people had been so thoroughly distracted by alien conspiracies and pluralist revisions. The United States therefore persisted with organized-crime-control methods that helped win a few battles but could do little to prevent the country from continuing to lose the war.

★

Not all the battles won by law enforcement against criminal syndicates were as clear-cut as they appeared at the time. In an environment that continued to be corrupt, US organized-crime control was often misdirected, inadequate and counter-productive.

In recent years the conduct of the FBI's Boston office since the 1960s has come under particularly damning scrutiny. Robert Kennedy and J. Edgar Hoover's drive against the Mafia in New England focused on the crime bosses Raymond Patriarca and Gennaro Angiulo. To help bring them down, the FBI relied on 'turning' some of their criminal associates against them, notably Joseph 'The Animal' Barboza. Barboza was a contract killer and, as it turned out, a compulsive liar, who was more than willing to give uncorroborated testimony to the government in return for lenient treatment by the courts. In 1968 the FBI allowed Barboza to commit perjury for the government in the case against Joseph Salvati and five others, accused of murdering a New Bedford gangster called Edward Deegan in 1965. Deegan was found dead in an alleyway in Chelsea, Massachusetts, slain, according to the newspapers, in 'gangland fashion'. Documents released in 2002 showed that the FBI agents were aware that five gangsters, including Barboza, were involved in the 'hit'. They decided to keep silent, however, and allowed Barboza to testify against several innocent men, including Joseph Salvati, who served nearly three decades for the crime, separated from his wife and four young children.

Salvati's lawyer, Victor Garo, later summarized the case: 'The FBI determined who got liberty, the FBI determined who got justice, and justice was not for all . . . What Constitution? What Bill of Rights? What human rights? What human decency? We're the FBI. We don't have to adhere to these principles so long as we have a good press and so long as we get convictions. That will show that the ends justify the means.'[33]

Barboza then entered the newly created Witness Protection Program and was given a new identity and life in California. He briefly worked in a legitimate occupation but had a fall and as a result acquired $18,500 in workman's compensation. He used this money to traffic in drugs before killing a fellow drug trafficker and receiving a five-year sentence for the crime. While in prison he charged that he had proof that Frank Sinatra was a puppet of the Mafia, which was one of many conspiracy theories circulating in the right-wing media of the time. Barboza was invited by a government investigating committee to repeat his charges in Washington. His government handler, John Partington, clearly knew his man and said to him, 'Shit, Joe, you don't know nothing about Sinatra, you're just making that shit up!' Barboza, according to Partington, just laughed and said, 'It gets me out of the joint for a while, don't it?' At the committee's hearings Barboza testified that Sinatra was a front man for Patriarca in the ownership of the Sands casino in Las Vegas and a luxury hotel in Miami. Sinatra was forced to defend himself and made the point that Barboza was a 'bum . . . running off at the mouth'. No evidence was turned up to support Barboza's charges but mud tended to stick where Sinatra was concerned. After serving his sentence Barboza made some money extorting money from San Francisco bookmakers before being shot and killed in 1976.[34]

Barboza was only one of many gangster informants recruited by the FBI during their war against the Mafia. Others in Boston were James 'Whitey' Bulger and Stevie 'The Rifleman' Flemmi who were handled by FBI agent John Connolly. Between the 1970s and 1990s Bulger, in particular, used his protected status as an FBI informer effectively. He was able to run loan-sharking, gambling and drug rackets in South Boston with virtual immunity. He was told whenever his phone was about to be tapped or his operations were about to come under surveillance. Most disturbingly, he was also told who was informing on his crimes and several killings resulted. All the time his criminal competitors were being investigated, wiretapped and prosecuted by federal government officials. Eventually Bulger and Flemmi were charged with 21 murders, 11 of them committed while they were co-operating with the FBI (three of those killed had been talking to the FBI). Connolly was convicted in May 2002 on charges relating to his mutually enriching relationship with Bulger. In 1995 he had leaked word of a federal grand-jury indictment to Bulger who has not been seen since. Flemmi was convicted in 2004 on racketeering charges and admitted to his role in ten murders carried out by him and other members of the Bulger gang.[35]

The FBI tried to portray Connolly as a rogue agent but memos written between 1964 and 1987 showed that Bureau senior staff knew and condoned much of what Connolly and other Boston agents were doing. Evidence also suggests that Boston was just one of many cities where agents used and protected violent criminals as informants.[36]

New York's most prominent government-protected witness in recent years has been Sammy 'The Bull' Gravano, whose testimony helped put John Gotti in prison. Gravano admitted to participating in 19 murders and a lifetime of involvement in the rackets, but for his help in the Gotti prosecution he was rewarded with a greatly reduced prison sentence and a place on the FBI's Witness Protection Program.

Gravano resigned from the Witness Protection Program in 1998, having been relocated close to Phoenix, Arizona. He later told an *Arizona Republic* reporter that life was boring in the state except for the pleasure he got from giving advice to youngsters and from 'wheeling and dealing'. The 'wheeling and dealing' turned out to be in ecstasy and other drugs. State officials said that Gravano served as a mentor to a local gang known as the 'Devil Dogs' and that these provided the muscle for a network that trafficked in ecstasy, marijuana, steroids and amphetamines. In 2002 he was sentenced to 20 years.

The problem with protected witnesses in organized-crime cases is that the best witnesses are criminals themselves, who continue to be criminals after release. They talk to the government to get reduced sentences for their crimes, are then released and relocated to a different part of the country, sometimes with their criminal fortunes largely intact and sometimes with government seed money to set up businesses.

Another much trumpeted American organized-crime-control weapon is asset forfeiture, which itself has proved to have many problems. To begin with it has helped create a new form of commercial enterprise – informing for profit. Informants can now receive a salary and bonuses for information, whether or not it leads to convictions, and up to 25 per cent of forfeiture profits. Federal, state and local agencies now pay out hundred of millions of dollars to informants each year and some informants have been active enough to make up to a million dollars or more from their work with the government.

Anthony Tait, a Hell's Angel, for example, worked with the FBI as a co-operating witness between 1985 and 1988, earning nearly $1 million for informing during this time. Some $250,000 of this was his share of the value of assets forfeited as a result of his co-operation. Edward Vaughn of San Francisco was another to take advantage of the government's new largess. He ran a large, international drug smuggling ring during the 1980s and served two terms in prison before arranging an early parole and paid-informant deal with the government. From then he earned $40,000 in salary and expenses between August 1989 and October 1990 working for the Drug Enforcement Administration (DEA), and was promised a 25 per cent cut of any seizures. This information came out at a trial in Pittsburgh in 1990, in which Vaughn's testimony resulted in one man being found guilty of distributing marijuana. The other defendant in the case was acquitted because the jury felt Vaughn had entrapped him by pushing him too hard to make a drug deal.[37]

As the economic analyst R.T. Naylor has pointed out, information received from informants like Vaughn is not to be trusted. 'The criminal milieu', he argues 'has more than its share of pathological liars and acute paranoiacs, not to mention people who have lived so long in the shadow world of deceit and deception that they cease to recognize any border between fact and fantasy. The credibility of the information is especially dubious when informants have a vested interest (in terms of direct payment, license to continue their own rackets, or reduced sentences) in exaggerating the importance of the information they are peddling.'[38]

Asset forfeiture has also led to new forms of police corruption. There have been numerous cases of police agencies targeting assets with no regard for the rights of the suspects. One officer in Oakland, California, for example, admitted that his unit operated 'more or less like a wolf-pack', driving up in police vehicles and taking 'anything and everything we saw on the street corner'. In Louisiana, police illegally stopped and searched massive numbers of drivers, seizing money that was then diverted to police department skiing holidays and other unauthorized uses. In Los Angeles, a Sheriff's Department employee revealed that deputies routinely planted drugs and falsified police reports to establish probable cause for cash seizures. Many other disclosures in cities across the country indicated that police lawlessness can be the norm rather than the exception.[39]

The most publicized tragedy related to asset forfeiture to date involved a reclusive millionaire called Donald Scott, owner of a 250-acre estate in the Santa Monica mountains. On the morning of 2 October 1992, Scott and his wife woke up to the sound of someone pounding on their door. As his wife was attempting to answer the door, a team of Los Angeles County Sheriff's Department officers burst in. She cried out, 'Don't shoot me, don't kill me!' Her husband ran to her assistance, waving a revolver above his head. A deputy sheriff reacted by shooting and killing him. The raid had been justified by an alleged sighting from a police helicopter of marijuana plants growing on Scott's estate but a search of the estate found no drugs of any kind.[40]

A similar case of deadly police heavy-handedness happened in August 1999 when a 61-year-old man, Mario Paz, was sleeping in his home in Compton, near Los Angeles. He was awoken when a police SWAT team shot both the front and rear door locks, tossed in a stun grenade, and stormed inside. One of the SWAT officers entered Paz's bedroom and shot him twice in the back as he was kneeling by his bedside. Again the motive for the police raid was the possibility of asset seizure and again no drugs were found.[41]

Despite and in many ways, because of, the stepped-up enforcement, the war on drugs has continued to produce a world of institutionalized greed, chaos, corruption, betrayal and terror. Every president since Richard Nixon would rather tolerate corruption and trafficking on a massive scale than take part in a reasoned, well-informed debate that seriously considers alternatives to prohibition. Billions of dollars have been spent on enforcement but evidence of the corrupt and destructive consequences of drug prohibition continues to mount up. Witness-protection programmes, asset forfeiture and other organized-crime-control weapons have not come close to controlling organized crime while the American war on drugs remains as futile and destructive as it always was. The United States will, however, continue to invest in failed efforts at repression and, as we shall see in Chapter 9, persuade other countries to do the same.

There are good political reasons for the continued emphasis on prohibition of drugs. Above all it permits the public understanding of organized crime to remain fixed at the level established in the late 1950s. If organized crime is mainly associated with activity in *illegal* markets, criminal activity in *legal* markets is less politically intrusive. Hence the vast bulk of organized crime is shifted into innocuous sounding categories: 'white-collar crime' is committed by 'bad apples', often through boring-sounding methods like 'accounting irregularities', 'tax evasion' and 'transfer pricing'. The impression is given that 'bad apples' are encouraged to act criminally because of 'defective corporate governance', or 'failures in self-regulation'. The public thus cannot understand how criminal activity emerges in legally constituted institutions and they cannot appreciate how abuse of the public interest escapes from legal jurisdiction – they are discouraged from considering the identical impact of tax avoidance and tax evasion on national budgets, for example.

Organized crime as a category must include offences to the public interest, even when those offences are not punishable in statute. The move to make all institutions and individuals equally available for prosecution in the event of an offence against the public is an essentially political matter. Much can be done within the law-enforcement institutions of nations to end immunity for powerful interests – given sustained, reformist pressure from the public. But only reform of global institutions can match the challenge posed by the globalized, organized crime that we shall consider in Parts 2 and 3.

6

Capital Corruption

After the Nixon period, US prosecutors and police often used their new organized-crime control powers successfully against targeted gangsters or groups of gangsters. However, it is the contention of this book that the wars against the Mafia and other gangster groups were little more than an entertaining distraction from more significant developments that have returned America to a condition of gangster capitalism akin to that of the 1920s. These developments opened up criminal opportunities for corporate, professional and gangster crime on an unprecedented scale and the rot set in during Richard Nixon's administration.

In Nixon's first term he did little to impede the liberal legislative agenda of the Democratic-controlled Congress. Social Security payments and food-stamp funding were increased to help the poor. The Occupational Safety and Health Administration was established to reduce hazards in the work place and the Environmental Protection Agency was established to combat pollution. Nixon also reluctantly signed into law the Clean Air Act, the Clean Water Act and the Pesticide Control Act. Laws are one thing, however, enforcement is another. The promise of these agencies in terms of creating a safer, less polluted and fairer America was immediately undermined by those appointed to administer the new agencies. Nixon ensured that these were either weak managers or more responsive to the interests of business than the interests of workers.[1]

After the 1972 election Nixon began to show his true right-wing colours more openly. Things were going to be different, he hoped, in his second administration. He signalled this in his Second Inaugural Address with a commitment to two tendencies that were key parts of a decisive shift in American politics to the right: cutting taxes and cutting welfare. 'Government', he announced, 'must learn to take less from people so that people can do more for themselves. Let us remember that America was built not by government, but by people – not by welfare, but by work – not by shirking responsibility, but by seeking responsibility.'[2] In February 1973, he proposed a budget that cut deep into government programmes, including eliminating urban renewal and paring down grants for hospital construction, soil management for farmers and the Rural Electrification Administration. Cuts would also be made in spending on milk for school children, compensatory education for poor students and mental health facilities. In these and other ways he sought to change the direction of American domestic policy away from its post-Depression New Deal foundations.[3]

Nixon's thinking was in tune with a conservative intellectual revival. The work of Austrian economist Friedrich von Hayek came to be revered where once it had been ignored and others such as Milton Friedman and Jude Wanniski were producing bestselling polemics and prominent opinion pieces in the newspapers. These argued in essence the equation 'Free Market = Freedom of the Individual' and claimed that any departure from this equation was no less than *The Road to Serfdom* (1944), to quote the title of Hayek's most influential book.[4] Capitalism was not only efficient, it was moral, according to the thinking of Alan Greenspan, the man who, as Chairman of the Federal Reserve System, would be largely responsible for the direction of US national monetary policy from the Reagan era to the twenty-first century. In an early article that attacked government regulatory agencies such as the Pure Food and Drug Agency, the Securities and Exchange Commission, and those involved in welfare provision, Greenspan made the following claim:

> Capitalism is based on self-interest and self-esteem; it holds integrity and trust-worthiness as cardinal virtues and makes them pay off in the market place, thus demanding that men survive by means of virtues, not of vices. It is this superlatively moral system that the welfare statists propose to improve upon by means of preventive law, snooping bureaucrats, and the chronic goad of fear.[5]

American big business was quick to climb aboard and put hard cash in support of the updated versions of *laissez-faire* and Social Darwinism, and contributed to the setting up of such new right-wing think-tanks as the Heritage Foundation. Also, instead of directly funding the campaigns of corrupt politicians like Nixon, which could lead to bad publicity, business began setting up political action committees (PACS) to support policies deemed to be in its interest, rather than relying on the greed or ambition of individuals. These supported such various causes as: cutting taxes on profits and investment income; defeating pro-labour legislation; preventing the creation of a consumer protection agency; limiting the growth of government domestic spending and promoting deregulation of specific industries. They perfected the art of 'single-issue' politics by exploiting anti-civil rights, anti-welfare, anti-affirmative action, anti-tax, anti-busing and anti-gun control in middle and corporate America and forged strategic alliances with the National Rifle Association and various other pro-business and law-and-order lobbies.[6]

Nixon was forced to resign over the Watergate scandal in 1975, and was replaced by his vice-president, Gerald Ford, until the 1976 election. Jimmy Carter, although a Democrat, did not interrupt America's right-ward shift. The liberal left in America would gain little from Nixon's disgrace. By contrast the right had a packaged message that had enduring appeal. Government, they repeated endlessly, was the problem not the solution in all areas except defence, street crime and drugs. A new consensus was reached that has helped create an environment at least as conducive to organized criminal activity as the 1920s.

★

Although the New Right made gains during the 1970s and changed attitudes it had to wait until the election as president of its most charis-matic spokesman, Ronald Reagan, in 1980 to make real advances. Reagan built on the foundations laid by Nixon and ushered in a period of right-wing dominance not known since the 1920s. The year 1980 is as significant a date in American history as 1932 and Roosevelt's victory, marking the starting point of what became known as the Reagan Revolution.

Reagan confirmed his right-wing credentials in his inaugural address, speaking of the need to restore a 'dynamic economy'. He blamed the current recession on 'the intervention and intrusion in our lives that result from unnecessary and excessive growth of government', and pledged to roll back government bureaucracy, reduce tax and government spending. In February 1981 he unveiled his economic programme, which promised large tax cuts particularly to the rich, various cuts in help to the poor through welfare programmes and sweeping deregulation to 'unshackle' business.[7]

Reagan did not start the deregulation of the American economy but his administration took the process much further than that of his predecessor Jimmy Carter. Many of Reagan's appointees were more committed to *laissez-faire* ideology than to federal controls. Even the pro-business *Wall Street Journal* pointed out that the president was 'naming regulators who by virtue of attitude or inexperience are more likely to be nonregulators'.[8] The president and his officials argued that reducing enforcement of 'needless regulations' at both federal and state levels was necessary to reduce business costs, make American goods competitive in world markets, and set free the free market's benevolence as promised by Friedman and others. Partly as a result of Reagan's economic policy changes, business did boom for some in the 1980s, but there were downsides. As we shall see in the following section, America became less equal and the Reagan years had a particularly devastating impact on the poor. But deregulation had a more specific downside, increasing opportunities for large-scale and systematic corporate criminal activity.

Environmental protection was most noticeably affected initially. The consequences of the lack of environmental protection resulting from Reagan and his successors' lax approach were particularly severe. Private waste disposal companies, sometimes run by gangsters but more often by unethical businessmen, made themselves available to dispose of a corporation's toxic waste cheaply and often illegally. In 1991 a University of Tennessee study estimated that the number of sites in need of cleaning up exceeded 3,000 and that open pits, ponds and lagoons across the country were full of industrial poison. One extreme local consequence of lax federal and state oversight occurred in 1983, when most of the residents of Times Beach, Montana, were forced to flee from the town. They were told that a highly toxic substance, dioxin, had been sprayed on horse arenas, streets, parking lots and farms throughout the state by a local waste hauler. It cost the taxpayer $36.7 million to buy out virtually the entire town.[9]

Major corporations also continued to flout the environmental laws in more direct ways. Exxon was particularly criminally destructive. In 1991 Exxon Corporation and Exxon Shipping pleaded guilty to criminal violations of federal environmental laws and paid a $125 million fine related to the 11 million gallons of crude oil spilled from the *Valdez* oil tanker. This spillage polluted 700 miles of Alaska shoreline, killed vast amounts of marine life, and destroyed the way of life of thousands of native Americans. Exxon also joins a long list of corporations that have illegally poisoned American waterways, mostly with delayed consequences, but in the case of illegal discharges from a Marathon Oil refinery with explosive results. After a two-year investigation by the FBI, Marathon pleaded guilty to criminal charges in relation to an explosion and consequent house fire. The house had been situated downstream from the company's Indianapolis refinery, which had been illegally discharging explosive pollutants.[10]

The meat-packing and slaughter industries that were discussed in Chapter 1 have also contributed to America's water pollution problems. In 1997 Smithfield Foods and two of its subsidiaries were fined $12.6 million for discharging illegal pollutants into the Pagan River in Virginia. The ruling found that Smithfield had committed more than 5,000 violations of permit limits for phosphorus, cyanide and other contaminants including faecal coliform. Faecal coliform is an organism found in animal and human waste that is associated with bacteria known to cause serious problems in humans. The violations had continued over a five-year period and 'seriously degraded' two rivers and Chesapeake Bay. The ruling also found that Smithfield had routinely falsified documents and destroyed water quality records.[11]

Basing their conclusions on a confidential survey of the senior attorneys of more than 200 corporations, the *National Law Journal* found in 1993 that 66.8 per cent of the respondents said that their businesses have operated in violation of federal or state environmental laws at least some time in the previous year.[12] The overall impact on public health of these violations is unquantifiable but they have clearly contributed to the increased incidence of many cancer-related illnesses and other health problems. Many birth defects have, for example, been linked to contaminated water. In one case the number of babies born with congenital heart deformities rose sharply in the early 1980s after the Fairfield Camera and Instruments Company of San José, California, leaked an industrial solvent into one neighbourhood's drinking supply. The company agreed to a financial settlement in a lawsuit filed on behalf of 117 affected children.[13]

Although the Clinton administration's record on environmental enforcement was inhibited and came in for some scathing criticism from environmental activists, it was far better than Reagan's and George Bush Sr's. There were genuine efforts to cut industrial pollution and thus make America's air cleaner. The administration of the younger George Bush, however, has operated in ways that have made environmental law evasion easier for the polluters. Carol Browner, head of the Environmental Protection Agency during the Clinton years, claimed that Bush had sent a signal to the polluting community, 'You can get away with bad habits . . . state governments in the north-east were much tougher,' she elaborated, 'so the north-eastern power stations upgraded their emissions standards in the 90s whereas the mid-west guys, who are their competitors, didn't. Now they're not enforcing the law. So what they're saying to the companies is: Don't go early, don't comply with the law first. The rules might change.' Even companies that were willing to obey the emission laws had to think twice or risk losing out to dirtier competitors.

George W. Bush had followed the Reaganite line and promised to free business 'from the heavy hand of regulation' when campaigning for the presidency in 2000. During his administration America's water, as well as its air, has become dirtier, as $500 million was cut from the federal fund used to help communities meet water-quality standards. The American environment has never been more threatened due to population pressures, government laxity and corporate harm. Corporations routinely break environmental laws and thus endanger millions of Americans. 'This nation is devouring itself,' according to Phil Clapp of the National Environmental

Trust, and since America contributes a quarter of the world's carbon dioxide emissions, the rest of the world is also paying a heavy price.[14]

★

The Reagan era also opened up a flood of opportunities for large-scale and systematic corporate criminal activity in the financial world. The Garn-St Germain Depository Institutions Decontrol Act of 1982, for example, released 'the yoke of excessive regulation' from America's Savings and Loans (S & L) institutions and started a race to attract new business and, at the same time, freely loot outrageous sums of money. This act was the culmination of a series of administrative and legislative changes recommended by thrift businesses and intended to 'deregulate' S & L institutions, allowing them to compete for more business. Garn-St Germain allowed S & Ls to go beyond their established and well-regulated role since the nineteenth century, of offering affordable mortgages to ordinary people. Officers could now invest up to 40 per cent of their assets in almost any ventures they liked the look of with deposits that were insured by a government agency, the Federal Savings and Loan Insurance Corporation (FSLIC).

S & L operators took their government-insured deposits and went on a wild spending and embezzlement spree. They spent vast amounts of other people's money to cultivate legislators and keep them away from effective regulatory measures. Don Dixon of Vernon Savings, for example, made his Potomac River yacht and fleet of six aircraft available to a number of congressmen. Other thrift executives had their own ties with politicians as high up as Jim Wright, Speaker of the House of Representatives. These ties were replicated throughout the country but most prominently in California, Texas, Arkansas and Florida, where the most bankruptcies occurred. One senior official in Florida reported that, to his knowledge, every Florida thrift that managed to stay open after insolvency did so with the help of their owners' and operators' well-placed political connections.[15]

Vernon Savings' financial difficulties were disguised for some time through the use of some creative practices including the use of 'participation loans'. This involved selling off loans that were likely to go into default. When examiners were expected, Vernon executives tended to farm out bad loans to other troubled S & Ls until the heat was off, making the company look more solvent than it actually was. In one case, 19 of the largest thrifts in Texas sent representatives to a secret meeting in Houston in 1985 to exchange bad assets, 'dead horses for dead cows' as they put it, for the purpose of keeping regulators in the dark. Vernon's insolvency would cost taxpayers an estimated $1.3 billion.[16]

Many S & L officials used their new freedoms to embezzle staggering sums of money. One type of deal involved 'land flips', which were transfers of land between related parties, which in the process artificially inflated its value. One condominium project in Lake Tahoe, Nevada, was bought for less than $4 million and sold back and forth until it cost $40 million. The transactions often took place in the same room.[17] Loan broker J. William Oldenburg bought some property in California in 1979 for $874,000, 'flipped' it back and forth, then, in 1981, had the land appraised at $83.5 million. He then bought State Saving and Loan in Salt Lake City, Utah, for $10.5 million and sold his property to his newly acquired thrift for $26.5 million. The S & L soon went bankrupt, leaving $416 million in outstanding debts, insured by FSLIC.[18]

A report on the Savings and Loans scandal by the Government Accounting Office (GAO) summed up the wider extent of the criminality. It found that

> Extensive, repeated and blatant violations of laws and regulations characterized the failed thrifts that we reviewed in each and every case. Virtually every one of the thrifts was operating in an unsafe and unsound manner and was exposed to risks far beyond what was prudent . . . fraud or insider abuse existed at each and every one of the failed thrifts and allegations of criminal misconduct abounded . . . despite the fact that examination reports revealed critical problems at the failed thrifts, federal regulators did not always obtain agreements for corrective action. When they obtained them, they were in many cases violated, ignored, and in many cases it was years before resolutions were taken. The failed thrifts were not responsive to the concerns of the regulators.[19]

In other words, effective government oversight had ceased, with predictable consequences.

As of 31 December 1999, the thrift crisis had cost taxpayers around $124 billion and the thrift industry another $29 billion, an estimated total loss of around $153 billion.[20] Each taxpayer thus had to pay out hundreds of dollars to pay for what amounts to wholesale theft. The average prison terms for convicted S & L fraudsters were around two years to be served in minimum security federal prisons.[21]

Little noticed at the time but of great significance in later years was Reagan's lifting of federal controls on natural gas markets. This was a move favoured by Ken Lay, whose company Enron would become synonymous with corporate fraud.[22]

The proliferation of white-collar criminal opportunities was attributable to changes of legislation which weakened regulation, made largely as a result of high-pressure lobbying in the interests of the business-community industry. Few lessons, however, were learnt from these costly débâcles. Reagan's mantra that government was the problem not the solution was not seriously challenged by any of his successors.

Reaganomics did not make America more economically secure. In fact, thanks partly to the S & L thefts and bailout and more to an immense boost to defence spending, the nation went from being the world's largest creditor to being the world's largest debtor. Reagan's vice-president, the first George Bush, won the 1988 election but inherited a slowing economy on its way into a deep recession. Despite the foreign policy success that drove Saddam Hussain out of Kuwait in the first Gulf War, Bush served just one term.

★

In 1993 Bill Clinton took office as the first Democratic president since Carter in the 1970s. He tried but failed to reform America's corrupt and expensive health-care system. Initially he also tried to distance himself from what he called 'a bunch of fucking bond traders in Wall Street'. It was not long, however, before Clinton was moving closer to the right and espousing free-market ideology or neo-liberalism, as it began to be called.[23] His speeches began to echo such themes as individual responsibility, free enterprise and the dangers of big government, and he committed his administration to continue the deregulatory policies of the Republicans. During his two terms of office the Securities and Exchange Commission and the Department of Justice were notably ineffective in pursuing criminal prosecutions for financial fraud. Federal regulators, for example, uncovered a 'mountain of damning evidence' indicating fraud in the Bankers Trust group, according to Frank Partnoy in *Infectious Greed* (2004). He quoted a Bankers Trust employee describing the derivatives business thus, 'Funny business, you know? Lure people into that calm and then just totally fuck 'em.' Despite the evidence, punishment was minimal and most of the people involved in the case continued to work in Wall Street.[24]

America's continuing rightward shift was also reflected after the November 1994 elections when, the following January, Congress convened, committed to the 'Contract with America' agenda of Republican speaker Newt Gingrich and his allies including Tom DeLay and Phil Gramm. These made statements to the effect that their main goal was to deregulate corporate America.[25]

Despite his move to the right, Clinton did have reservations, however, about the Private Securities Litigation Reform Act (PSLRA) but Congress passed it anyway in 1995, overriding the president's veto. The act made securities-fraud suits more difficult for plaintiffs to sustain. According to one observer, it allowed 'dishonest managements to lie with impunity' and shielded 'underwriters and accountants from the consequences of lax performance'. And so the benign attitude of the Clinton administration, combined with new limits on plaintiffs' lawyers, ensured that corporations would be scarcely governed by any legal restraint. This was at a time when the widespread use of stock options to reward corporate executives had greatly increased the scope and opportunity for financial fraud.[26]

Stock options had been around for a long time but they began to take off as the preferred form of corporate compensation in the 1980s and 1990s. It began to be widely believed that if Chief Executive Officers (CEOs) owned options on stock in the companies they ran they would act less like bureaucrats and more like successful entrepreneurs. Executives were able to demand and get more and more options alongside their already large salaries. In 1993 the government's Financial Accounting Standards Board (FASB) recommended a rule to require companies to deduct the cost of options from their reported earnings. As the economic historian Roger Lowenstein has explained, the FASB did not propose to outlaw, or even limit, only to require companies to book or disclose their costs. An intense corporate-sponsored lobbying effort, spearheaded by the prominent Democratic party politician, Joe Lieberman, scuppered this small reform which would have let in some light on corporate compensation had it been implemented. Lieberman's argument that the reform would hurt the chances of ordinary workers to share in the American dream was 'simply untrue', according, to Lowenstein. Although many companies were distributing a small number of options to the rank and file, 75 per cent of options went to people who ranked in the top five in their companies. More than half of the remainder went to the next 50. Senior executives were clearly having most of the pie to themselves as the total number of options was rising during the 1990s, from 5 per cent to around 15 per cent of the ownership of corporate America. This amounted to an 'unprecedented accumulation of private wealth'.[27]

'Stock options', according to Joseph Stiglitz in *The Roaring Nineties* (2003), 'meant that executive pay depended on stock prices in the short run, and in the short run, it was easier to improve the appearances of profits than to increase true profits.' Executives found many fraudulent ways to boost their earnings. They could invent transactions allowing them to book revenues even if they didn't really have them. They could move expenses off their books or use one-time write-offs to fake the appearance of profits that were normally robust. Their objective, wrote Stiglitz, 'was to give the appearance of alluring success – or at least, of alluring promise – and cash out before the world discovered the truth. Thus did one form of deception give rise to many others.'[28]

Meanwhile, as America's fat cats were becoming fatter, Congress opened up more opportunities for them in 1996 when it passed the Telecommunications Act and made an even greater move towards deregulation. Marcy Kaptur, a Democratic party congresswoman and one of the few dissenters to the passing of this Act, called the process leading up to the Act 'living proof of what unlimited money can do to buy influence and the Congress of the United States'.[29] It was written, according to journalist Molly Ivins, 'by lobbyists for telecom, and lobbyists for telecom bought it through Congress'.[30] The new law removed certain longstanding restrictions on ownership of media properties and was meant to allow new companies and forms of competition to flourish. Instead the telecommunications industry began a series of buyouts and monopoly building, with, in the words of one commentator, 'telephone and cable systems merging and converging in a whirling tangle of free-market ebullience'.[31]

The 1996 law boosted the prospects of a number of new companies such as WorldCom, Global Crossing and Quest, intending to capitalize on what they claimed would be an unprecedented growth of demand, generated by the unlimited promise of the world wide web.[32] Their strategy was focusing on the stock market and finance and its short-term success was guaranteed by another major deregulatory move.

An intense lobbying effort by banking interests who spent more than $300 million in the process helped push through the repeal of the Glass-Steagall Act in 1999.[33] This Depression-era banking reform forbade commercial banks from engaging in the investment business and thus removed major sources for conflict of interest. Banks had been investing their own assets in securities with consequent risks to commercial and savings deposits. They had also been making unsound loans in order to shore up the price of securities or the financial position of companies in which they had invested. Finally, commercial banks with financial interests in the ownership, price, or distribution of securities tempted bank officials to press their customers into investing in securities which the banks themselves were under pressure to sell because of their own financial stake in the transaction.[34] These conflicts of interest, of course, often led to fraud or at the very least forms of interest-serving deception. Repealing such an important check on criminal behaviour would in rational times not be seriously considered but efforts to defend it were weak because, as Stiglitz noted, 'in the deregulatory fervor of the Roaring Nineties, neither the legislative nor the executive branch of government had any stomach for such an effort'.[35] The end of Glass-Steagall, along with the other business-interest-serving developments since Reagan, allowed the corruption of the late 1990s to encompass the entire American financial community. The financial markets now resembled 'Swiss cheese', as Frank Partnoy put it, 'with the holes – the unregulated places – getting bigger every year'.[36] Bankers, brokers, lawyers, auditors, analysts joined in a feast of fraud that began to be partially revealed when one of the shining stars of the so-called New Economy went bust in 2002.

Enron was first set up in 1985 from the merger of two energy companies, Houston Natural Gas and InterNorth. Its CEO Kenneth Lay was an ardent deregulator who hoped to gain from the new opportunities made possible by the Reagan administration's moves to loosen government controls. Lay's talents were political and he developed a close relationship with the Republican party, cultivating both George Bushes in particular. Lay's personal and political talents were not matched by administrative competence, however, and his lax management was exposed at the beginning of Enron's existence.

Part of the newly merged company was an oil-trading business in Valhalla, New York, which speculated in crude oil and refined products. The Valhalla group was headed by a trader, Louis Borget, who with others was profiting from manipulating the company's books. They set up a series of sham corporations in Panama, which they used to create phoney transactions. These transactions were made to look like money-making enterprises and Borget's group were paid millions of dollars' worth of bonuses. Lay was apprised of the dishonest bookkeeping involved in the scams but decided not to sack Borget and his colleagues because they were bringing in such useful profits. Even after the frauds were exposed and Borget convicted, Lay chose not to explain the episode to shareholders in subsequent annual reports, probably because the company's image might have been tarnished.[37] With hindsight the episode's combination of greed and deception prefigured much of what was to follow.

After surviving this expensive fraud, Lay chose to continue his policy of minimal supervision while Enron was refashioned by another free-market enthusiast, Jeffrey Skilling, so effectively that it rose to become the seventh-largest US company in terms of revenue by the end of the 1990s. Skilling became first president and then CEO of Enron and with a new vice-president of finance, Andy Fastow, plus scores of the best and the brightest young analysts and associates, accumulated millions of dollars in salary, bonuses and, of course, stock options. Things were going so well that an enormous banner was put up at the firm's state-of-the-art skyscraper headquarters in Houston. It claimed in big letters that

Enron was 'The World's Greatest Energy Company on the Way to Becoming the World's Greatest Company'.[38]

All the while Enron was greasing the wheels of the political process by donating freely to both political parties. In 2000, $2.4 million of Enron's money was spent supporting candidates for public office in the US, most for the Republicans but with large amounts going to Democrat fellow-travelling free-market supporters.[39] These kind of sums put Enron in the vanguard of the successful effort to deregulate California's energy grid which was so poorly managed as to end in widespread black-outs and exorbitant prices for Californian consumers during the state's energy crisis of 2000–1. According to transcripts of telephone calls released in 2004, Enron traders joked about stealing from grandmothers and talked openly about manipulating the electricity market by creating congestion on transmission lines and taking generating units offline to pump up electricity prices.[40]

Fastow was the company's chief financial officer and thus the architect of the thousands of convoluted offshore partnerships that contributed significantly to Enron's final collapse. The partnerships were given names from *Star Wars* and other films, names like Chewbacca, Jedi, Braveheart, Raptor and Condor. Some of the deals involving these partnerships can best be described as outright theft, according to Lowenstein. In one case, Enron was trying hard to sell three barges that were generating power off the coast of Nigeria in order to boost its earnings for the 1999 fourth quarter. The company eventually persuaded Merrill Lynch to buy the barges on the verbal understanding that Enron would later unwind the deal after Merrill had collected its profits. Merrill bought the barges at a price that netted Merrill, as promised, a 15 per cent annualized return. Enron had to pay one of its partnerships a hefty fee for this, but as far as the public was concerned, Enron got to record a profit. Enron's proposition and Merrill Lynch's willingness to implement it represented a much more general sense of corporate corruption.[41] There were many more of these corrupt deals. Enron was using its offshore partnerships to report profits it never made and cover up enormous losses. Between July 2000 and October 2001, for example, Enron recorded $1 billion of profit it did not really earn.[42] It was confidence tricksterism on a grand scale but actually proving fraud in the courts has so far proved difficult partly because Enron's accountants, Arthur Andersen, shredded a number of possibly damning documents. Revelations about Andersen's complicity in Enron's deceptions did at least shed some light on the widespread and often corrupt collusion between executives and their accountants.

Following shortly after Enron's collapse came a string of revelations, disclosures and bankruptcies that made very clear the fact that the Texas company was not the only rotten apple in the barrel. In fact it became clear that the whole barrel was rotten. By the end of 2002 companies were regularly admitting that their reported earnings were not as they should have been and there was the collapse of a billion-dollar company every few weeks. The range of financial malfeasance and manipulation was vast, according to Frank Partnoy's account: 'Energy companies, such as Dynergy, El Paso, and Williams, did the same complex financial deals Andy Fastow had engineered at Enron. Telecommunications firms, such as Global Crossing and WorldCom, fell into bankruptcy after it became clear that they, too, had been cooking their books.' These top energy and telecommunications firms did the most notorious transactions, Partnoy continued, 'including questionable round-trip swaps with each other, many of which were arranged by Wall Street's top banks and blessed by Big Five accounting firms'.[43] Whether or not these practices were technically legal they were clearly economically unsound and investors dumped the companies' stocks as soon as they heard about them.

WorldCom's collapse in June 2002 was the most spectacular of many corporate crashes. As its name suggested, WorldCom was a global company which served more than 20 million customers. It was the nation's second-largest long-distance provider, the largest carrier of international traffic, and the world's largest Internet carrier with operations on six continents. The company's contracts with the US government affected 80 million Social Security recipients, air-traffic-control applications for the Federal Aviation Administration, network management for the Department of Defense and critical data-network services for the United States Postal Service, plus much more. It had grown from a small long-distance telecommunications provider into a global force by making more than 60 acquisitions in only 15 years.[44] On 27 June 2002 WorldCom admitted to overstating its earnings between 1999 and 2001 by nearly $4 billion and later raised the figure to $9 billion, a fraud so immense as to immediately get the label of the greatest accounting fraud in history. The fraud was achieved largely by treating expenditures on day-to-day items like wages as if they were payments for capital goods. WorldCom could then put off into the future their appearances as costs on their balance sheet. According to an investigation conducted by Richard Thornburgh, a bankruptcy examiner, WorldCom's ability to borrow monies and acquire other companies was facilitated by this massive accountancy fraud which allowed the company to present itself as credit-worthy when it clearly wasn't. Thornburgh also felt that 'the company's ability to borrow vast sums allowed it to perpetuate the illusion of financial health created by its accounting fraud.' He noted that World-Com's treasurer even admitted to him that the company simply 'robbed Peter to pay Paul'.[45]

While some individual WorldCom executives have been tried and convicted, notably the company's Chief Executive Officer, Bernard Ebbers, the company itself got off very lightly. The company changed its name to MCI, kept many of its lucrative, federal contracts and was even granted more. It escaped any significant financial penalty for its crimes. Victims of the various frauds have got next to nothing in compensation at the time of writing. The company even sought a $300 million refund from the Internal Revenue Service for taxes paid on its fraudulently overstated earnings. A legal representative for a rival telecommunications company asked a Senate committee this rhetorical question: 'Have the enforcement authorities taken any action to strip away the fruits of the crime?' The answer was no. 'In fact', he elaborated, 'they have left this company with virtually all of the fruits of the crime intact to deploy against law-abiding companies in the marketplace.'[46]

Wall Street's accounting norms were a crucial ingredient in the development of the criminal corporate culture laid bare by the Enron, WorldCom and other scandals. According to the economist Robert Bremner, these norms legitimated virtually any trick in the book to pump-up 'pro-forma' earnings – those that are reported quarterly to stockholders and the financial community. It was only later that regulatory agencies required more realistic figures. 'Needless to say', Bremmer added, 'this system of dual reporting invited abuses – for instance, exaggerating short-term earnings just long enough to sustain equity prices while corporate insiders unload their stock.'

Corporate organized crime contributed hugely to a mountainous redistribution of wealth achieved by American corporate leaders during the 1990s. Between 1995 and 1999 the value of stock options granted to US executives more than quadrupled, from $26.5 billion to $110 billion. In 1992, corporate CEOs held 2 per cent of the equity of US corporations; 10 years later they owned 12 per cent. Between 1997 and 2001 insiders cashed in some $18 billion in shares, unloading more than half this total in 2000 at the peak of the telecoms bubble and thus avoiding the massive hits taken by less well-connected investors. This all ranks, Bremner rightly concluded, amongst the most spectacular acts of expropriation in the history of capitalism.[47] Stock options had been designed by executives to benefit themselves and they show how self-regulation fails even when there is a clear conflict between two groups within the institution itself (in this case the shareholders and senior managers). The formal ownership power of institutional investors and private individuals was no match for the superior knowledge of senior managers. Stock-option schemes themselves were not of course criminal but the riches they offered certainly provided motives for those with means and opportunity.

There have been a large number of trials and convictions for the wave of corporate crime that began to unravel after Enron and many of these are still unresolved at the time of writing. However, one thing is certain, the effort against corporate crime is mainly directed against individual transgressors and the intention is to put as many of these behind bars to deter others. There have been some cosmetic rather than structural reforms. These are unlikely to be an adequate response to a crisis that, in the words of political scientist Justin O'Brien, 'is not the result of deviance but rather the inevitable out-workings of a political and economic system, which pivots on the malign power of money to distort the deliberative process ... It is the system itself', O'Brien continued, 'that now stands accused of creating the circumstances for the morally challenged executives to thrive.' It is not in the interests of the system to draw attention to this failure.[48]

There will be trials and more trials and they have probably made a short-term impact. The Justice Department's Corporate Crime Task Force, set up by President Bush soon after the WorldCom scandal, had obtained more than 500 corporate-fraud convictions or guilty pleas by June 2004 and the SEC had been equally active.[49] But the punishments have hardly fitted the scale of the crimes. There are now a number of convicted corporate executives on the business school lecture circuit who, having served short sentences, talk about their misdeeds for up to $5,000 a lecture.[50] Perhaps, however, a greater number will share their criminal know-how and explain where they went wrong to a new generation.

Deregulation and inadequate enforcement by the appropriate authorities meant that the system of checks and balances established by the New Deal had broken down. The system that had partly kept the lid on organized, corporate crime was destroyed by endless claims that the market knows best made by well-financed and well-connected lobbyists. Many business experts now claim that the Sarbanes-Oxley Act of 2002 and other corporate-governance reforms since Enron and WorldCom have set up a new system of checks and balances. Now independent company directors have more power, outside auditors have fewer conflicts of interests and there is greater transparency in reporting.[51] Corporate lobbyists however claim that reform has gone far enough and the re-election of President Bush in 2004 ensures Washington will be receptive to that argument.

The rise in market power of Enron, WorldCom and the rest owed a great deal to criminal activities. Their crimes had many victims, including shareholders who lost money and workers who lost jobs when revelations of fraud caused bankruptcies or 'downsizing'. WorldCom investors alone lost more than $200 billion in equity and bonds from the company's bankruptcy and workers' pension funds lost at least $70 billion in equity alone. Added to this more than 22 states lost more than $2.6 billion in their public employee retirement funds as a result of the bankruptcy. Local government funds lost billions more at a time when state and local governments were already facing fiscal crises, thus threatening the retirement security of teachers, firefighters, police and other state and local government employees.[52] The winners were few; the losers were many.

Although there has been some effort to curb corporate crime of the Enron and WorldCom type, there has been little effort to pass laws that attack abusive tax shelters or finance a serious hunt for America's many big time tax cheats. One tax consultant estimated that around $18 billion was lost to cheats in 2000 but this figure, according to David Cay Johnston writing in the *New York Times*, may be conservative because it is based on indicators of tax cheating that could be detected through statistical analysis, rather than actual investigation of cheating that is designed to slip past Internal Revenue Service (IRS) computer-screening programmes. As an example, Johnston cites, the tax shelters sold by major accounting firms that use multilayered partnerships so that the figures that flow from the bottom layer onto corporate or individual tax returns appear proper. 'The IRS,' he states, 'only audits one in 400 partnership returns, making them an efficient vehicle for tax cheats, especially when used in layers.' American tax policies and enforcement have become a disaster, according to Johnston, because of discreet lobbying by the political donor class. Nearly 30,000 more auditors and investigators needed to be added to the IRS to curb cheating, according to one former commissioner of the agency, and the Bush administration has little intention of meeting this minimum requirement.[53]

Even without the wholesale cheating, American corporations have been paying progressively less of their share of income tax since the 1950s. Corporate income taxes reached a peak of 32 per cent of federal income tax receipts in 1952. By the 1960s this percentage had declined to an average 21 per cent of federal revenues, by the 1970s down further to 15 per cent, and by the 1980s to less than 10 per cent. In 2003, they were just over 7 per cent of federal revenues. Meanwhile, the tax burden on American workers has gone the other way and they have been paying a higher proportion of their income on taxes since the 1950s. Payroll taxes represented about 10 per cent of all federal tax receipts in 1952, but 40 per cent in 2003.[54]

In large part because of corporate income tax cuts, allied to tax breaks and large-scale tax evasion, America's playing field has become increasingly uneven. The gaps between high-income and low- and middle-income families have widened since the 1970s. According to Jared Bernstein of the Economic Policy Institute in Washington, DC, 'If you go back to 1979, prior to the period when the growth in inequality really took off in the United States, the top 5 percent on average had 11 times the average income of the bottom 20 percent. If you fast forward to the year 2000 . . . you find that that ratio increased to 19 times. So over the course of those two decades, the gap between the wealthiest and the lowest income families grew from 11 times to 19 times.'[55] The 400 richest Americans pay less and less of their income in taxes while the middle class pays more and more. While the income of the big rich skyrocketed, the average income for the bottom 90 per cent of American society has fallen.[56] In terms of wealth inequality America is returning to the socially and economically disastrous levels of inequality of the 1920s.

This trend had been a consequence of the dominance of free-market thinking since Nixon. Welfare for the poor has been cut back while deregulation has increased the fortunes of corporate executives. Few pointed out the burgeoning inequalities and social breakdown that unregulated markets engendered.[57] Instead a large part of the response to this breakdown has been a policy of mass imprisonment, mainly affecting the African-American and recent immigrant poor. But, mass imprisonment, as we shall see next, has become more a part of the problem of organized crime than its solution.

7

Zero Tolerance and the Rise of the Gangs

Crime has played an increasingly large part in American local, state and presidential elections since the 1960s. Nixon's cynical and successful exploitation of the issue during his time in office has made it essential for all candidates for high office to appear tough on crime. Any suggestion of 'softness' is political death, as shown by the failed campaigns of George McGovern in 1972 and Michael Dukakis in 1988. The political right has benefited most from the widely held belief that the poor are out of control in America and that the only viable response is increasingly draconian punishment for even minor offences. This has led to the phenomenon of 'governing through crime', according to the criminologist Jonathan Simon, as the United States and other advanced industrial societies have prioritized crime and punishment as the preferred contexts for governance.[1] Phrases like 'tough on crime', 'zero tolerance', and 'three strikes and you're out' were endlessly turned out to give the impression that the government is sincerely anti-crime.

Paradoxically, therefore, just as right-wing politicians have been committed to rolling back the state in terms of business regulation and allowing the corporate crime wave that has just been described, they have been simultaneously committed to building a state apparatus that is stronger and more authoritarian than ever before.[2] This is particularly the case in the area of drug control.

No accurate statistics exist but illegal drug use has certainly pervaded all strata of Western industrialized society since the 1970s. A good host in some middle- and upper-class circles would be expected to offer marijuana or cocaine as well as or instead of the best malt Scotch to his guests.[3] Amphetamine was the drug of choice for many working-class youths, manufactured in the United States or across the border in Mexico. Hallucinogens such as LSD and an almost infinite variety of synthetic drugs such as ecstasy go in and out of fashion as frequently as clothes. Heroin use is common at all levels of society. However, at the lowest levels, the reality of heroin use amongst the poor is dependency, misery and early death.

In the mid-1980s, crack, a derivative of cocaine and 'the narcotic equivalent of fast food', hit the streets.[4] Hospital and police statistics registered the terrible and immediate impact. Emergency room admissions for cocaine trauma doubled, 15 per cent of babies in public hospitals were diagnosed as addicted to cocaine, the number of arrests for dealing multiplied and the number of 'gang-related' slayings averaged one a day in the city area. The media coverage was sensationalized and mainly unhelpful but it could not be denied that crack was a commodity that did an immense amount of harm and deserved the *Los Angeles Times*' description as 'the most devastating of all the monster drugs to afflict any American adolescent generation thus far'.[5]

As the market for drugs increased, so did the efforts of federal, state and local governments to suppress it. In 1969, $65 million was spent by the Nixon administration on the drug war. In 1982 the Reagan administration increased this commitment to $1.65 *billion*. In 2000 the Clinton administration massively increased this figure to $17.9 billion. In 2002 the Bush administration spent more than $18.822 billion.[6] After adjusting for inflation, federal drug enforcement now costs more than ten times as much as Prohibition enforcement did during the 1920s. States, cities, and local governments also spend massive amounts to supplement the federal efforts.

The result of this effort has been a massive increase in arrests for drug violations. In 1973, there were 328,670 arrests for drug law violations, according to the FBI Uniform Crime Reports. In 1989, there were 1,361,700 drug arrests, nearly 10 per cent of all arrests. In 2002, that number rose to 1,538,813. Forty-five per cent of the 2002 arrests were for marijuana rather than for the more dangerous drugs. Most of these arrests were for simple possession offences rather than sale or manufacture.[7]

More than any other single factor, the succession of Nixon-style wars on drugs declared by presidents Reagan and Bush Sr fuelled the largest and most rapid expansion of the US prison population in its history. Between 1980 and 1994, the prison population tripled from 500,000 to 1.5 million. In 2002 the United States incarcerated 2,166,260 persons, and it retained its status as having the highest prison population rate in the world, some 701 per 100,000 of the national population. This compares with the United Kingdom's rate of 141 per 100,000 of the national population, which is the highest rate among European Union countries.[8]

Francis Ianni observed in *Black Mafia* (1976) that 'prisons and the prison experience are the most important loci for establishing the social relationships that form the basis for partnerships in organized crime.' It had long been known that prisons were self-perpetuating institutions because they reinforced existing criminal attitudes and because they provided many opportunities for learning new criminal techniques. Ianni's studies revealed the great extent to which criminal partnerships were formed in prison and some of the mechanisms that operated in prison which promoted the formation of these partnerships.[9]

Predictably, however, Ianni's research was ignored and the policy of mass imprisonment multiplied gangster partnerships. US prison gangs fight over prostitution, protection and drug-trafficking rackets in systems based on brutality, informants and staff corruption. Most of the gangs are organized along racial and ethnic lines and spend as much time fighting each other in wars based on race hate as in commercial ventures. During the 1970s and 1980s some, like the Aryan Brotherhood, the Black Guerillas, the Mexican Mafia, the Texas Syndicate and La Nuestra Familia, achieved state-wide and even inter-state influence, but since that time there has been evidence of an increasing splintering of prison groupings.[10] Of the larger groups mentioned above, for example, the Aryan Brotherhood have spawned other white supremacist gangs such as the Nazi Low Riders, which was said to be the fastest-growing white gang in California and is heavily involved in the production and trade of methamphetamine. The origins of this neo-fascist wave can thus be traced back directly to the forces created and sustained by drug prohibition.[11]

The influence of prison gangs has often extended beyond the prison gates. This was famously illustrated by the fate of three consultants for the Edward James Olmos film, *American Me*, on the rise of the Mexican Mafia. The film portrayed one founder of the gang as having been raped as a young man. In retribution, the film's consultants were machine-gunned to death in their homes by hit men and Olmos himself was forced into hiding.[12]

There are of course hierarchies amongst prison gangs and clearly some organization but the overall picture of the phenomenon is one of chaos, betrayal and race hate, stirred up and even encouraged by prison guards and officials. One study of the Californian prison system, for example, suggested that guards sometimes encouraged the development and establishment of gangs for a variety of reasons. First, guards were keen to create 'threats to security', which necessitated increased surveillance and therefore more overtime. Second, some actually participated in the gangs' enterprises, bringing knives, drugs, food and other commodities in for sale to their literally captive market. Finally, and most importantly, gang conflict was encouraged in order to control the inmates more effectively. According to one inmate,

> They perpetuated the friction because, for instance, what they would do is . . . give false information to different groups . . . Something to put the fear so that then the Latino would prepare himself for a conflict . . . And so everybody's on point and the next thing you know a fight would break out and the shit would come down. So it was to their interest to perpetuate division among the inmates so that they would be able to better control the institution. Because if you are spending your time fighting each other you have no time to fight the establishment.

Many other inmates confirmed the existence of a divide-and-rule policy, helping to ignite the already existing racial tensions.[13]

The prison race war is not limited to the yards. As Christian Parenti puts it in *Lockdown America* (2000), 'the hate factory discharges 90 percent of its product back to the streets.' He cites an example from the late 1990s of a conflict between Latinos and African-Americans in the Venice, Santa Monica and Culver City parts of Los Angeles, in which over a dozen people were killed and three African-American families had their homes firebombed. It was believed that these racial vendettas were a direct extension of mayhem originating in the Californian prison system.[14]

Parenti also explains how the violence, corruption and general failure of the system, like many law-enforcement defeats, serve the bureaucracy of control better than victory ever could, 'mayhem in prison is parlayed into empire-building . . . The more "deviance" the big house excretes . . . the more the guards and administrators need new prisons . . . more gang investigators, further expansion into outside communities, closer cooperation with other agencies, better computers, more dossiers, new tracking software, better guns, more tear gas, more body armor . . . and so on. Thus corrections bureaucracies grow, like most others.'[15]

Politicians from both major parties have been reluctant to address a problem that is directly related to the great expansion of drug arrests and convictions that have stretched penal institutions to breaking point. Although the full consequences of putting hundreds of thousands of young people in with career criminals will not be known until well into the twenty-first century, the American prison gang phenomenon has already added spectacular substance to the observation that prison serves best to train more efficient and determined criminals. The public has been well trained by politicians and media and therefore few question a crime-control solution, based largely on locking up the poor, that will continue to have disastrously counter-productive results.

Today, many thousands of young men and women, whose mobility is blocked by failing school systems and whose insecurity is heightened by draconian welfare regimes, choose to join gangs, up to 35 per cent of high school drop-outs in Chicago for example. The gangs have a presence in 94 per cent of all US cities with populations greater than 100,000. Los Angeles alone has over 950 different gangs, with more than 100,000 members.[16]

While demographic and other factors including more intensive policing have caused an overall decrease in violent crime over the past decades, gang homicides rose more than 50 per cent from 1999 to 2002, according to government figures. The FBI's 2003 annual report on national crime statistics found that youth-gang homicides had jumped to more than 1,100 in 2002, up from 692 in 1999. Chicago's Police Superintendent, Philip J. Cline, indicating the severity of the problem to a national conference of gang violence, compared the 1,300 killings by street gangs in Chicago in the previous five years with around 1,000 killings in total over a period of over 80 years by 'members of the Mafia, or traditional organized-crime figures'.[17]

Street gangs participate in a variety of entrepreneurial activities but mainly in the drug trade according to Steven Wiley, Chief of the FBI's Violent Crimes and Major Offenders Section. Wiley told a Senate committee in 1997 that gangs have been involved with the lower levels of the drug trade for many years, but their participation skyrocketed with the arrival of 'crack' cocaine in the 1980s. 'Almost overnight,' he continued,

> a major industry was born, with major outlets in every neighbourhood, tens of thousands of potential new customers and thousands of sales jobs available. In slightly over a decade, street gangs have become highly involved in drug trafficking at all levels. Intelligence developed through investigations has revealed extensive interaction among individuals belonging to gangs across the Nation. This interaction . . . is more a loose network of contacts and associations that come together as needed to support individual business ventures.[18]

These young gangsters are killing each other with guns mostly corruptly supplied by American manufacturers. In February 2003 a former, senior firearms-industry executive made this point when testifying in support of claims by 12 California cities and counties suing the gun makers and their wholesalers and retail dealers. The cities and counties contended that the gun industry maintained a distribution system that allowed many guns to fall into the hands of criminals and juveniles. Robert A. Ricker lost his post as executive director of the American

Shooting Sports Council in 1999 after discussing ways to prevent more school shootings such as the slaughter at Columbine High School in Colorado. He testified that gun makers had long known that 'the diversion of firearms from legal channels of commerce to the black market' takes place 'principally at the distributor/dealer level'. Corrupt dealers, he said, make it easy for criminals and juveniles to buy guns by allowing practices like 'straw sales', in which an individual buys a gun on behalf of someone who is prohibited from purchasing a gun because of age or a criminal conviction. 'Leaders in the industry have long known that greater industry action to prevent illegal transactions is possible,' Ricker continued but industry officials 'resisted taking constructive voluntary action' and 'have sought to silence others within the industry'. His conclusion was that this resulted in 'a culture of evasion of firearms laws and regulations'. As a gun-control advocate said of Ricker's testimony, 'The consummate insider has now exposed the dirty little secret of the gun industry – that is, the underground market is supplied by corrupt gun dealers, and the industry punishes anyone who tried to stop it.'[19]

Later in 2003, in a case that confirmed Ricker's testimony, James Dillard, an Ohio gun dealer, was charged with fostering the flow of arms to the New Jersey Double ii Bloods street gang. He was accused of allowing Ohio college students to act as the straw buyers in the transactions.[20]

Los Angeles has experienced one of the most devastating upsurges in gang violence in recent years – between 2001 and 2002, for example, homicides, mostly gang-related, jumped by 52 per cent. Many factors have been put forward to explain such a precipitous rise but Father Gregory Boyle, a priest from one of the worst affected parts of the city, points to the counter-productive effects of the policy of mass imprisonment. Particularly after the 1992 riots that burnt down large parts of the city, city and Californian state authorities jailed tens of thousands of young people, often for trivial offences. After the riots, according to Father Boyle, 'we jailed a whole generation of people. They're now back out on the streets. And they've come to no family and no network of helpers. So those people from the riots – they've just gone back to the only thing they know: the gangs. That, alongside the slump in the economy, has led to the rise in murders here. If it shows anything, it shows that jailing kids doesn't work.'[21]

America has even begun to export at least some of its youth-gang problems. From the early 1980s people came to America illegally in the hundreds and thousands from neighbouring countries damaged by war and poverty such as Jamaica, Honduras, El Salvador, Colombia, Mexico, Guatemala and the Dominican Republic. Many came with children who grew up more on American city streets than the unprepared and under-equipped city schools. Not surprisingly the children frequently got involved in gangs and the underground economy of the cities and, equally not surprisingly, got arrested. Since 1992 the US Immigration and Naturalization Service has been rounding them up and deporting them en masse to countries they often don't know. When they arrive in their native countries the deportees, often educated in the worst aspects of US criminal culture, bring a new criminal element to countries that are already unstable and violent.[22] Gang 'franchises' have taken hold in El Salvador, Honduras and Guatemala, in particular. According to Rupert Widdicombe and Duncan Campbell, writing in the *Guardian*,

> The influence of US gang culture is evident in poor neighbourhoods or barrios across Central America. There are local variations on a dress code of baggy clothes, baseball caps and chains, a defined taste in music (much of it Latino rap and hip-hop), a semiology in tattoos, graffiti and hand signs, and a slang peppered with imported words like *broderes* (brothers) and 'homies'. Most damaging is a fashion for extreme violence that has found an easy home in countries with violent histories.[23]

Children as young as seven join the gangs in a country where one in three people is a victim of violent crime.[24] Americans cannot even be reassured that at least exported gang crime is no longer their problem since the deportees frequently and illegally cross the border and come back to the country they know best.[25]

WorldCom, Enron, much of the rest of corporate America and the thousands of splintered gangster groups are proof that US organized-crime and drug-control methods do not work. Yet such is the strength and effectiveness of the US government that it has managed to sell them to the rest of the world.

PART 2

The United States and Setting the Global Agenda on Organized Crime

The world belongs to the strong. It always has – it always will.

Harry J. Anslinger, Federal Bureau of Narcotics, 1945

[We must] accept whole-heartedly our duty and our opportunity as the most powerful and vital nation in the world and in consequence to exert upon the world the full impact of our influence, for such purposes as we see fit and by such means as we see fit.

Henry Robinson Luce, 'The American Century', *Life*, 1941

8

The Broken Promise of Roosevelt's Global Freedoms

In 1941 Franklin Roosevelt offered the peoples of the world, then embroiled in the Second World War, an alternative to the brutalities of fascist and militarist regimes, just as he had offered Americans an alternative to the brutalities and corruption of unregulated capitalism. There was 'nothing mysterious about the foundations of a healthy and strong democracy', he argued. 'The basic things expected by our people of their political and economic systems are simple. They are: Equality of opportunity for youth and for others. Jobs for those who can work. Security for those who need it. The ending of special privilege for the few. The preservation of civil liberties for all. The enjoyment of the fruits of scientific progress in a wider and constantly rising standard of living.' Although a distant hope in his own country for African-Americans, Roosevelt sought to spread these laudable aspirations throughout the world. 'In future days,' he announced, 'which we seek to make secure, we look forward to a world founded upon four essential human freedoms.' These he listed:

> The first is freedom of speech and expression – everywhere in the world. The second is freedom of every person to worship God in his own way – everywhere in the world. The third is freedom from want, which, translated into world terms, means economic understandings which will secure to every nation a healthy peacetime life for its inhabitants – everywhere in the world. The fourth is freedom from fear, which translated into world terms, means a world-wide reduction of armaments to such a point and in such a thorough fashion that no nation will be in a position to commit an act of physical aggression against any neighbour – anywhere in the world.[1]

Roosevelt was of course a pragmatic politician committed to America's business system and thus at least as committed to making the world safe for American business as to the democratic interests of the world's peoples. However, his words were based on the foundation of the New Deal's democratic response to economic crisis and its moves towards a more equitable, honest and less violent America. He had also reaffirmed his commitment to social justice by choosing as his vice-president Henry Wallace against the strong opposition of right-wing Democrats and by encouraging his Treasury Secretary Henry Morgenthau to pursue a radical agenda while planning international economy policy for the post-war world.

To complement Roosevelt's effort to inform the fighting of the Second World War with a moral purpose, Vice-President Wallace delivered a powerful speech on 8 May 1942. Wallace was responding to the un-ashamedly imperialist 'American Century' editorial by Henry Luce, the owner of *Time* magazine.[2] While Luce's twentieth century was to be the century of General Motors, Standard Oil, Pan-Am and his own Time-Life-Fortune, entrenched everywhere in the world with the protection of American military power, Wallace demanded that the century which came out of the war must be 'the century of the common man . . . Victory for the Allies', he said, 'must lift the men and women of all nations from the bonds of military, political and economic tyranny.' It is fair to assume that by economic tyranny he was referring to the kind of corporate power lionized by Luce.[3]

Wallace attempted to go further than this rhetoric and use American strength to further the interests of ordinary people everywhere. He tried to use his position as chair of the Board of Economic Warfare (BEW) as much more than a purchasing agent for critical war materials, as one of the principal mechanisms for reshaping the post-war world. He intended to use the leverage of the BEW's funds to promote progressive reform in the nations with which they were doing business. For example, a nation in South America that wished to sell material to the United States would be required to allow trade unions or bar business monopolies or lose their BEW contracts. The BEW's efforts to bring liberal reform to the rest of the world were, however, stymied by intense opposition from the business community and the government's more business-friendly Secretary of Commerce, Jesse H. Jones.[4]

At the Treasury, Roosevelt's commitment to a more equitable world was represented by Henry Morgenthau. Morgenthau had announced his intention to use the post-war planning effort to build 'a New Deal in inter-national economics', curbing the power of bankers at home and abroad that had dominated and damaged international finance in the 1920s and 1930s.[5] To help create a new, international, financial order, Morgenthau chose Harry Dexter White, someone who was far from being tied to the orthodox financial thinking that had supported the power of the bankers.

Morgenthau and White ensured that American leaders were motivated by more than simple self-interest when it came to laying the foundations of a new economic world order. All of those present during the creation of this order at Bretton Woods, New Hampshire, in 1944 were keenly aware that international co-operation was essential to prevent a recurrence of the previous decades of war, depression, tyranny and international anarchy. Roosevelt was at one with his Treasury negotiators in believing that no country could maintain its own prosperity unless other countries prospered as well. They also believed that it was equally necessary that the 'common people' or 'ordinary men and women' of all countries should share in this prosperity.[6] Governments should not tolerate prolonged and widespread unemployment and anything less than reasonable standards of living. As Roosevelt put it in his message to Congress on the Bretton Woods agreements, the hope was

> for a secure and fruitful world, a world in which plain people in all countries can work at tasks which they do well, exchange in peace the products of their labor and work out their several destinies in security and peace; a world in which Governments, as their major contribution to the common welfare, are highly and effectively resolved to work together in practical affairs.[7]

From Bretton Woods emerged a new framework for international economic and financial relations and a new monetary system pegged to the dollar as the world's strongest currency. The International Monetary Fund (IMF) and the International Bank for Reconstruction and Development (later called the World Bank) were to be the key institutions whose first task was to rebuild a world whose infrastructure and productive capacity had been shattered by war.

Although the American and British negotiators at Bretton Woods differed on many issues they agreed that there could not be a return to the pre-First World War situation where capital was free to move all over the world. With the commitment to free trade was a determination not to allow the movement of capital to disrupt trade and currency relationships. Governments, they felt, should regulate capitalism, which would include limiting the control that a small number of private bankers had once exercised over international finance.

Morgenthau memorably echoed Roosevelt's 1933 condemnation of the financial community. Establishing a world bank to provide long-term financial aid at reasonable rates to those countries whose industry and agriculture had been destroyed, he explained, would help ensure global stability and 'drive only the usurious money lenders out of the temple of international finance'.[8] Crucially, the thinking behind the Bretton Woods agreements conceded an important role to the nation state in economic development, and promised minimum social and economic guarantees to citizens.

Therefore the IMF and the World Bank were originally progressive institutions, surprisingly, given their record in recent decades. According to the economist Susan George, 'their mandate was to help prevent future conflicts by lending for reconstruction and development and by smoothing out temporary balance of payments problems.' 'They had', she concluded, 'no control over individual governments' economic decisions nor did their mandate include a licence to intervene in national policy.'

The memory of the market-based causes of the Great Depression allied to the New Deal background of America's post-war economic planners justified Karl Polanyi's optimism in *The Great Transformation* (1944). 'We are witnessing', he wrote, 'a development under which the economic system ceases to lay down the law to society and the primacy of society over that system is secured.' However, Polanyi's great study of the failures of nineteenth-century *laissez-faire* industrial society also led him to warn that 'To allow the market mechanism to be the sole director of the fate of human beings and their natural environment . . . would result in the demolition of society.'[9] As we shall see, once the IMF, the World Bank and the international economic agenda as a whole were captured by neo-liberals, this proved to be a tragically accurate prediction. As long as the Bretton Woods consensus prevailed, however, it acted as a check on the ambitions of those private financial interests more committed to profits than the interests of foreign governments and citizens.

America's international economic policy was phenomenally successful in the two decades that followed Bretton Woods. America had in effect built what it called a Free World in Western Europe, Japan and other parts of the world based on the dollar and backed by a nuclear capacity that ensured that there would be no serious overt conflict between the United States and the Soviet Union. Economic success lifted the United States to a trillion-dollar economy and brought devastated Japan and Western Europe to new heights of prosperity, leading one British prime minister to tell his electorate quite correctly in 1959 that 'you've never had it so good'.[10]

Although these economic success stories happened mostly in the developed capitalist countries, less developed countries or what became known as the Third World also shared in the overall increase in prosperity. Third World countries in Africa, Asia and the Americas had gained their independence from colonial powers such as Britain and France in the post-Second World War period. Many of them attempted to develop systems based on protectionism, preferences and planned international trade that would benefit both their producers and provide jobs for their peoples. In other words they tried to control their own development in ways that had been successfully employed by Britain, the United States and other industrialized nations. Under the Bretton Woods system individual countries had policy autonomy and all Third World countries chose to shun economic liberalism when it came to trade and financial policy. They established customs barriers to shield infant industries from competition, and imposed foreign-exchange controls to prevent capital flight. Many developing countries were able to achieve reasonable growth between the 1950s and the 1980s.

The economist Ha-Joon Chang has calculated that the per capita income in developing countries grew at 3 per cent per annum between 1960 and 1980. He argues that poor nations were able to achieve this by pursuing growth policies similar to those used historically by nations such as Britain and the United States, which had successfully protected their infant industries from foreign competition using interventionist industrial, trade and technology policies. During the 1970s, and particularly during the administration of President Richard Nixon, however, the old Bretton Woods system was broken down, replaced by a global order that actively promoted economic liberalism in trade and financial matters. Few poor countries have since been able to resist pressures from developed countries, represented most visibly by the World Bank and the IMF, to liberalize, deregulate and privatize their economies. The thinking behind the international financial system that replaced the Bretton Woods consensus from the 1970s onwards denied an important role to the less developed nation states in economic development and offered few protections from the brutal realities of the free market. By removing the ability of poor countries to control and protect their economies, rich countries, to use Chang's appropriate description, have 'kicked away the ladders' that they themselves used as they developed. Largely as a result, per capita income in developing countries grew at only 1.5 per cent between 1980 and 2000 and problems associated with global poverty have increased.[11] At the same time, the usurious money lenders and a host of other parasites were let back into the temple. The good intentions of America's post-war planners were to be undermined and the world was to be closer to Luce's vision than Wallace's. Appropriately, as we shall see in Chapter 10, Richard Nixon opened the door.

★

'Bretton Woods', according to historian Hugh Brogan, 'was a civilized arrangement . . . that had been properly and reasonably negotiated.'[12] The economic ordering of the world was a key part of a panoply of understanding and agreements beginning with the Atlantic Charter of 1941, continuing through the establishment of the United Nations in 1945, and including conventions on such crucial issues as refugees, human rights, genocide, arms control and war crimes. 'Behind the new ordering of the world', as the historian Tony Judt has explained, 'lay the memory of thirty calamitous years of war, depression, domestic tyranny, and international anarchy, as those who were present at the creation fully understood.'[13]

But in the decades that followed the combination of an interventionist foreign policy with expansionist corporate enterprise led America a long way from the spirit of the Atlantic Charter and support for human freedom as Roosevelt had explained it. Blinded by a rigid and often ill-informed anti-communist ideology, Americans were led into many murderous and corrupt dealings with other countries.

George Kennan, the State Department's expert on Soviet Affairs, had first articulated the rationale behind America's post-war foreign policy in 1946. According to Kennan, the Soviet Union was an imperial empire, expansionist and hostile, but an all-out clash for the United States could be avoided through 'containment'. Containment required 'the adroit and vigilant application of counterforce at a series of constantly shifting geographical and political points'. The following year President Harry Truman made containment the cornerstone of American foreign policy over the following decades when he articulated the Truman Doctrine. 'I believe', Truman announced, 'that it must be the policy of the United States to support free peoples who are resisting attempted subjugation by armed minorities or by outside pressures.'[14]

H.W. Brands, in the *Wages of Globalism* (1997), has accurately described the language of the Truman Doctrine as loose since it made containment applicable almost anywhere in the world, and implied a vast over-commitment of American resources. Because the message of containment was so simple and morally reassuring it was used time and again to mobilize American public and congressional support. It was not just used for the protracted effort of waging the Cold War against communism but also for crushing movements that were inspired by legitimate nationalist aspirations and sought only moderate social and economic reforms.[15] The doctrine would justify the American government's Faustian arrangements with brutal and opportunist criminals of every variety, and locked the United States into a foreign policy that culminated in the quagmire of the Vietnam War.

Although rhetorical commitments to human rights and democracy were frequently made, the overriding aim of American foreign policy since the Second World War has been to keep the world safe for capitalism, especially American capitalism. CIA, State Department and armed-service activity has been consistently directed towards an aim that was never openly admitted but can be found in unreleased documents. George Kennan, already mentioned as the author of America's post-war policy for the containment of communism, for example, wrote confidentially in 1948:

> We have about 50 percent of the world's wealth, but only 6.3 per cent of its population . . . In this situation, we cannot fail to be the object of envy and resentment. Our real task in the coming period is to devise a pattern of relationships which will permit us to maintain this position of disparity . . . We need not deceive ourselves that we can afford the luxury of altruism and world-benefaction . . . We should cease to talk about vague and . . . unreal objectives such as human rights, the raising of living standards, and democratization.[16]

From the Eisenhower administration onwards, the covert side of American foreign policy consistently favoured the interests of Western corporations over 'vague and . . . unreal objectives such as human rights, the raising of living standards, and democratization', as the following accounts of CIA operations demonstrate.

In 1953, Operation Ajax, run jointly with British intelligence, facilitated the removal of Iranian Prime Minister Mohammed Mossadegh and the return to power of the monarchy in the figure of Reza Shah Pahlavi. Two years earlier Mossadegh had pushed through the nationalization of his country's oil industry. Mossadegh's action was a blow not only to the British-owned Anglo-Iranian Company (later to become British Petroleum) but also to American oil companies with ambitions to exploit the vast reserves of Middle Eastern oil. The British and Americans then co-operated in organizing a boycott of Iranian oil and, according to William Blum's account, plunging 'the already impoverished country into near destitution'.[17] Mossadegh's response involved looking to the Soviet Union for support and this provided the rationale for the involvement of the British and American intelligence communities. These provided financial and logistical aid for Mossadegh's opponents to affect a *coup d'état* and restore the Shah to power. In the words of one of Operation Ajax's planners it created 'a situation and an atmosphere in Tehran that forced the people to choose between an established institution, the monarchy, and the unknown future offered by Mossadegh'.[18] After the operation, Iran remained firmly in the West's orbit for the next two and a half decades while Reza Shah Pahlavi's regime was maintained with torture and police terror. Much of the revenue for the country's oil went to a consortium dominated by British Petroleum, Royal Dutch Shell and a number of US corporations, including Gulf, Mobil, Standard Oil of New

Jersey and Standard Oil of California.[19] The American officials and agents, according to Mark Lytle, a historian of the episode, knew very little about Iran before they acted in concert with British imperialists to overthrow a nationalist and respected leader. After that time, the Shah was always beholden to the United States and, as a result, mistrusted by his own people. He was always a target for nationalists and Muslim fundamentalists who eventually led the revolution that saw him removed from power in 1979. It was, Lytle concluded, 'interventionism of the worst kind'.[20]

In 1954 Operation Success in Guatemala preserved that small country as the principal Central American destination for United States trade and capital. It served the interests of several US corporations – notably the United Fruit Company.

The company has prospered there for more than 50 years because as one of its own executives put it, 'the country contained prime banana land and because at the time we entered Central America, Guatemala's government was the region's weakest, most corrupt and most pliable . . . In short', he continued, the country offered an 'ideal investment climate.'[21] By the middle of the century United Fruit owned much of the small Central American country, including large landholdings and its railroad, its major port, its telephone and telegraph service. The company was known locally as *El Pulpo*, the Octopus, since it had interests in every significant enterprise and company executives could decide how much tax they were prepared to pay and how they treated their workers without interference from the government. For years the company reported only a fraction of the value of its land and exports for tax purposes and resisted any worker demands for better wages and conditions.[22]

During the Second World War, many Guatemalans became aware of American promises of democracy and human rights. Franklin Roosevelt had become a hero in the country after his Four Freedoms speech and, in particular, his advocacy of trade unions in a country where the workers were beginning to make a collective response to the power of their employers. Inspired by the New Deal, Guatemalans felt that their government should promote the public good rather than the narrow and often corrupt interests of the few.[23] In 1951 they voted for a nationalist, Jacobo Arbenz, to bring them a New Deal of their own.

Arbenz soon threatened United Fruit dominance by attempting to implement a programme of land reform and building alternative communications services to those owned by the company. The company responded by hiring a corps of publicists and influential lobbyists to convince the US government that Arbenz was a threat to freedom and therefore had to be deposed. President Eisenhower's Secretary of State

John Foster Dulles, as a former United Fruit legal representative, needed little convincing that the company interests needed protection. His brother Allen Dulles, as head of the CIA, was given the task of toppling Arbenz and Operation Success was launched at the beginning of 1954. At an estimated cost of around $20 million, an invasion force of mercenaries, trained by the CIA at military bases in Honduras and Nicaragua, was organized under the leadership of Colonel Carlos Castillo Armas. With American air support, the invasion was successful and Armas became the first of a series of Guatemalan military dictators acceptable to and even trained by the United States. In the decades that followed Arbenz's downfall, the country remained impoverished while tens of thousands of dissidents were murdered by official or semi-official death squads. By 1970 the 'machinery of murder' in Guatemala was 'concentrated in the hands of the military, and civilian terrorist groups acted only under its orders', according to Nick Cullather, a historian given access to previously secret CIA files. The army in effect became an organized criminal enterprise. 'Officers received subsidized housing and consumer goods, and soft loans; as they rose through the ranks, the perks and opportunities for graft increased.'[24]

CIA planning, finance and organization also contributed to several efforts to assassinate foreign leaders, such as Cuba's Fidel Castro and Ernesto 'Che' Guevara, and Patrice Lumumba, president of the Congo. The agency failed in the case of Guevara and Lumumba (others beat them to it) and Castro to date has survived several assassination efforts. More serious, however, was the CIA's involvement in Operation Phoenix during the Vietnam war. This was a programme, in association with military intelligence and America's South Vietnamese allies, to identify and then remove communist personnel hidden within the civilian personnel of South Vietnam. It soon became more of a campaign of mass assassination, carried out by the South Vietnamese but made possible and condoned by the Americans. Between 20,000 and 60,000 communists or suspected communists were assassinated in the period between 1968 and 1972 but many were, as a CIA analyst put it, 'the wrong damn people'. There were many examples of South Vietnamese reporting people to whom they owed money or with whom they were feuding. These individuals were then 'neutralized', to use an intelligence community euphemism for assassinated.

The CIA's connection with this operation as well as evidence coming out about its assassination efforts against foreign leaders led to the public perception that the agency was a rogue elephant, uncontrolled and uncontrollable. John Ranelagh, in his history of the agency, makes the important point that it was 'a presidential tool, acting under the direction and in coordination with other U.S. government agencies – in this case the armed forces'. In other words, the CIA was a loyal servant involved in the pursuit of foreign policy goals and accountable to the US government.[25] The US government may not have intended the mass murder of innocent civilians during these years but its blinkered anti-communism made them happen. It is also possible to claim that these and other examples of American corruption and brutality during the Cold War, in Indonesia, the Philippines and the Congo, as discussed in Part 3, actually discredited the United States in Asia, Latin America and within the communist world itself and thus helped preserve communist regimes as well as shoring up pro-American dictatorships.

★

While there is little evidence that American interventionism made the world a better place for people, there is plenty that it made the world a better place for corporations.

From the 1950s and 1960s, corporations began to see and exploit the profit potential of the underdeveloped world. Apart from sources of raw materials on or under the earth in poor countries, there was an abundance of cheap, non-unionized labour and an even greater abundance of potential consumers in their rapidly expanding populations. The institutions that supported labour and capital in underdeveloped countries were too weak to prevent the pervasive penetration of multinationals throughout key sectors of their economies and only governments, as we have suggested earlier, could put limits on foreign corporate power by, for example, protecting infant industries. If corporations had an interest in improving the lives of the people in underdeveloped countries then their economic power could have had a positive impact. Unfortunately, this was not the case. Their primary interest was always profit maximization. In terms of improving people's lives, the multinationals claimed that by enriching themselves they were enriching the whole world. They thus internationalized the rationale of the original American robber barons. 'Millionaires are the bees that make the most honey', to repeat Andrew Carnegie's self-serving analysis, 'and contribute most to the hive even after they have gorged themselves full.'[26]

In the case of poor countries, the practice of 'transfer pricing' meant that the corporate bees contributed as little as possible to the hive. Transfer pricing involves multinationals buying and selling to their own subsidiaries and had become standard business practice by the 1970s. One common technique described by the economists Richard Barnett and Ronald Muller was to ship underpriced exports or overpriced imports to a tax haven such as the Bahamas and then re-export the goods at their normal market value, or even an inflated price, to another subsidiary in the country where they were to be sold. The economists also noted another more obviously fraudulent practice. In Colombia, for example, foreign firms would often collect the 15 per cent subsidy paid by the government on all exports on the basis of empty crates shipped to Panama. The result of all this was that the countries that needed it most were fleeced out of vast amounts of foreign exchange and taxes. Company accountants ensured that the figures reported to the local government or the US Treasury bore little relation to the true profits earned by the companies in poor countries.[27]

Corporations also frequently argued that their presence in poor countries was in many ways improving the health and welfare of local populations. Many cases showed, however, that corporate behaviour often harmed the populations of poor countries, literally from the cradle.

An investigation by *New Internationalist* magazine and the charity War on Want in the early 1970s found, for example, that Nestlé's aggressive and irresponsible marketing techniques for their baby feeding products were partly responsible for the premature deaths of thousand of babies. The magazine published interviews with two professors of child health with long experience dealing with infant malnutrition in Africa. The doctors revealed that Nestlé encouraged African mothers to abandon breastfeeding their children in favour of formula-milk feeding despite the known benefits of breastfeeding in terms of providing immunity from disease. Nestlé were also advising mothers to wash their hands and sterilize the bottle before feeding the baby in areas where 66 per cent of the households had no washing facilities and an even greater percentage had only rudimentary cooking facilities involving stones supporting a pot above a wood fire. As the charity's report noted, 'The pot that must be used to sterilize the baby's bottle also has to serve to cook the family's meal – so sterilizing and boiling of water will probably be forgotten.' Nestlé claimed that their products had instruction leaflets in the main languages of the country but failed to acknowledge that these were often useless in countries where the majority of the population was illiterate. 'The baby food industry stands accused', according to the War on Want report, 'of promoting their products in communities which cannot afford to use them properly' and noted in particular the practice of using sales girls dressed up in nurses uniforms going around maternity hospitals and clinics to demonstrate the use of Nestlé products. The doctors concluded that 'undoubtedly, the increase of malnutrition in the young baby and the many deaths which occur from this must have some relationship to the increased mis-use of artificial feeding.'[28]

These corporate practices, whether or not they were legal, were moving the world ever further from the freedom from want that Roosevelt had promised. At the same time corporate pressure was putting corporate freedom at the top of the global agenda.

9

Nixon and the New World Economic Disorder

When Richard Nixon took over the presidency in 1969 he had no intention of spending much time on economic matters, which he thought were both 'boring and baffling'. But, despite wanting to play to his strengths and concentrate on domestic politics and foreign policy, he soon faced an avalanche of economic problems and had to respond. At home jobs were being lost, prices and interest rates were going up, and the stock market was more than usually jittery. In an international context he was the incumbent when America faced losing its dominance in the global economy, challenged by Japan and West Germany, in particular. 'Somehow,' as Allen Matusow puts it in *Nixon's Economy* (1998), 'he had to make the economy hum by 1972 or face likely defeat in his quest for reelection.'[1] The ways in which Nixon responded to the economic challenges of the period initiated changes in international monetary and financial affairs that took away many of the checks on capitalism established at Bretton Woods. These changes also helped open up a world of criminal opportunity in ways that were inadvertent but grimly appropriate given the nature of the man.

Initially Nixon assumed that the affluence of the 1960s would continue under his stewardship. He soon found he had to face up to a messy economic situation inherited from his predecessor Lyndon B. Johnson. Johnson's commitment to help both the poor and the American middle class with his Great Society programmes could perhaps have been paid for if the United States had remained at peace. But Johnson's escalation of the war in Vietnam was immensely expensive, approaching $900 billion dollars according to estimates.[2] Even the richest nation in history could not pay for the war in Asia, along with America's many other global defence commitments, and the great increase in spending required to fund Great Society programmes. Americans were spending more than they could afford and this caused more people to doubt that the world's economy could continue to rest on the dollar. In 1971, after trade figures revealed that the United States had imported more goods than it had been able to export, Americans and investors across the world started to cash in their dollars for gold and other securities.[3] Nationally and internationally there was an air of panic.

Nixon had to choose from several options in his response to the monetary crisis. First, he could save dollars by reducing US defence commitments. But he was determined to expand rather than reduce the nation's influence. Second, he could limit US investment abroad and thus force American corporations to invest more at home and therefore bring more dollars back to the USA. Nixon, however, would never interfere in the market place unless there was a clear political advantage, and in any case he knew that corporations could safely ignore his demands by operating out of overseas offices and thus out of America's reach. Third, he could raise taxes to pay for both welfare and warfare but that would risk alienating American voters. Finally, he could force America's allies to help the US economy by devaluing the dollar and forcing other countries to appreciate their currencies. Not coincidentally this would help secure his own re-election in 1972.[4]

Nixon chose the latter course of action, largely because finding a way to maintain both America's global financial and military dominance and himself in power was uppermost in his thinking. Offending America's allies was preferable to offending voters and corporations. The president was strongly influenced by a new and aggressively America-first Secretary of the Treasury, John Connally. Connally's approach to international economic policy was summed up in his remarks to a group of Treasury consultants soon after taking charge. 'My basic approach is that the foreigners are out to screw us,' he said. 'Our job is to screw them first.'[5] Guided by this philosophy, Nixon initiated a sequence of events that effectively dismantled the old Bretton Woods system without establishing a system capable of regulating global finance.

On 13 and 14 August 1971, Nixon and Connally summoned ten advisers to the president's retreat at Camp David to make a decision that was as momentous in its own way as those made at Bretton Woods nearly three decades earlier. In contrast to the integrity and intensity of the discussions at the earlier meeting, Camp David was an exercise in short-term expediency. According to Matusow's account,

> The agenda had emerged mainly from the private conversations of Nixon and Connally. The regular departments were excluded; the usual staff work had not been completed; and everything had to be decided in two days, leaving scant time for analysis. Despite the gravity of the issues, Nixon cared less for the particulars of the decisions he would make than for the image of action they would project, action that he would dramatize at the

climax of the weekend in a televised speech to restore his leadership and dispel the gloom enveloping his administration.

The domestic measures that came out of this meeting need not concern us here; the decision that mattered in the long term was the decision to 'close the gold window' by repudiating the international obligation of the United States to redeem its dollar in gold. Although Arthur Burns, Chairman of the Federal Reserve, warned of the potentially devastating consequences of this action, noting that other countries would retaliate and global capitalism would be destabilized, Nixon in the end took the view of Connally, 'So the other countries don't like it, so what?'[6]

In Nixon's televised speech outlining a 'new economic policy', he announced that 'we must protect the position of the dollar as a pillar of monetary stability around the world' from 'speculators' who have been 'waging an all-out war on the American dollar'. 'I have', he continued, 'directed Secretary Connally to suspend temporarily the convertibility of the dollar into gold or other reserve assets, except in amounts and conditions determined to be in the interest of monetary stability and in the best interests of the United States.' Referring to the renewed economic strength of the major industrial nations of Europe and Asia after the devastation of the Second World War, he announced that 'the time has come for them to bear their fair share of the burden of defending freedom around the world. The time has come for exchange rates to be set straight and for the major nations to compete as equals. There is no longer any need for the United States to compete with one hand tied behind her back.' His new measures would, he said, 'make it possible for us to compete fairly with the rest of the world, to open the door to new prosperity'.

Nixon gave no idea of the type of international monetary system he envisioned would replace the Bretton Woods system. He just noted that in 'full cooperation with the International Monetary Fund and those who trade with us, we will press for the necessary reforms to set up an urgently needed new international monetary system'. The question of a new international monetary system never came up at the Camp David meeting. 'We were winging it,' said William Safire, one of the participants.[7] This, given the momentous nature of the decision taken at Camp David, says as much about the Nixon administration as the Watergate revelations. August 1971 was a historical moment, and economic statesmanship on a level with that on display at Bretton Woods in 1944 was required. Instead, the world got reckless opportunism and short-term self-interest.

On the foreign front, the allies came round to accepting first a devalued dollar and finally to the change of the international monetary system from one based on fixed exchange rates to one based on flexible rates. Subsequent international efforts in the following decades to develop a new system failed, and the US shares the responsibility for these failures with the world's other main economic powers. Robert Gilpin has described the situation that emerged as a 'nonsystem' because 'there were no generally accepted rules to guide the flexible rates or any other decisions on international monetary affairs.'[8] Governments no longer regulated capitalism; the market would now rule and capital's freedoms and opportunities tended to override individual freedoms and opportunities. Globalization, as we know it today, was built on this flimsy foundation, and crooks inside and outside the corporate, financial and governmental worlds would take full advantage.

★

Among its many illegalities, President Nixon's administration was involved in corrupt alliances with the giant multinational International Telephone and Telegraph (ITT) in an episode that had devastating consequences for the people of Chile. The story of Nixon–ITT illuminates some of the costs involved when the world's greatest power puts the interests of capital over the rights of humans.

ITT were amongst Nixon's largest financial supporters and clearly expected special treatment in return. In 1971 ITT offered a large contribution to Nixon's campaign effort at the same time as it was engaged in negotiations over whether the corporation had violated the antitrust laws. On 19 April of that year Nixon made the following revealing point to his main domestic policy adviser, John Ehrlichman, recorded by the White House taping system: 'I don't know whether ITT is bad, good or indifferent . . . But there is not going to be any more antitrust actions as long as I am in this chair . . . goddam it, we are going to stop it.'[9]

Nixon continued to act in ITT's interests in helping to remove Chilean president Salvatore Allende in 1973. ITT and other American multinationals had become increasingly worried about their Chilean interests from the late 1960s when it became apparent that Allende and his Socialist party were capable of winning electoral power and harming corporate interests through programmes of nationalization. In 1970, John McClone, a member of the ITT board of directors and former CIA head, contacted the agency to offer $1 million in anti-Allende efforts. Without directly accepting the money, the CIA advised the company on 'secure' funding channels to Allende opponents. Despite these efforts, Allende narrowly won the 1970 elections. ITT then urged the CIA to take tough action against Allende, traded information with the agency, and tried to persuade other US corporations to bring economic pressure to bear against Chile.[10] A government-corporate assault on the Chilean economy began, involving such tactics as asking banks to delay credits and perhaps it was no coincidence that five US banks, Chase Manhattan, Chemical, First National City, Manufactures Hanover and Morgan Guaranty, did cut off short-term credit to Chile after Allende came to power. This action made it very difficult for the country to afford to pay for essential imports such as food. The Nixon government also asked other companies to drag their feet in shipping supplies necessary for Chile's industry. In the words of President Nixon, the intention was to 'make the economy scream'. The assault succeeded in destabilizing the Chilean economy and preparing the way for the coup of 11 September 1973 and the murder of President Allende.

A brutal and repressive military regime was set up under the leadership of one of the coup's plotters, Augusto Pinochet, who presided over a reign that can best be described as free-market terror.[11] With the aid of the Americans, Chile was subjected to one of South America's worst military regimes, experiencing mass killings, 'disappearance' or exile for dissenters, and the systematic torture of prisoners.[12] Pinochet remained in power for 17 years, which he used to introduce a policy of Chicago-school inspired economic neo-liberalism to his country. In Chile it was called *el tratamiento de choque*, 'shock treatment', and was essentially based on freedom for business but repression for labour.[13] The anti-democratic brutalities of Chile's experience serve as an apt precursor of much of the rest of the world's experience with neo-liberalism.

Revelations about ITT's role in this coup and many other multinational abuses shocked the international community, represented by the United Nations, to the extent of including corporate crime in its early deliberations over the problem of transnational organized crime. These deliberations considered the complexities of organized crime in ways that ran counter to America's misleadingly simplistic concentration on supercriminal organizations. Most significantly the international organization's early thought on the subject emphasized organized criminal *activity* and the involvement of otherwise respectable business institutions or persons in the problem rather than the actions of distinct 'organized criminal groups'.

Discussions at the 5th United Nations Congress on the Prevention of Crime in 1975, for example, were concerned about ways to curtail such illegal activities as bribery, price-fixing, smuggling, violation of regulatory laws by private companies, currency offences such as transfer pricing involving the evasion or avoidance of tax (see page 126–7)[14] and the behaviour of transnational corporations as much as that of more conventionally understood organized criminal groups. In a section entitled 'Crime as Business', which clearly recognized that much corporate crime was organized crime, the Congress recommended further study of the following:

> The variation that might exist in different countries regarding (a) the scope of the criminal law relating to 'crime as business' and (b) the techniques used to control harmful forms of behaviour. For example, in some countries price-fixing was now regarded as criminal, whereas in others it was merely the subject of civil remedies. It was argued that it was also important to study value systems in relation to legislation, especially in respect of differences in the class structure of different societies. It was pointed out by several delegates that crime as business had its origins in class conflict, and that businessmen, managers, administrators and other economically powerful middle-class or upper-class persons might tend to control the machinery of criminal justice so as to succeed in getting their own deviant and economically harmful behaviour defined as non-criminal.

The delegates making the latter point were in fact offering a prescient description of what happened with deregulation world-wide in the 1980s and 1990s.

Participants at the Congress also discussed what techniques might best be used to control crime as business. It was strongly argued by some participants that criminal law and imprisonment should be an integral part of business-crime control rather than the trend towards decriminalization of many harmful business activities such as price-fixing and bribery. Criminal law and imprisonment would, it was argued, 'have a definite deterrent effect in relation to businessmen-criminals, even though they might not be effective for other crimes'.[15]

The United Nations had already showed its commitment to controlling the behaviour of powerful transnational business interests by establishing the United Nations Centre for Transnational Corporations (UNCTC) in 1974. The UNCTC began by investigating the activities and economic strength of transnational corporations, concluding in 1985 that the 350 largest transnational organizations, about half of them based in the United States, had combined sales of $2.7 trillion. This figure amounted to one-third of the combined industrial market economies and was far larger than the combined GNP of all the developing countries, including China. In the wake of revelations about ITT's role in ousting the democratically elected president of Chile, and clearly concerned about other possibilities for the abuse of such concentrated forms of power, the UNCTC also set out to elaborate codes of conduct for transnational corporations, most notably codes attempting to check corruption, ensure respect for human rights and for consumer and environmental protection objectives.

By the 1990s, however, the United Nations itself and the UNCTC in particular had come in for intense criticism from the administrations of presidents Ronald Reagan and George Bush Sr and pro-business think-tanks such as the Heritage Foundation, accompanied by the US refusal to pay UN dues. To remedy what the Americans argued was UN 'waste and inefficiency', Bush's former Attorney General Richard Thornburgh was appointed Under Secretary General of the international organization in 1992. The following year, largely as a result of his efforts, the UNCTC was abolished and UN attempts to establish more effective controls over transnational corporations were largely abandoned.[16] Thornburgh's role, according to Ian Williams in *The Nation*, had been not just to cut the organization to the smaller size the United States wanted 'but also to carve it into the shape the American right wants'.[17]

From the 1990s discussion of the problem of organized crime under the auspices of the United Nations narrowed in ways that suited the world view of the American right. It downplayed the criminal involvement of otherwise respectable business institutions or persons in the problem. Far from the concern showed in the 1975 meeting about the involvement of multinational corporations in harmful organized criminal activities, they were now threatened by 'crime multinationals'. These, according to the new line as presented by UN Secretary General Boutros Boutros-Ghali in 1994 and in the background literature to the Convention against Trans-national Organized Crime, poison, pollute and infiltrate legitimate business. This dumbing of organized-crime discourse was no coincidence since by the 1990s the dominance of neo-liberal ideology was assured, affecting not just the World Bank and the IMF but also the United Nations. The term 'neo-liberal' now represented the transference of the pro-market, anti-welfare, deregulatory and monetarist Reagan economic programme from its American homeland to the global arena. UN Secretary General Boutros-Ghali and his successor, Kofi Annan, did little to impede neo-liberalism's global advance since they both wanted big business approval for UN policies and objectives. For these and other reasons analyses of organized crime that included multinational corporations in particular and misguided laws and policies in general as part of the problem were no longer acceptable. Transnational corporate criminality was therefore off the UN agenda by the new millennium, replaced by a global commitment to support American dreams of a global drug-prohibition regime and a hopelessly misleading and inadequate understanding of transnational organized crime.

10

The War on Drugs and the Rise of International Drug Traffic

Although US drug-control policy changed in the early 1960s, there was no fundamental break with the essence of past policy, which was based on the irrational moral righteousness of early twentieth-century America. Education, treatment and rehabilitation programmes were simply added to the policy of bare repression of drug use and sale. Richard Nixon, as we have seen, preserved the old illusion that a drug-free country could be achieved. Relentless enforcement at home, he felt, should be combined with relentless enforcement abroad. Nixon's position as president of the most powerful nation on earth allowed him to bring the early moral crusaders' dream of a global drug-prohibition regime closer to reality.

Throughout his time at the White House, Nixon made the war on drugs one of his highest priorities, regularly calling top-level meetings on the issue. These could include his cabinet, top administration officials, ambassadors and even, on 3 June 1971, Chairman of the Joint Chiefs of Staff Admiral Thomas H. Moorer, plus General William Westmoreland, commander of US forces in Vietnam and three other top-level military chiefs. The purpose of this meeting, according to the president's background briefing memo, was, 'To indicate your [Nixon's] determination to attack drug abuse in a comprehensive manner'. The memo advised Nixon in his closing remarks to 'expect the fullest cooperation and support from all involved departments and agencies' or as a summary of the meeting put it, 'President told group that . . . Crapping around will not be tolerated.' The contribution and reaction of the military chiefs was not recorded.[1] One can speculate, however, that a kind of respectful bemusement and embarrassment was the likely reaction from men whose whole careers had been spent organizing the nation's machinery of war to fight armed adversaries as opposed to the powders and pills that so concerned their commander-in-chief. They were also likely to be embarrassed because they were called in response to press reports about the large number of active servicemen known to be addicted to heroin.

Even before his first year of office was complete President Nixon had shown that he had no intention of confining his war against drugs within American borders. On 29 September 1969 his national security adviser Henry Kissinger sent a memo to Secretary of State William Rogers and Attorney General Mitchell that contained in it the essence of the stick-and-carrot approach of American drug-control diplomacy as it exists at the present day:

> The President is convinced that the problem of narcotics addiction in the U.S. has reached proportions constituting a threat to our national stability. Most narcotics are grown and processed in foreign countries and smuggled into the U.S.: this is particularly true of heroin. Under these circumstances, the President considers that any country facilitating, or in any way contributing to, international traffic in heroin is committing an act inimical to the United States.

Rogers and Mitchell were then directed 'to study this problem on an urgent basis' and

> Recommend as soon as possible an action program that will make emphatically clear to those countries growing opium poppies that their non-medicinal cultivation must be stopped; and to those countries manufacturing finished heroin that their illicit laboratories must be closed ... In your study you should consider methods of positive persuasion, including financial incentives for cooperation on the control of heroin traffic, as well as those of retaliation, in the event that any country refuses to cooperate in this program.[2]

In brief, from then on, efforts to bully or bribe other countries into acceptance of an American-based global drug-control regime would be intensified.

By the time Kissinger sent his memo, the administration's international effort had already begun. On 21 September 1969 an attempt was made by Customs and Immigration officers to curb the importation of illegal drugs from Mexico by stopping and searching over 2 million people crossing the United States–Mexico border. Operation Intercept, as it was called, involved 'a 100 percent inspection of all persons and vehicles crossing into the United States' with 'no exceptions'. Officers thoroughly searched the trunk and engine areas, under the seats and behind the cushions and door panels of every car and truck in a process that took far longer than normal Customs procedure. To emphasize the military aspects of the operation, planes, boats and radar were also involved in what was accurately acknowledged as the most extensive attempt in United States history to curb the importation of illegal drugs. Although Customs and

Immigration officers worked round the clock along the 2,500 miles of the United States–Mexico border, the hopelessness of their task was made clear by the comment of a Texas border scout, 'There are areas out there where a small army could cross without detection.'[3] After three weeks the operation was called off after complaints by business interests both sides of the border. Operation Intercept in sum resulted in the seizure of a negligible amount of drug contraband and the creation of immense traffic jams.[4]

Another expensive international intervention began in 1971 and could be judged a pyrrhic victory of sorts for the stick-and-carrot policy. Turkey was thought to be the major source of heroin and was vulnerable to diplomatic pressure because of its dependence on massive US economic and military aid. The Turkish government therefore agreed to ban all opium-growing for a three-year period in return for a payment of $35 million – intended to assist the development of alternative crops to replace opium. Little of the money reached the tens of thousands of farmers who lost income because of the ban. Most accounts agree, however, that Turkey did cease being a significant source of heroin on American streets. Supply was soon resumed by increased Mexican production (despite Intercept and its successors) and new routes from South-East Asia's Golden Triangle, as well as Afghanistan, Pakistan and elsewhere. It should have become clear that the ending of production in one country could not come close to eliminating the supply. The hopelessness of the Turkish episode was revealed when an economist calculated that the US demand for heroin could be met by the amount of opium poppies growing on a 10- to 20-square-mile patch of land, roughly equivalent to the island of Manhattan.[5] Politicians and drug-control bureaucrats have never faced up to this kind of logic.

While the Mexican and Turkish interventions were playing out, Nixon was opening up two other fronts in his war on drugs. The first of these involved the use of US diplomatic power through the United Nations. John E. Ingersoll, Director of the Bureau of Narcotics and Dangerous Drugs, was sent to a special session of the UN Commission on Narcotic Drugs in the autumn of 1970. His brief was to point out the weaknesses of the 1961 UN Single Convention and initiate the first part of a United Nations plan which, in Ingersoll's words 'could develop into an effective worldwide program'.[6] The 1961 Convention's primary weakness, according to the American delegation, was the fact that it rested 'essentially upon faithful cooperation by all parties in the context of their national decision rather than upon effective international measures'. The United States decided that the Single Convention had to be amended to 'curb and, eventually prevent entirely' the illicit drug traffic. The proposed amendments had two basic objectives: firstly 'to establish enforceable controls and appropriate international machinery to assure compliance, and, secondly, to provide inducements to Parties to perform faithfully all their treaty obligations'. Ingersoll's delegation bluntly told the UN's Division of Narcotic Drugs that it 'will be expected to pursue their present activities more vigorously but will have to assume new and important responsibilities'. These new responsibilities were to include 'a capacity for the planning and implementing of technical assistance programs to assist countries . . . in the establishment and improvement of national drug control administrations and enforcement machinery, the training of personnel required for these services'.[7] The hubris of these demands was staggering. Just two years earlier America's premier drug-law-enforcement agency had had to be abolished due to endemic corruption.[8]

To make sure their proposals for strengthening the global drug-prohibition regime stayed high on the UN agenda, the Americans were prepared to pay. They made an initial pledge of $2 million to help establish the United Nations Fund for Drug Abuse Control.[9] Other nations, foundations and private individuals were expected to feed into this fund. From then on the US made sure that, however starved of American contributions the UN might otherwise be, the funding for the international war on drugs would remain flush.

The second of Nixon's new fronts on the war on drugs involved the use of US diplomatic power directly to ensure the compliance of other countries. On 14 June 1971 he called in top State Department officials and ambassadors to South Vietnam, France, Turkey, Thailand and Luxembourg. These five countries were described in the background memo to the meeting as 'directly involved in the illicit international drug traffic' and the purpose of the meeting was to stress 'the need for a tougher stance abroad'. According to the summary of this meeting, the President stated that he considered the 'Ambassadors' most important diplomatic mission' to be 'discussions with those countries on the drug problem'. He then 'ordered the Ambassadors to convey to their host governments that the U.S. means business', concluding with the blunt point that 'stopping the drug traffic is more important than good tempo-rized relations'.[10] From then on the State Department pushed American ambassadors to deliver results on international drug control. If it was considered that they weren't doing this they were replaced.

To complement the high-level work of the ambassadors, US drug-control agents were expected to do much more at operational level. As Ethan Nadelmann has explained in *Cops Across Borders* (1993) they also had to act as drug-enforcement diplomats and advocates: 'to push for structural changes in drug enforcement wherever they were stationed, to lobby for tougher laws, to train local police in drug enforcement techniques, to sensitize local officials to U.S. concerns in this area, and so on'.[11] During the Nixon era, a small overseas complement of American narcotics agents grew into the 'first global law enforcement agency with operational capabilities', Nadelmann concluded. Nixon's administration more than doubled the corps of drug-control officers assigned to United States embassies and missions abroad and their numbers have since continued to expand. By 1976, the Drug Enforcement Agency's overall budget was $161.1 million, with more than 10 per cent of its 2,141 agents stationed overseas, in 68 offices in 43 countries. Today, the agency has more than 5,000 agents and a budget of $2,150.9 million.[12]

The Nixon administration also secured the passage of the Narcotics Control Trade Act of 1974, which would have a damaging international impact in the decades that followed. Essentially the terms of this new law meant that those drug-producing or drug-transit countries that failed to co-operate with United States drug-prohibition policies would be subject to various sanctions, including the withdrawal of American aid and increases in duties and tariffs. In other words, small countries had to comply with American demands on drugs or be economically squeezed.

Other countries could thus be bullied to make futile, often cynical, drug-control gestures on America's behalf. American consumers continued to pay whatever price was necessary to buy drugs and the effort only revealed that plants that could be processed into drugs grow everywhere and that foreign drug enforcers accept bribes just as enthusiastically as their counterparts in the United States. Under Nixon, drugs as well as organized crime were redefined as national-security threats, and were repeatedly said to warrant an approach based mainly on repression at home and the continued export of failed policies abroad. Meanwhile, the sorry story of alcohol and drug prohibition at home became the more tragic and continuing story of drug prohibition globally.

The most authoritative conclusions about the impact of alcohol prohibition on the United States came from a government commission in 1931. The Wickersham Commission's verdict on alcohol prohibition nationally could equally be applied to the more recent international wars on drugs:

> The constant cheapening and simplification of production of alcohol and of alcoholic drinks, the improvement of quality of what may be made by illicit means, the diffusion of knowledge as to how to produce liquor and the perfection of organization of unlawful manufacture and distribution have

developed faster than the means of enforcement. But of even more significance is the margin of profit in smuggling liquor, in diversion of alcohol, in illicit distilling and brewing, in bootlegging, and in the manufacture and sale of products of which the bulk goes into illicit or doubtfully lawful making of liquor. This profit makes possible systematic and organized violation of the National Prohibition Act on a large scale and offers rewards on a par with the most important legitimate industries. It makes lavish expenditure in corruption possible. It puts heavy temptation in the way of everyone engaged in enforcement and administration of the law. It affords a financial basis for organized crime.[13]

The story of global drug prohibition since the Nixon era follows a very similar pattern. While enforcement efforts have greatly intensified, the production of prohibited drugs has been simplified, rationalized and considerably cheapened. The diffusion of knowledge as to how to produce, refine, adulterate and distribute these drugs has developed far faster than the means of enforcement. Most significantly the margin of profit in the production, smuggling and distribution of drugs has made fortunes for a few at the top end of the drug-trafficking pyramid, particularly in countries whose governments are weakened by conflict and corruption. And, of course, global drug prohibition provides a financial basis for organized crime across borders. This will be demonstrated by the following case studies of some of the most prominent participants.

The most notable of many South-East Asian warlords to gain from drug prohibition was Khun Sa, who played an important part in the decades of fighting that have characterized the Golden Triangle opium territory bordering Laos, Thailand and Burma. Originally armed by the CIA and its allies, the anti-communist Chinese nationalist Kuomintang (KMT), Khun Sa's operations were protected by both the Burmese and Thai governments and expanded exponentially from the 1970s and 1980s. By the end of the 1980s he controlled many opium-growing areas, as well as the trade routes within Burma and the refineries that converted the raw material into heroin.[14] By the early 1990s his army numbered more than 20,000 men, equipped with advanced weaponry, doing battle with other insurgent groups also armed with the latest M16s, AK47s, grenade launchers, artillery and mortars. Khun Sa's armies were trained along strict military lines and his decisions were based on military-intelligence-gathering techniques. In 1996 a DEA agent in a television interview described Khun Sa without exaggeration as the 'world's most heavily armed gang leader' with 'an organization that has enriched itself beyond anything we'd ever seen'. The interview then put the warlord's organization in the following context of corruption:

[it] relied on violence and murders and assassinations and bribery to keep its whole infrastructure in place. And, as they did what they wanted within Burma, which is grow the opium and produce the heroin, they then had to market it internationally and the front door was Thailand.

[A]nd inside Thailand they built up a network . . . who had done a number of things. [O]ne, they had built up a great international clientele until they had penetrated some of the Thai organizations that were supposed to be out there combating this problem. And so they had a very cozy, tight relationship. In fact, over twenty years we know of nobody of any significance that went to jail. A few would get arrested but they were right back there again.[15]

Khun Sa participated in a heavily publicized 'surrender' in January 1996. In front of television cameras he supervised the laying down of weapons by nearly 2,000 of his troops and announced with staggering hypocrisy that he and the Burmese government should 'now work together to . . . eradicate the opium and narcotics drugs, which endanger the entire humanity of our country'. He was then taken to a luxurious villa and allowed to continue his legal and illegal business. His 'downfall' made little impact on the flow of heroin out of the Golden Triangle.[16]

As Alfred McCoy has shown, America's long and corrupt involvement in the quagmire of the Vietnam war and in particular, CIA complicity in the Golden Triangle drug trade was largely responsible for the success of Khun Sa and other drug-trafficking warlords. McCoy also charted America's involvement in South-West Asia and the development of the world's other main source area for the supply of heroin.

American involvement in the region took a new turn in 1979. In response to the Soviet invasion of Afghanistan in 1979, President Jimmy Carter used his diplomatic and covert-action resources to mobilize military aid for the mujahedin guerrillas, and these with the help of both the CIA and the Pakistan Inter-Services Intelligence (ISI) agency took the lead in fighting the Soviets. Among those mujahedin helped by the ISI and the CIA was Gulbuddin Hekmatyar, who led a group called the Hezbi-i Islami, which would become the largest guerrilla army. Hekmatyar, according to a *New York Times* report, had established his reputation for brutality by, among other things, dispatching followers to throw vials of acid into the faces of women students who refused to wear veils. During the 1980s, Hekmatyar, with the active assistance of the ISI and the tacit support of the CIA, used his army to become Afghanistan's leading drug trafficker, controlling six heroin refineries that processed the large opium harvest from the Helmand valley. By 1990, McCoy concluded, 'the CIA's Afghan operation had proved doubly disastrous. After ten years of covert operations at a cost of $2 billion, America was left with mujahedin warlords whose skill as drug dealers exceeded their competence as military commanders.'[17]

Hekmatyar's power was temporarily ended when he was forced to leave Afghanistan for Iran when the Taliban took control of the country in 1996. Now that the Taliban themselves have been driven from power by the American invasion of 2002, Hekmatyar continues to embarrass the US. According to one account, the CIA attempted to deal with this embarrassment after reportedly spotting him in the Shegal Gorge, near Kabal, by firing a Hellfire missile from an unmanned Predator spy plane, but missed him. Hekmatyar's Hezb-i Islami movement was involved in battles with US forces in January 2003 and was suspected of terrorist activity including the death of nine minibus passengers the same month. According to a message distributed along the Afghan-Pakistan border to attract recruits, his group has promised to fight 'our jihad until foreign troops are gone from Afghanistan and Afghans have set up an Islamic government'.[18]

Meanwhile, according to the UN, the cultivation of opium poppies in Afghanistan has reached record levels by the time of writing. The administration of President Hamid Karzai, interim leader of the country from 2001 and democratically elected in 2004, has included known drug traffickers or those in their pay.[19]

Sicilian and Calabrian mafias also prospered thanks again largely to American and other western demand and the inflated prices that heroin consignments were able to fetch. In fact, according to an authoritative study by Letizia Paoli, *Mafia Brotherhoods: Organized Crime, Italian Style* (2003), it was only in the 1970s that 'drug trafficking became an ongoing and economically significant activity for a large number of mafia families and single members'. Although some mafia members had organized drug deals since the 1940s, much more money began to be made from the importing and processing of morphine and the export of heroin from the late 1970s. Paoli quoted a Mafia turncoat, Antonino Calderone, as testifying that drug trafficking was vastly more profitable than other illegal activities such as cigarette smuggling, 'richness came, we all became rich. With cigarettes we had earned well but it was not a strong source [of income]; what changed Cosa Nostra's life has been drugs, which drove them crazy and allowed them to earn a huge amount of money.'[20]

The craziness that went with excess drug profits helps to explain the contempt that mafiosi held for the Italian state during the early 1980s. The year 1980, for example, saw three so-called 'eminent corpses': a police captain, the president of the Sicilian Region and the chief prosecutor in Palermo. Then 1981 saw the violence escalate. Bodies were left near police headquarters or simply burned in the street. According to John Dickie's account in *Cosa Nostra* (2004) the carnage peaked at the end of 1982 when General Carlo Alberto Dalla Chiesa was killed in Palermo, along with his wife and their escort. A party of about a dozen mafiosi blocked the road in front of his car in via Carini and machine-gunned them to death. Dalla Chiesa was the Italian state's response to the violence and his death, according to Dickie, showed that Cosa Nostra, 'with its new heroin wealth ... simply did not take the Italian state seriously'.[21]

Profitable as heroin was, cocaine rapidly became more so during the 1970s, thanks initially to an upsurge in American demand. After decades of obscurity, its use increased within all classes of Americans, but was most noticeable amongst athletes, entertainers and 'young, upwardly mobiles' in well-paid professions. Much of the drug's new-found glamour and 'forbidden fruit' mystique was related to its outlaw status, and its popularity was if anything increased by sensationalized news-media coverage of the dangers of excessive use.

Like opium, the coca plant is a relatively easy crop to grow – hardy, disease-resistant and long-lived. The major known growing areas are in remote parts of South America. According to 1979 estimates, a peasant farmer could hope to realize $250 from the sale of 500 kilos of coca leaves in regions where the average monthly wage was around $50. This same amount – not taking account of the costs of refining, smuggling and distribution – might realize $80,000 in the United States.[22] This level of profit, not the drug itself, has caused devastation in several South American countries, particularly in Brazil, Peru, Bolivia and Colombia.

In Bolivia, the growing of coca expanded rapidly from the 1970s. Dozens of drug-trafficking organizations evolved to co-ordinate coca paste purchases, coca base and cocaine refining, and sales of most of their cocaine base to foreigners, mainly Colombians, associated with trafficking groups based mainly in the cities of Medellin and Cali. Of the Bolivian traffickers, Roberto Suarez became the main Bolivian supplier to the Colombians. Suarez owned a number of remote ranches in the Beni Department and first prospered as a cocaine trafficker during the dictatorship of his friend General Hugo Banzer. Through Banzer, according to Clare Hargreaves' account in *Snowfields: The War on Cocaine in the Andes* (1992), Suarez linked up with Klaus Barbie, once the head of the Gestapo in Lyons and known as the 'Butcher of Lyons' for his Second World War crimes. Barbie had made himself useful to Banzer and the country's other rulers by advising on torture, the setting-up and running of concentration camps and the organization of squads whose main purpose was killing and intimidation. In 1978 Barbie became security consultant for Roberto Suarez. For Suarez he helped organize a paramilitary squad to protect operations. This squad, which called itself the Fiancés of Death, after a French Foreign Legion song, played an active part in the campaign of terror initiated by the leaders of a 1980 military coup, one of whom was Colonel Luis Arce Gomez, a cousin of Suarez. The new regime immediately murdered many of the trade union leaders who had led the opposition to their takeover. With the help of the Fiancés they also took virtual control of the cocaine trade, driving the smaller operators out of business and 'taxing' the shipments of the major traffickers. The 13 months of this 'narco-government's' existence were, according to Hargreaves' account, 'paradise for Suarez'. He built up his empire into a multi-million dollar business. He profited from an arrangement set up by Gomez, 'whereby cocaine seized from traffickers who were not paying protection was delivered to traffickers who were'. Hargreaves quotes one analyst as saying, 'It is impossible to calculate the money [the drug barons] made. Think of a preposterous figure, double it and know damned well that you've made a gross underestimate.' Suarez' luck finally ran out in July 1988 when he was arrested on one of his Beni ranches and sentenced to 15 years in prison.[23]

One of Suarez' most important contacts in the export of his product was Pablo Escobar, a drug trafficker from the Colombian city of Medellin who became the best known of the misnamed Medellin cartel. The US authorities described Escobar and his associates as a cartel despite the fact that their group, like the Cali equivalent, was not a cartel in the traditional economic sense since it did not control raw material production and most distribution systems in their main markets.[24] However, Escobar's group did achieve both immense wealth and an exceptional degree of gangster power. From the early 1980s it killed judges and police officers and even those at the top of Colombia's government hierarchies, including Rodrigo Lara Bonilla, the Justice Minister in 1984. When President Belisario Betancur responded to the assassination by agreeing to extradite traffickers to the United States, Escobar and his fellow traffickers responded in turn with a campaign of extreme and disruptive violence. Bombs were detonated in public places and any who opposed the drug trade became targets for assassination, adding journalists, military personnel, presidential candidates to the government officials already under threat.[25] These atrocities peaked in August 1989 when a bomb was planted on an Avianca airliner in an effort to kill presidential candidate Cesar Gaviria. The intended target was not on the plane but the explosion killed 110 innocent people.[26] By being involved in these assassinations Escobar made himself literally a target for both the US and the Colombian governments. He was shot down on the roof of a house in Medellin trying to escape from police on 2 December 1993.[27]

Throughout the 1970s and 1980s and into the 1990s, the Escobar group competed mainly with drug traffickers from the Colombian city of Cali, most notably Gilberto and Miguel Rodriguez Orejuela, Fanor Arizabaleta, Helmer Herrera-Buitrago, Henry Loiaza, Victor Patino and Jose Santacruz Londono. These, like their Medellin counterparts, organized the smuggling of large amounts of cocaine to the United States and Europe hidden in the bodies of 'mules' or in other more sophisticated ways, such as shipments of flowers, lumber and concrete fence posts. It took impressive police work by both the Drug Enforcement Agency and Colombian police to bring down the group's leaders, but the group fell because the loyalty of the various groups of accountants, contract killers, realtors, bankers and other professionals that it had to associate with could not be guaranteed.

Harold Ackerman was one of the first and most significant to turn against the Cali group. Ackerman oversaw Cali operations in Miami until the early 1990s and, as he later testified,

> My cooperation with the United States provided a detailed, minute and true narrative of my activities in narcotics smuggling. I was involved with the Rodriguez Orejuela organization. This cooperation also included the explanation of the organizational's flow chart, the structure of the Cali Cartel organization, its operation methods, as well as providing the positive identification of other persons involved in the organization, the identification of other routes of importation and distribution of cocaine in the United States, and a precise and exact analysis of the participation and the activities of the U.S. attorneys who worked on behalf of the cartel. And as a result of this information, a number of investigations and operations were begun against the Cali Cartel.[28]

Effective policing and the inherent limitations of illegal business groups had therefore effectively broken up the Cali group by the late 1990s, yet as Ron Chepesiuk, the chronicler of these efforts, concludes, nothing much was really accomplished. Other groups have filled any vacuums created. 'Colombia is still at the center of the drug trafficking universe', Chesesiuk wrote, 'while it teeters politically on the verge of disintegration.'[29] The careers of Medellin and Cali traffickers show that involvement in illegal markets can bring political power to the most successful actors, but this power is highly unstable and rarely lasts. Such gangster power does, however, place huge strains on the state in countries with small economic bases.

Francisco E. Thoumi's *Illegal Drugs, Economy, and Society in the Andes* (2003) confirms the findings of other researchers that the drug industry tends to be fluid and opportunistic rather than rigid and bureau-cratically structured. On the illegal drug industry in Colombia, for example, he writes, 'Drug organizations are continually changing in their attempts to foil law enforcement efforts, and they are constantly searching for new raw material and intermediate good sources, export routes, and markets. The secrecy imposed by illegality precludes a highly structured and transparent organization in which workers know their bosses, what they do, and how they operate.' The profits from the drug industry are great and they thus attract independent operators that continuously spring up at various stages of the business. Thoumi also details the increasing involvement of guerrilla and paramilitary organiza-tions and their links with international organized criminal operations involved in illegal-weapons trafficking.[30] Prohibition thus not only spurs production, it also creates new forms of political power, usually military or paramilitary power.

Another recent book details American complicity in grave human rights abuses by the Colombian military, which are excused and perpetu-ated by the continuing fruitless efforts against the drug trade. Robin Kirk in *More Terrible than Death: Violence, Drugs, and America's War in Colombia* (2003) writes that the Colombian military began accepting more money and advice from the American government in the name of the war on drugs from 1990 and then directed the system more against people they suspected of 'subversion'.

A new navy intelligence network based in Barracaberja began to recruit professional killers and paramilitaries as a 'hunter-killer' squad that col-lected information used to murder ... peasant leaders, human rights defenders, and people who made the mistake of getting in their way. Called Network 7, its commander, Colonel Rodrigo Quinones, was later linked by government investigators to at least fifty-seven murders, including the sidewalk execution of the secretary of the main human rights group in the region. Network 7 also set up paramilitary groups that used the name MAS to threaten and kill in the surrounding countryside.

In response to details of human rights atrocities such as these, US officials rejected proposals to put human rights conditions on aid, arguing that they would be counter-productive and that Colombian officers would eventually behave better once they followed the good examples of their American counterparts. One high-ranking State Department official put it like this to an unconcerned Congressional committee, 'Denying aid or imposing conditions impossible to meet defeats the goals of improving human rights. In the real world, the perfect is the enemy of the good.'[31] The lawless crusade against drugs survives on this kind of logic. Human rights violations are as high as ever in Colombia at the time of writing but American politicians are as reluctant as they have been since the Nixon era to confront these and other catastrophic results of drug-prohibition campaigns.

Khun Sa, Hekmatyar, Suarez, Escobar and the host of other large and small-time operators involved in the drug traffic would never have existed without prohibition. And, over the past three decades, changes in the structure of the global economy and in the ease of transportation in particular have actually made contraband drugs easier to smuggle.

11

Dumbing the International Response to Drugs and Organized Crime

The United States has played a central role in the treaties and organizations dealing with drugs and drug trafficking since the early twentieth century and, as we have seen, Nixon accelerated the process of establishing global drug prohibition. To institutionalize this process the Bureau of International Narcotic Matters (INM) was created in 1978 in the State Department. INM existed first and foremost as a 'policy shop', representing America at international level, with the DEA and other drug-enforcement agencies. It also helped organize crop eradication and other anti-drug measures and prepared the annual International Narcotics Control Strategy Report on global drug production, traffic and abuse. This report and the drug-control certification process that INM managed decided whether other countries were taking measures in line with prohibition policies. Essentially the INM helped manage the effort to persuade or bully other countries into attempting to stop their citizens supplying the richest market in the world. Mainly through the INM the State Department spent tens of millions of dollars each year on crop eradication or substitution programmes. They also used the United Nations and other international organizations to spread the gospel of US drug-control policy, holding it up as a model for other countries to follow.

All the INM's work continues to this day but in the early 1990s its remit was expanded to include money laundering, arms or other contraband, human trafficking and other forms of transnational crime. Accordingly its name was changed to the Bureau of International Narcotics and Law Enforcement (INL) in 1995. Today, the INL's main task is to work towards the implementation of America's International Crime Control Strategy. It developed this with other agencies in 1998 'as a roadmap for a coordinated, effective, long-term attack on international crime'. In the pursuit of this aim American diplomats work incessantly through multilateral and bilateral forums to define what the INL calls 'global norms for effective criminal laws', which are in effect American norms. The INL also 'actively' encourages 'foreign governments to enact and enforce laws based on these norms'.[1] Today, the INL organizes and sponsors law-enforcement training for police officers, judges, investigators, prosecutors, court reporters, and customs and border officials in more than 95 countries world-wide.[2]

The INM/INL played and continues to play a key role in the 'Americanization' of law-enforcement systems of the international community. Professor Ethan Nadelmann chronicled this process most comprehensively in *Cops Across Borders*:

> The modern era of international law enforcement is one in which U.S. criminal justice priorities and U.S. models of criminalization and criminal investigation have been exported abroad. Foreign governments have responded to U.S. pressures, inducements, and examples by enacting new criminal laws regarding drug trafficking, money laundering, insider trading, and organized crime and by changing financial and corporate secrecy laws as well as their codes of criminal procedure to better accommodate U.S. requests for assistance. Foreign police have adopted U.S. investigative techniques, and foreign courts and legislatures have followed up with the requisite legal authorizations. And foreign governments have devoted substantial police and even military resources to curtailing illicit drug production and trafficking . . . By and large, the United States has provided the models, and other governments have done the accommodating.[3]

To provide the models that Nadelmann refers to, American government officials needed the rest of the world to accept American-inspired analyses of drugs and organized-crime 'threats' and also needed to maintain the false perception that American drug-control and organized-crime-control methods work. The intention was always to gain an international acceptance of the need for collaboration along the lines prescribed by the United States.

The INM first made a significant impact in the early 1980s as the US belief that the control of drug production at source was essential led it to intervene more directly in the affairs of producer countries. It was charged with managing and ensuring the enforcement of new US laws that required source countries to achieve 'the maximum reduction in illicit production determined to be achievable'. The intention was to do this mainly by crop eradication at first, but also by getting other countries to enact legislation concerning the extradition of drug traffickers, money laundering and the refining of raw materials. If the source countries failed to satisfy American requirements in these areas, they would lose American aid money and face a number of sanctions involving measures that would stifle their export trade. They would also face the likely failure to obtain development loans from the World Bank and other multilateral banks.[4] Most developing countries therefore have little choice but to comply with American demands.

The international strategies Americans have forced on producer countries have shown little sign of succeeding despite the claims of US officials. Eradication campaigns have characterized drug control in the Andean countries, for example, for the past two decades. These usually involve the spraying of herbicides or the use of military force to oversee the cutting down of trees or plants. The first of these methods has often had damaging environmental consequences, perhaps even catastrophic in the long term, since the chemical war on drugs has contributed to the deforestation of the Amazon basin and the high Andean forests. The second, involving the more environmentally friendly direct removal of plants, has often been violently divisive, given the peasant farmers' economic dependence on the illegal cash crops.[5]

For most decades from the 1980s, successful eradication campaigns in some areas were marked by the so-called 'balloon effect', where huge fields of coca emerge in one region after being eradicated in another. Increased American and home-country effort has perhaps seen the balloon effect coming under control with increased spraying but there is now an 'atomization' of drug farms into many smaller plots, often in isolated areas that would be almost impossible to detect. Growers have also adapted to the new conditions by creating coca plants that are resistant to chemicals, adaptable to different climates and yield more cocaine from fewer plants.[6]

Crop substitution programmes in Asia and Latin America – whereby farmers are encouraged to grow alternative cash crops, such as sugar beet, coffee, or potatoes – have also failed. Growers are often far away from markets for legitimate crops and the cash return does not compensate for their effort. Opium and coca, by contrast, are profitable crops even for the most exploited farmers. There is no need, for example, to pay for transportation since the traffickers come to them.

It was clear by the mid-1980s that US international efforts to stem the flow of drugs from producer countries had failed. A 1984 congressional report, for example, noted that 'in most of the major producing countries, illicit narcotic production, manufacture and traffic had dramatically increased'.[7] Instead of re-examining drug-control policy the Reagan administration used the INM and other agencies to globalize the failed policy of prohibition ever further. Because of the new intensified American effort most governments across the world expanded and stiffened their penalties for drug trafficking and related activities. Many governments decided to adopt American-inspired legislation permitting the seizure and forfeiture of drug-trafficker assets and international organizations, notably Interpol and the United Nations' drug-control organs, promoted American-inspired model legislation and drug prohibition policies. Most important of all was the successful negotiation of the United Nations Convention Against Illicit Traffic in Narcotics and Psychotropic Substances in 1988. This extended the scope of measures against trafficking, introduced provisions to control money laundering and seize the assets of drug traffickers, to allow for extradition of major traffickers and improved legal co-operation between countries. It also proposed criminalization of purchase and possession by users. Although the Convention did allow for the treatment or rehabilitation of addicts as an alternative to a penal sentence, it was effectively an acknowledgement that America's drug prohibition regime would now be applied in every other country that signed up to the Convention. Rather than risk American disapproval most countries did sign up and it came into force in November 1990.[8]

Among other things the 1988 Convention gave another stick to the Americans to beat producer countries with. Each country that received INM assistance in the previous two years was required to submit a report on the extent to which it had 'met the goals and objectives of the United Nations Convention Against Illicit Traffic in Narcotic Drugs and Psychotropic Substances'. This included action on such issues as illicit cultivation, production, distribution, sale, transport and financing, and money laundering, asset seizure, extradition, mutual legal assistance, law enforcement and transit co-operation, precursor chemical control, and demand reduction.

By 1996, 136 countries had ratified the 1988 Convention and could no longer simply pay lip-service to American prohibitionist dreams. It was the global equivalent of the Volstead Act being passed to enforce alcohol prohibition in the 1920s and just as doomed to produce nothing more than violence, corruption and overriding failure. The United Nations' own statistics demonstrated continued failure very clearly. In 1986 world opium production was around 2,000 tons. By 1994 this had trebled to over 6,000 tons. There were an estimated 141 million drug abusers globally, including 8 million heroin addicts, 30 million amphetamine users and 13 million cocaine users.[9] Because of prohibition these people were paying inflated prices for drugs that remained cheap to produce. A multitude of growers, smugglers, distributors, corrupt officials and professionals – such as lawyers, accountants and bankers – were sharing the resultant profit. There was a need to explain this failure, which involved dumbing down international discourse on organized crime. In the process the Americanization of international law enforcement was continued.

★

The most prominent popularizer of a new understanding of organized crime was Claire Sterling, an American reporter based in Italy. Sterling had originally become known during the 1980s for publicizing material that probably originated from her sources in the American intelligence community. Parts of the CIA certainly liked her claim that the Soviets controlled global terrorism at a time when President Reagan was ratcheting up Cold War tension with 'evil empire' rhetoric. There were links between Soviet agents and terrorist groups, just as the CIA often kept undesirable company, but Sterling's thesis was wildly overstated. However, the support of such notables as Secretary of State Alexander Haig and CIA chief William Casey did help boost the sales of her book, *The Terror Network: The Secret War of International Terrorism* (1981).

By the end of the Cold War, Sterling, like her sources in intelligence, was looking for new conspiratorial threats and found them in the world of organized crime. She argued in *Octopus: The Long Reach of the International Sicilian Mafia* (1990) that the Sicilian Mafia controlled the world's supply of heroin in co-operation with terrorists and various other crime organizations such as the Colombian drug 'cartels'. Four years later she updated her work on organized crime by producing *Thieves' World: The Threat of the New Global Network of Organized Crime* (1994). This claimed that the Sicilian and American Mafias, Colombian drug cartels, Chinese Triads and Japanese Yakusa had joined with the Russian Mafia to mount a full-scale attack on Russia and Europe to plunder both.[10] Both these books fit Richard Hofstadter's description of conspiracy theories, notably their tendency to jump from the undeniable to the unbelievable and their claims that nebulous forces threatened the whole of civilization. Few serious researchers find her work credible. Unsurprisingly, however, the American intelligence community lauded her. In many ways Sterling was the founder of mainstream, transnational organized-crime analysis, influencing high-level American opinion on the subject. She helped give US government officials a line that could be sold to the United Nations. Given the authority of the United Nations, more and more nations have chosen to adopt an approach to the problem of organized crime that was as conveniently blame-shifting as the American approach has proved to be.

The American intelligence community certainly thought highly enough of Sterling to invite her to chair a panel on Russian organized crime at a

Washington, DC, conference of high-level American law-enforcement and intelligence community personnel in September 1994. Conference organizer Arnaud de Borchgrave introduced her by praising *Thieves' World* and making the questionable claim that her previous book, *The Terror Network*, had been 'vindicated . . . by the miles upon miles of files pouring out of the archives of former Communist intelligence services'.[11]

Sterling was invited because her outlandish theories closely reflected those of the American intelligence community's at the time. The title of the conference – Global Organized Crime: The New Empire of Evil – and the speeches delivered were classic conspiracy theory, involving not only jumps from the undeniable to the unbelievable, but also mythical statistics and claims that the future of civilization was threatened by outside forces. The executive summary of the conference set the tone: 'The dimensions of global organized crime present a greater international security challenge than anything Western democracies had to cope with during the Cold War. World-wide alliances are being forged in every criminal field from money laundering and currency counterfeiting to trafficking in drugs and nuclear materials. Global organized crime is the world's fastest growing business, with profits estimated at $1 trillion.' The keynote speaker at the conference was FBI Director Louis Freeh who stressed that 'the ravages of transnational crime' were the greatest long-term threat to the security of the United States and warned that the very fabric of democratic society was at risk everywhere. CIA Director R. James Woolsey followed up by noting that 'the threats from organized crime transcend traditional law enforcement concerns. They affect critical national security interests . . . some governments find their authority besieged at home and their foreign policy interests imperiled abroad.'[12]

Woolsey's speech included the most revealing indication that the new shared understanding of organized crime was designed to fit with a neoliberal worldview. He singled out President Boris Yeltsin's efforts to counter 'the threat from organized crime' towards Russia's privatization process for praise. Russia was then undergoing a wide-ranging reform effort to transform its economy from a communist to a capitalist model. Yeltsin, according to Woolsey, was protecting this 'positive transformation' by signing various new laws which brought Russian organized-crime control more into line with American methods. However, the reality of the Russian privatization suggests that the process was itself corrupt from the beginning rather than being threatened and imperilled by Woolsey's estimate of the 5,700 organized-crime groups then operating in Russia. The way privatization was organized by Yeltsin's government resulted in rampant corruption and a system of capitalism that enriched a new breed of Russian robber barons on a spectacular scale. As one academic put it, the government securities and loans-for-share schemes, in particular, proved to be 'a gargantuan government-sponsored pyramid scheme that predictably collapsed and in doing so put the savings of millions of ordinary Russians into the pockets of those robber barons'.[13] Russian privatization therefore proved to be economically, politically and socially disastrous to the vast majority of the population and immensely enriching to a few. These few were mostly brutal and corrupt, but always well-placed individuals. The corrupt implementation of neo-liberal inspired reforms was therefore more responsible for the creation of a new hybrid of gangster capitalism and the thousands of Russian organized-crime groups were more a symptom of mismanaged privatization rather than a cause of privatization's problems.

The message that came from the New Empire of Evil conference and from a co-operative media was that this new global threat of organized crime required a tougher and more collaborative international response. More specifically the threat required more thorough information sharing amongst police and intelligence officials in different countries and improved methods of transcending jurisdictional frontiers in pursuing and prosecuting malefactors.

By the early 1990s American diplomats were already pushing hard. Two months after the Washington conference, the United Nations held the World Ministerial Conference on Organized Transnational Crime in Naples. It is clear from studies of the background to this conference that it represented a coincidence of the interests of the US, the member states of the European Union and the internal politics of the UN itself.[14] It provided an international forum for the global conspiracy theory of organized crime.

The UN conference was attended by high-level governmental representatives from 138 countries. The rhetoric and analysis was essentially the same as that employed by Freeh, Woolsey and Sterling. According to the UN's press release, participants at the conference recognized the growing threat of organized crime, with its 'highly destabilizing and corrupting influence on fundamental social, economic and political institutions'. This represented a challenge demanding increased and more effective international co-operation. 'The challenge posed by transnational organized crime', the document continued, 'can only be met if law enforcement authorities are able to display the same ingenuity and innovation, organizational flexibility and cooperation that characterize the criminal organizations themselves.'[15] This was essentially the same analysis as that produced by American politicians and government officials since the 1960s.

United Nations Secretary-General Boutros Boutros-Ghali set the tone of the conference and gave probably the best exposition of the new conventional wisdom on organized crime with his opening address.

> Organized crime has . . . become a world phenomenon. In Europe, in Asia, in Africa and in America, the forces of darkness are at work and no society is spared . . . it scoffs at frontiers and becomes a universal force. Traditional crime organizations have, in a very short time, succeeded in adapting to the new international context to become veritable crime multinationals . . . Transnational crime . . . undermines the very foundations of the international democratic order. Transnational crime poisons the business climate, corrupts political leaders and undermines human rights. It weakens the effectiveness and credibility of institutions and thus undermines democratic life.

He concluded with what was already becoming a familiar call to international action: 'We also know, however, that when the States decide to take effective, voluntary steps to combat transnational crime, and when they decide to cooperate with each other and harmonize their efforts, legitimate society regains all its power and strength. It is on behalf of this effort to promote the rule of law and to combat transnational crime that we are meeting here in Naples.'[16]

Boutros-Ghali was followed by a series of speakers echoing the same themes: the threat posed by organized crime to societies and governmental institutions across the globe and the need for more international co-operation to meet this threat. The seriousness of the perceived threat was emphasized in the language of many of the speeches. For example, Elias Jassan, Secretary of Justice in Argentina, described organized crime as 'a new monster . . . the Anti-State' and Silvio Berlusconi, Prime Minister of Italy, described crime organizations as 'armies of evil' that could be defeated 'only by international collaboration'.[17] Melchior Wathelet, Deputy Prime Minister and Minister of Justice of Belgium, claimed that no region of the world 'was safe from the large criminal networks' and favoured the proposal to elaborate a binding legal instrument along the lines of the precedent set by the 1988 anti-drug treaty.[18] There was no significant dissent from this line at the conference, discussion of organized crime at the highest international level had been frozen by images that effectively excluded discussion.

Many speakers at Naples implicitly or explicitly emphasized the success of US-approved organized-crime-control strategies. This deferential consensus was most clearly reflected in a background document for this conference, which singled out the 1970 Racketeer Influenced and Corrupt Organizations (RICO) statute as 'an example of "dynamic" legislation able to adapt itself to . . . developments'. The document then elaborated,

'In the United States, the RICO statute is generally considered to be the starting point of a new process of awareness of organized crime by the United States Government and its criminal justice system. Its effectiveness has been demonstrated in the many indictments and convictions of members of organized crime groups that have resulted since the legislation was passed.'[19] In the newsletter that reported on the conference the UN Crime Prevention and Criminal Justice Division illuminated the new line on transnational organized crime with a series of graphic profiles of organized-crime networks which included maps to locate such criminal groups as the Sicilian and US Cosa Nostras, the Camorra, 'Ndrangeta and United Sacred Crown from mainland Italy, Triads from China, Colombian Cartels, Japanese Yakusa and the Russian Mafia. The maps and profiles were accompanied with unsubstantiated and nonsensical claims such as 'the worldwide business of all the world's Mafias amounts to 1 billion United States dollars' and gave the impression that the world was threatened by these clearly identifiable 'armies of evil'. Significantly in the 'Size and structure' sections of the profiles, only the United States was credited with any success, with the information that 20 out of 25 US Cosa Nostra bosses were in prison along with 300 New York soldiers.[20]

The main result of the conference was to put the elaboration of the United Nations Convention against Transnational Organized Crime (UNTOC) at the centre of discussion. This process culminated in December 2000, when representatives of more than a hundred countries met in Palermo, Sicily, to sign up to the Convention in principle, and 23 September 2003 when it came into force, having been ratified by the required number of states. The UNTOC defined an 'organized crime group' as 'a structured group of three or more persons existing for a period of time and having the aim of committing one or more serious crimes or offences established in accordance with this Convention in order to obtain, directly or indirectly, a financial or other material benefit.[21] The UN chose not to explain this significant departure from the organization's previous thinking on the subject, which considered the problem of organized crime in terms of *activity* rather than distinct groups of people and emphasized the need to curb the activities of transnational corporations.

Nations that ratify the UNTOC Convention commit themselves to the type of American measures deemed to be effective in combating organized crime by the UN. Articles 12 to 14, for example, commit states to adopt measures as may be necessary to enable the confiscation and seizure of the proceeds of crime derived from offences covered by the Convention. Article 20 commits each state, if 'permitted by the basic principles of its domestic legal system' to 'take the necessary measures to allow for the appropriate use of controlled delivery and, where it deems appropriate, for the use of other special investigative techniques such as electronic and other forms of surveillance, and undercover operations, by its competent authorities in its territory for the purpose of effectively combating organized crime'. 'Controlled delivery' had been defined earlier as meaning the 'technique of allowing illicit or suspect consignments to pass out of, through or into the territory of one or more States, with the knowledge and under the supervision of their competent authorities, with a view to the investigation of an offence and the identification of persons involved in the commission of the offence'. Most controlled deliveries would consist of illegal drugs. Article 26 on 'Measures to enhance cooperation with law enforcement authorities' commits states to take 'appropriate measures to encourage persons who participate or who have participated in organized crime groups'. Under this article states 'shall consider providing for the possibility in appropriate cases, of mitigating punishment of an accused person who provides substantial cooperation in the investigation or prosecution of an offence covered by this Convention'. Such witnesses would be covered by protection measures outlined in Article 20.

There are many problems associated with these US recommended strategies, as discussed in Chapter 5. The main problem, however, is that they are exclusively concerned with arresting and punishing harmful people rather than a more strategic approach that reduces the opportunities for harmful activity. These methods, as we have seen, have been in use in the United States, locally and nationally, for decades. Although they have helped secure many important convictions they have not significantly affected the extent of organized-crime activity in any measurable way while other factors have actually exacerbated American organized-crime problems.

Amongst other things it was hoped that the Convention would finally make global drug prohibition effective. This was implied when an attachment to a draft of the convention put the 'illicit traffic in narcotic drugs or psychotropic substances and money-laundering', as defined in the 1988 UN Convention, at the top of its list of serious crimes.[22] The hope was made explicit when US Assistant Secretary of State Rand Beers announced that the convention would go to the Senate for review and ratification in February 2001, and made it clear that the new Convention was a 'follow-on' to the 1988 drug convention.[23] Had American drug-control policies actually worked there may have been some logic to the international community's adoption of these policies but, as we have seen, the evidence suggests otherwise. Meanwhile, the war on drugs internationally, according to the UN's own admission, has failed in equal measure to the American version. Recent UN estimates show the use of prohibited drugs has increased significantly over recent decades and drug prices generally have fallen sharply. The United Nations International Drug Control Programme (UNDCP) estimated in 2003 that the total number of drug abusers was around 200 million people, equivalent to 3.4 per cent of the global population or 4.7 per cent of the population aged 15 and above. These figures included 160 million for cannabis, 34 million for amphetamines, 8 million for ecstasy, and around 14 million each for cocaine and heroin.[24] Given the immense cost of this crusade and avalanche of crime and corruption that accompanied it, the comment of Senator Robert Wagner in 1931 on the prohibition of alcohol is worth recalling. 'Why heap more sacrifice upon the altar of hopelessness?'

Just as early twentieth-century American business interests had managed to divert the reform element in society away from corruption in the system towards attempting to eliminate aspects of the personal behaviour of individuals, American diplomats and bureaucrats had successfully achieved an equivalent diversion at the United Nations. The UN's early analysis had been out of line with the dominant neo-liberal agenda, the new emphasis on comic book supercriminal organizations allowed it to get back in step. The international organization now recommends that every country should set up rat traps on the American model at the same time as the neo-liberal and morally hypocritical conditions that breed rats continue to worsen.

PART 3

A World of
Criminal Opportunity
1965–

There is always somebody who pays, and international business is generally the main source of corruption.

George Soros, *Financial Times*, 8 December 1998

Introduction

As we saw in Chapter 9, Nixon's unilateral decision to terminate the Bretton Woods system for governing international money in the 1970s and the failure of efforts to find a workable alternative system were important parts of the process that led to profound changes in the global political economy. These changes have resulted in an explosion of opportunity for organized criminal activity across the globe while governments continued to follow the blueprints for failure favoured by the US government.

Nixon's decision to end the restrictive Bretton Woods order allowed private international financial activity to grow at a phenomenal rate, giving market actors such as banks and corporations a degree of freedom they had not held since the 1920s.[1] Coincidentally, the fourfold rise in oil prices in the early 1970s meant that American banks, in particular, were flush with petrodollars from the newly rich Organization of Petroleum Exporting Countries (OPEC). The flow of OPEC money into the banks was soon followed by an unprecedented rush of very risky bank lending to countries in the Third World, often led by brutal and corrupt dictators, and equally greedy local elites. These leaders bought tanks and fighter planes, nuclear plants, huge dams, and many other unproductive products while stealing billions of dollars for themselves to be smuggled out of their countries and into the banks of richer nations.[2] American and other Western governments enthusiastically encouraged the lending and claimed that it demonstrated the superior efficiency of the free market over intervention and official programmes of development aid.[3] The debts of many countries mushroomed out of control from the late 1970s as the impact of rapidly rising interest rates hit the poorest countries the hardest. Paul Volcker, then chairman of the US Federal Reserve, responding to pressure from corporate interests to fight inflation, was chiefly responsible for this interest-rate hike.

While interest rates were reaching the kind of levels demanded by neighbourhood loan-sharks, commodity prices were falling fast due to 1980s recessions in Europe and North America. A basket of 28 commodities which included lead, zinc, sugar, coffee and tea was worth 48 per

cent less in 1988 than in 1974.[4] Countries expected to export their way
out of their debt crisis were in a no-win situation.

In August 1982 the Mexican government threatened to default on its
debts and Brazil, Argentina and Venezuela were likely to follow suit. If
they had, international financial and trading systems might well have
collapsed, even taking down top US banks such as Chase Manhattan and
Citibank. The rescue package needed co-ordination by a public agency
since there were many lenders with their own terms and conditions and
the IMF was called in to provide this important new function. The IMF's
response to the Mexican crisis served as a precedent to be repeated many
times in following years. It had three fundamental points: first, the
commercial banks agreed to reschedule outstanding debt and make some
new lending available; second, IMF money would supplement this package; third, the provision of extra funding was to be conditional on the
implementation of an austerity package by the debtor.[5]

By this time, the thinking behind IMF and World Bank policy was
dominated by neo-liberalism and neo-liberal principles dominate the
management of the international economy to this day. The paramount
neo-liberal principle, as we have seen, is the 'sanctity and importance of
the market'. Neo-liberals assert that the role of the state in the economy
should be minimized and, if possible, eliminated. Neo-liberals promote
reducing tariffs and trade barriers, deregulation and privatization on the
American model already discussed in Chapter 6. They also claim that
the way forward for Third World countries is export-oriented industrial-
ization. As a corollary to these positions, neo-liberals usually oppose
labour and environmental standards in international trade deals and have
little to say about crimes that affect working people in particular and the
environment in general.[6] Neo-liberals emphasize wealth creation as a
positive outcome of the increasing economic integration of the world.
They either ignore or find someone or something to blame for the
downsides of globalization, because, as they constantly reiterate, 'there is
no alternative'.

Reflecting neo-liberal principles, the IMF and World Bank began to
exchange any help they were prepared to offer indebted countries for
certain 'free-market' reforms. The IMF established a formal Structural
Adjustment Facility in 1986 designed to facilitate closer co-operation
between itself and the World Bank in the control of debtor countries'
economies. These countries were essentially told to earn more and spend
less in order to qualify for help and the process was institutionalized by
what became known as Structural Adjustment Programmes (SAPs). First,
they were required to cut public spending, even on health, education and
welfare, on the grounds that this spending was inflationary and generated

an unsustainable demand for imports of goods and capital. Second, they were told to cut wages to reduce inflationary pressures and make exports cheaper. Third, they were told to eliminate subsidies and price controls. Fourth, they had to open the domestic markets to imports and remove restrictions on foreign investment in industry and financial services, on the grounds that this liberalization would encourage more competition and therefore more efficiency. Fifth, there had to be more emphasis on export-oriented industry and agriculture, partly through devaluation and partly through tax changes. Finally, Structural Adjustment Loan recipients were told to set about privatizing state-owned enterprises on the grounds that free enterprise was better at allocating resources between producers and consumers than the public sector.[7]

At the same time as the IMF and World Bank were forcing such conformity to market forces on the Third World, the Second World was opening up to capitalism. China had already begun to turn towards a market-based model of economic development after the death of Mao Zedong in 1976. The Soviet Union's collapse in 1991 led to a new commitment to market reform in Russia and other former Soviet states, such as the Ukraine and Georgia, as well as former Soviet satellite states such as Poland, Hungary and the new Czech and Slovak republics. The challenges faced by these former socialist nations were formidable. In Joseph Stiglitz's words they

> had to move from one price system – the distorted price system that prevailed under communism – to a market price system; they had to create markets and the institutional infrastructure that underlies it; and they had to privatize all the property which previously had belonged to the state. They had to create a new kind of entrepreneurship – not just the kind that was good at circumventing government rules and laws – and new enterprises to help redeploy the resources that had previously been so inefficiently used.[8]

China chose a gradualist approach to such fundamental reforms, the former Soviet Union states, strongly encouraged by the US Treasury and the IMF, chose the 'shock therapy' of a rapid move towards *laissez-faire* capitalism.[9]

Neo-liberals had promised that a world opened up to private capital would deliver goods and services more efficiently to more people. Privatization, they claimed, would reduce the 'rent-seeking' activity of government officials who either skim off the profits of government enterprises or award contracts and jobs to their friends. But, as we have already seen, this was not the result of Russian privatization. In fact, as Stiglitz has pointed out, privatization made matters so much worse in many countries that it was jokingly referred to as 'briberization'. Privatization was unlikely to solve the problem of corrupt governments. 'After all,' he continued,

> the same corrupt government that mismanaged the firm will also handle the privatization.
>
> In country after country, government officials have realized that privatization meant they no longer needed to be limited to annual profit skimming. By selling a government enterprise at below market price, they could get a significant chunk of the asset value for themselves rather than leaving it for subsequent officeholders. In effect, they could steal today much of what would have been skimmed off by future politicians. Not surprisingly, the rigged privatization process was designed to maximize the amount government ministers could appropriate for themselves, not the amount that would accrue to the government's treasury, let alone the overall efficiency of the economy.[10]

A United Nations report described the process more simply. It was 'outright theft'.[11]

Second and Third World states have now surrendered to a kind of *laissez-faire* capitalism that resembles the United States of the 1920s. This proved to be predictably disastrous, opening up vast new areas of criminal opportunity and placing intolerable burdens on the peoples of these countries.

A world-wide market therefore now exists, linked by the instant communications made possible by the world wide web and techno-logically enhanced air, sea and land transport. The main movers and shakers in this market are those representing the multinational firms and financial corporations whose wealth and power has grown exponentially in the last three decades. Hundreds of millions of North Americans, Europeans, Australians and East Asians have benefited from the changes brought about by globalization in terms of consumer choice and increasing affluence. But the downside of globalization is felt mainly by the less well-off in rich countries and the multitudes of poor in less privileged countries. The global economy is volatile and the rules that govern it are unfair. The volatility is constant but financial crises surfaced most prominently in 1990 and 2002 in Japan, in 1994 in Mexico, in 1997 in Thailand, Indonesia and South Korea, in 1998 in Russia and in 2002 in Argentina. The rules that govern trade and financial transactions in today's international economic system were devised by the United States and other wealthy nations and discriminate against poorer nations. The General Agreement on Tariffs and Trade (GATT), the World Trade Organization (WTO), the World Bank and the IMF are led by representatives of wealthy nations and support multinational corporate and banking interests more than those of the less developed countries. 'The result', as Scott Newton writes in *The Global Economy* (2004), has been 'a financial regime that subordinated national development programmes to the whims of the international financial markets and a set of rules governing trade and investment that denied export markets and cheap drugs to Third World countries while opening up their markets to foreign ownership'.[12] For this reason, many hundreds of millions in less privileged countries have suffered from increasing inequality in their societies, accompanied of course by high rates of poverty, disease, violent crime and corruption.

Global economic liberalization has not been accompanied by adequate control of international financial and business transactions. Unmanaged globalization and the crime-friendly world it created tended to make the rich richer and the poor more desperate, as the case studies that follow in the remaining chapters show. It is important to bear in mind that the activities described are best understood in terms of organized crime. The many ongoing conspiracies against the public that use fraud and force to achieve their ends are outlined. In their present immunity from criminal law the key actors in these conspiracies resemble the robber barons. In scale their plots far exceed those of late nineteenth-century industrialists.

12

Suharto and the Looting
of Indonesia

During its long Cold War conflicts with the Soviet Union and China, the United States made a practice of supporting systems of government that delivered them what they wanted. In the industrialized West and in Japan this meant liberal democracies that were free to decide on a range of matters in the domestic sphere but tended to obey American dictates when it came to foreign policy. Even faced with evidence of American brutality in the Vietnam War, for example, British governments rarely went further than expressing mild disapproval. In the developing world, this often meant support for greedy and corrupt dictators so long as they were subordinate to US interests. Years of support for these dictatorships were invariably followed by a pattern of violence, corruption, capital flight, debt and social disintegration.

In Indonesia, during the 1950s and early 1960s, the country's leader Achmed Sukarno represented communism in American eyes. Sukarno was not a communist but he nationalized foreign holdings in the country's vast reserves of oil, tin, nickel, copper and bauxite, favoured land reform and governed the country in alliance with the country's large communist party, the PKI.

In the late 1950s the Ford Foundation began to work with some of the leading US universities, notably the University of California, Berkeley, to study aspects of Indonesian society, including 'political obstacles' to development. By this time the foundation, which had been set up by the famous union buster Henry Ford in 1936, was led by John McCloy, whose diplomatic, political and corporate credentials made him, in one historian's words, 'the archetype of twentieth-century American power and influence'. McCloy had been Assistant Secretary of War, president of the World Bank and chairman of the Chase Manhattan Bank amongst other high-level positions.[1] Under McCloy the foundation also lavishly funded programmes that sent young aristocratic Indonesians to American universities, where they would most commonly learn American business methods and economic analysis: 'You can't have a modernizing country without a modernizing elite,' as one Ford official put it.[2] After studying at Berkeley and the other universities, many of these young economists became advisers for the Indonesian army. At the same time, thousands of army officers were being trained at US military bases and universities.

In the mid-1960s these students, along with students from Indonesia's elite universities and other youth groups, were in the vanguard of efforts to eliminate communist influence first and bring about Sukarno's downfall shortly afterwards. According to a *New York Times* report of May 1966, quoting a schoolteacher in a village near Jogjakarta, 'My students went right out with the army. They pointed out P.K.I. members. The army shot them on the spot along with their whole family; women, children. It was horrible.'[3] Estimates of the total number of communists or suspected communists murdered in the following years ranged from 500,000 to one million. A CIA study ranked it as one of the worst mass murders of the twentieth century, 'along with the Soviet purges of the 1930s, the Nazi mass murders during the Second World War, and the Maoist bloodbath of the early 1950s', but was less forthcoming about the agency's own involvement in the Indonesian purges.[4]

By 1966 Sukarno was deposed and replaced the following year by General Mohammed Suharto, all of whose ministers had PhDs from the US. From that time until he was himself deposed in 1998, Suharto, his ministers, his army officers and a number of home-grown or foreign corporate interests carved up the nation's abundant natural resources amongst themselves while ordinary Indonesians remained some of the world's poorest. Land reform, which Sukarno had called 'an indispensable part of the Indonesian revolution', had, of course, been ended.[5] Suharto and his ministers were regularly re-elected in a system of controlled and indirect election that was anything but democratic. For decades death squads operated at will, killing not just 'subversives' but 'suspected criminals' by the thousands. The torture and wrongful imprisonment of political prisoners became routine.[6]

America's interest in Indonesia further increased after the oil crisis of October 1973 and American banks and corporations lined up to do business with Suharto on the strength of Indonesia's rapidly increasing oil revenue, which went from $232 million in 1966 to $5.2 billion in 1974. Western firms enthusiastically sold the General telecommunications systems, steel mills, tanker fleets and, most cynically, weapons – jets, landing ships, tanks, submarines and rifles – to a country not seriously threatened by the possibility of invasion. Even oil profits could not cover the cost of these purchases and so Western banks lined up to lend Indonesia money.[7]

One of Suharto's first acts had been to create Pertamina, a state-owned oil company that was given sole rights to the country's oil, gas and related ventures, and became the fountainhead of Indonesian corruption. To run Pertamina, Suharto appointed General Ibnu Sutowo who operated international shakedowns that no ordinary gangster could contemplate. In one, Sutowo sent out letters on Pertamina letterhead soliciting 'investments' in a New York restaurant he was about to open. The solicitations went only to companies that were either doing business with or trying to do business with Pertamina. US corporate giants such as Mobil, Atlantic Richfield, Monsanto and Dresser dutifully paid up and made Sutowo and Suharto that much richer.[8] In 1976, with Pertamina deeply in debt to Western banks and unable to pay, Suharto was forced to remove Sutowo as head of the company, but the corruption continued with Suharto's family and friends becoming involved in every stage of oil production and marketing, siphoning off money at every opportunity. The amount of money Suharto alone stole from his country is staggering. Transparency International, a non-governmental organization devoted to combating corruption, put him at the top of their corruption league with an alleged haul of between $15 and 35 billion in his 31-year rule.[9] All carefully spirited away to Western and off-shore banks.

The debt accumulated during the graft-ridden Suharto years had still to be paid off and the IMF has ensured that the people of Indonesia will be paying for the Western-backed corruption of Suharto and his family for years to come. During the 1980s the IMF told Suharto that food and fuel subsidies had to be eliminated to help service the debts to Western banking interests. These subsidies allowed Indonesians to pay for the essentials of life for less money than the government would get selling the goods for export. Thanks to the IMF, bills for food and fuel rose by 90 per cent.[10] Very little of Indonesia's natural wealth in raw materials had helped the majority of the country's population, who remained mired in poverty.

13

Marcos Takes the Philippines

Ferdinand Marcos, President of the Philippines between 1965 and 1986, was another American-backed dictator who organized brutality and corruption and stole many millions of dollars from his country. Transparency International estimated that Marcos looted between $5 billion and $10 billion during his time in power.

In the case of the Philippines there was no need for American corporate interests to educate an elite on the Indonesian model. From the US–Philippine war of 1898 and America's subsequent decades of colonial power, a succession of US administrations had made sure to pamper the 60 or so ruling families, helping to perpetuate the feudal oligarchy that persists to the present. Even the date chosen for the country's independence showed an elite attachment to their former colonizers: 4 July 1946.

Marcos's rise up the new nation's political hierarchy was swift and at least partly based on deception. His claim to have led a guerrilla unit against the Japanese wartime occupiers was later found to be false. In 1965 he was elected president, having promised improved living standards for average Filipinos and land reform. A large public-works programme helped to fulfil the first promise but elite opposition put paid to the latter. In 1969 he was re-elected president but he was now faced with a growing communist movement capitalizing on the country's wide gap between rich and poor. In 1972 he used a series of terrorist bombings, some of which were caused by his henchmen, to declare martial law, outlawing demonstrations, strikes and boycotts. He then established a dictatorship.[1] From then on, Marcos and his associates took control of the economy in close collaboration with the IMF, which sought to 'liberalize' the country's financial system, and the World Bank, which began to implement a new strategic plan for the country's economic development.

By this time American and Japanese corporations were seeking to cut labour costs and Filipino labour was cheap thanks partly to Marcos's anti-trade-union attitude. Some of these corporations allegedly sweetened Marcos with payoffs, funnelled via Switzerland if the corporations were American, and Hong Kong if they were Japanese.

Marcos used his political control to establish crony control of large parts of the economy. Foreign bank loans, guaranteed by the state-owned development banks, were made available to selected entrepreneurs who would run businesses that tended to benefit from presidential decrees raising or lowering tariffs. It is thought that many of the loans were for far more than the project required, with Marcos and his favoured borrowers pocketing the difference.

The most famous of these favoured entrepreneurs was the president's wife, Imelda Marcos, who ran 30 government-owned corporations. She was also Minister for Human Settlements, through which American economic aid was channelled. The settlements helped during Imelda's term of office tended to be for the rich, such as convention centres and lavish hotels, rather than settlements for poor people. They were funded by borrowing abroad under government guarantee or by diverting the rent paid by the US government for its military bases. 'This aspect of the development strategy', noted one economist wryly, 'was so successful that by 1985 Manila was estimated to provide employment for 20,000 underage prostitutes.'[2] As well as servicing the needs of American military personnel, these prostitutes were routinely supplied to the mainly young American bankers whose promotion prospects during these years depended on lending money to the suspect projects of Third World business interests.[3]

During the same period, tens of thousands of political prisoners were routinely rounded up by the military. Hundreds were 'disappeared'; thousands were tortured. In 1981, Ronald Reagan's Vice-President George Bush Sr reaffirmed American commitment to Marcos at a function by toasting him for his 'adherence to democratic principles and to the democratic processes'.[4]

Perhaps Marcos's most flagrant and potentially dangerous corrupt activity concerned the spending of over $2.2 billion on the building of a nuclear power plant in Bataan. He personally intervened in the contest between Westinghouse and General Electric to give the building contract for the plant to the former. Critics later claimed that the astronomical cost of the project added around 8 per cent to its total foreign debt, and out of that Marcos collected millions of dollars for his efforts. In the end, fortunately, the plant wasn't completed. It had been situated close to a range of volcanoes![5]

The economist R.T. Naylor has summarized Marcos's corrupt methods and subsequent money moving:

> The government-owned development banks borrowed money abroad and 'lent' it to favored companies; their owners would divert some of that

money through Hong Kong bank accounts held in the same or Panamanian ghost companies or through the peekaboo centers of the Caribbean. The take, along with whatever could be skimmed from more than 300 government-owned and largely unaudited companies, would come to rest in Swiss bank-accounts – sometimes through the intermediation of Liechtenstein 'foundations' – or in ownership of California banks, Texas and New York real estate, and shares of corporations listed on the Zurich or Luxembourg stock exchanges ... And Imelda Marcos built a handsome New York real estate empire through a Netherlands Antilles shell company.[6]

The people of the Philippines were left with poverty and billions of dollars' worth of debt.

14

Mobutu and Debt in Africa

While Suharto and Marcos were doing incalculable damage to Asian countries, their closest equivalent in Africa was Mobutu Sese Seko.

Mobutu took control of the Congo's state machinery in 1965, changed the country's name to Zaire in the early 1970s and looted it until 1997. The Congo's strategic economic importance suddenly increased in the early 1960s when the new age of jet travel began to shrink the world. The new planes required cobalt and the Congo held nearly 70 per cent of the world's known cobalt ore. In fact the newly independent country should have been on the brink of unprecedented African prosperity as it also held plentiful reserves of copper, chromium, zinc, gold, tin, platinum, cadmium, uranium and even diamonds. Much of this mineral wealth was crucial to the aeronautical and rocket-manufacturing industries of Western powers and the United States was prepared to do anything it could, including assassination, to keep the Congo in the Western camp and away from Soviet influence.[1] The Senate Investigating Committee chaired by Frank Church in 1976 found strong evidence to indicate that President Dwight Eisenhower actually approved the attempted assassination of Patrice Lumumba, the Congo's first leader after it gained independence from Belgium in 1960. Lumumba's main offence was to attempt to pursue a non-aligned foreign policy. The American-sponsored assassination attempt failed but Lumumba was killed the following year by unknown assassins.[2]

After some years of political uncertainty and a civil war between 1963 and 1965, Mobutu assumed power in the Congo and proved to be much more accommodating to Western interests. To begin with this was because of straightforward bribery. Former US National Security Council official Roger Morris estimated that Mobutu received around $150 million in 'straight old fashioned boodle' from the United States, 'unaccountable money spent by the CIA'.[3]

From the late 1960s, however, Mobutu began to spend money to make money. He bribed or gave lucrative contracts to a former Belgian prime minister, members of the family of French President Valéry Giscard d'Estaing and to politically influential Americans. He also came to an arrangement with the Belgian-owned Société Générale de Belgique to manage the state-owned firm that controlled the nation's export economy. A proportion of the royalties were kicked back directly to Mobutu. By the time Mobutu had ended his kleptocratic rule he had amassed around $5 billion, while his country remained overwhelmingly poor. He was alleged to have diverted diamonds from the state mining monopoly for private sale in London, smuggled gold to Europe, sold strategic minerals through South Africa, engaged in profitable manipulation of the exchange rate and, of course, to have taken bribes from corporations. He then sent the proceeds of this grandiose theft to his foreign, mainly Swiss, bank accounts and acquired lavish European and African real estate holdings, including eight houses and two chateaux, a Swiss estate, a large apartment in Paris, three hotels in Dakar, and villas throughout Africa.[4]

During the whole of this period Mobutu was killing and torturing his people on a grand scale as reported by a former political aide, Mungal-Diaka, in April 1982. Mungal-Diaka noted the unexplained killing of thousands of people including:

The hanging of four cabinet ministers, without the right of self-defence, after an alleged plot against Mobutu in 1966.

The killing of several thousand Katangese soldiers by burning or burying alive or jettisoning from helicopters in 1967.

The killing of several hundred peacefully demonstrating students at the national university in Kinshasa in 1969.

The massacre of more than 500 innocent people in several villages in May 1970, in reprisal for the killing of a soldier who had tried to steal a chicken.

The massacre of 2,000 to 2,500 religious sect members in Kitawala in January 1978.

The massacre of 150 people in Eastern Kasai on 6 October 1981, after some villagers challenged some army officers who were dealing illegally in ivory.[5]

The slaughter continued, as did the West's support for Mobutu's regime. Writing in 2003, the economist John Kay summarized the history of Western involvement in the Congo as entirely disgraceful:

Western countries destabilized its politics, supported terrorist governments and armed oppositions, and gave criminals the trappings of statesmen . . . The Congo is an anarchy, mineral production has collapsed and large amounts of money have been handed to thieves by international agencies and commercial banks. It is hardly credible that the World Bank continued to lend to the Mobutu regime for over twenty years.[6]

Mobutu remained in control of Zaire for 31 years until 1997, when forced out by an invading army from neighbouring Rwanda. He stayed in power so long mainly by organizing corruption from the top down. Lower down the governmental hierarchy, judges, civil servants, customs agents, even nurses and midwives, regularly took bribes to supplement inadequate salaries. 'Smuggling, barter . . . speculation and middleman activity, theft, usury . . . embezzlement and extortion' were, according to a World Bank study, 'more important than formal employment as an income source for urban families'. But they got little compared to those at the top. Almost all of Zaire's wealth was siphoned off by him or by an elite of politicians and politically connected businessmen, who followed Mobutu's lead and let their capital take flight to foreign banks.[7]

In all the cases we have looked at – Indonesia, the Philippines, and Zaire – the IMF and the World Bank were well aware of severe human rights abuses, corruption at the top, capital flight out of these countries to Western financial institutions, and the poverty and squalor left for many millions of citizens at the bottom. However, instead of addressing these problems, these institutions and Western governments acted like gangster loan sharks. They continued to lend money to the corrupt regimes that ran these countries, thus allowing debt obligations to rise ever higher, and at the same time compounded the situation by demanding excessively high interest rates. Drained of resources, there was no way that the indebted countries could get out of the financial morass they were in and they were forced to accept the structural adjustment diktats of the international financial community, with catastrophic consequences as we shall see.

★

Gideon Burrows, in *The No-Nonsense Guide to the Arms Trade* (2002), has shown how high military spending in the poorest Third World countries reduced outlay on development and increased the occurrence of cross-border and internal conflicts. This created the need for more arms, which were bought using Western loans, thus increasing the debts of these countries. Since the end of the Cold War, the cycle has continued in many parts of Africa and Asia, as nations are weighed down by debts that they can never hope to pay off. As a report by the Campaign Against Arms Trade argued, 'Children not yet born will have to pay the price of debt for wars they did not fight, for ideas they did not hold, for a regional and global system that no longer exists and for decisions made by regional and world leaders no longer in power.' As we saw in the sections on Suharto, Marcos and Mobutu, these dictators made large-scale arms purchases, both to bolster their own power and to enrich themselves and their cronies at the expense of their people.

The situation is bad enough as it stands but, as Chapter 18 will detail, the arms companies of Western states are making it worse by continuing to sell to the same states already locked into this poverty trap. A US congressional report in 2001 made this clear and stated that 'countries of the South' which included war-torn regions such as sub-Saharan Africa accounted for 66 per cent of the value of all international arms deliveries in 2000. 'Money spent on arms, or money spent servicing debts', Gideon Burrows concluded, 'means less money is spent in social and developmental programs within the country.'[8] And the vicious cycle of arms, debt, poverty and war continues.

15

Bankers and International Crime

The Indonesia of Suharto, the Philippines of Marcos and the Zaire of Mobutu can accurately be termed 'kleptocracies' – regimes whose principal purpose was to enrich the rulers – and, as we have seen, kleptocrats feasted on the Third World lending boom of the 1970s and 1980s. For the Bank of Credit and Commerce International (BCCI), kleptocrats were a huge potential source of deposits and thus a business opportunity to be taken.

BCCI was only one of many international banks that collected money from corrupt dictators but, as Peter Truell and Larry Gurwin point out in *False Profits: The Inside Story of BCCI, the World's Most Corrupt Financial Empire* (1992), it stood out because of the number of kleptocrats on its client list. These included not just Marcos but Saddam Hussein of Iraq,[1] Manuel Noriega of Panama, Samuel Doe of Liberia, and a vast number of Persian Gulf oil sheikhs. They also note that BCCI stands out because of the intimate relationships it enjoyed with many of these rulers. Sometimes the bank helped these rulers enrich themselves by paying bribes and participating in frauds.[2] The BCCI was 'a chief accomplice in the looting of the Third World' as well as a provider of financial services to terrorists, drug traffickers, arms traffickers and government intelligence agencies, and a testament to the global opportunities for fraud made possible by the collapse of the Bretton Woods system. Its rise to prominence is therefore worth tracing.

Pakistani banker Agha Hasan Abedi founded BCCI in 1972, claiming that it would be a world bank acting as a bridge between the First and the Third World. It was first incorporated in Luxembourg and then, in 1974, set up another headquarters site in the Cayman Islands. Therefore from the beginning it operated in havens notable for their devotion to bank secrecy laws and lax or non-existent regulatory regimes. From there it expanded rapidly to the point where it had branches in over 70 countries. A US Senate investigatory committee, chaired by 2004 presidential candidate John Kerry, reported that its structure was made up of 'multiplying layers of entities, related to one another through an impenetrable series of holding companies, affiliates, subsidiaries, banks-within-banks, insider dealings and nominee relationships'. This complex 'family of entities' was able 'to evade ordinary legal restrictions on the movement of capital and goods as a matter of daily practice and routine'. The committee concluded that BCCI was thus 'created as a vehicle free from government control and one which would act as an ideal mechanism for facilitating illicit activity by others, including such activity by officials of many of the governments whose laws BCCI was breaking'.[3]

Although the Third World provided much of BCCI's deposit base it was able to expand into the world's major financial capitals, firstly London and Hong Kong. Its penetration of the City of London's financial world was eased by the support of many top-level British politicians who enjoyed BCCI's lavish hospitality, had accounts with its branches and even, allegedly, collected envelopes containing fresh pound notes from the bank's headquarters at 100 Leadenhall Street.[4]

Expansion into the United States was initially difficult but crucial for Abedi's ambition to make BCCI a genuine world bank, given the size and importance of the United States financial and banking markets and the country's status as one of the largest money havens for flight capital. BCCI's strategy for the United States was based first on acquiring two American banks: the National Bank of Georgia and FGB/First American. Then its strategy involved opening BCCI branch offices in regions with significant populations from the Third World engaged in transnational commercial activity, such as Miami, Houston, Los Angeles, San Francisco, New York and Chicago. BCCI's intention was to use these branch offices to feed depositors and banking activity to their two American banks. BCCI eventually acquired four banks, operating in seven states and the District of Columbia. Its techniques had already been perfected elsewhere in the world and included buying banks through nominees, and arranging to have its activities shielded by prestigious lawyers, accountants and public-relations firms. It was also crucial for BCCI's ambitions in the United States to have the support of those close to the centres of power in first Carter's and then Reagan's administration, notably former Defence Secretary Clark Clifford. 'Wittingly or not,' as the Kerry Report put it, 'these individuals provided essential assistance to BCCI through lending their names and their reputations to BCCI at critical moments.' BCCI's deceptions enabled it to infiltrate the United States but just as important was its use of political influence and the 'revolving door' in Washington between public and private service whereby serving the government at top level was inevitably followed by serving private interests.[5]

From the beginning of the 1980s, BCCI's American network came to serve drug dealers, arms merchants and their money launderers as well as those involved in capital flight from the Third World. 'The problem that we are having in dealing with this bank', as former Senate investigator Jack Blum put it, 'is that it had 3,000 criminal customers and every one of those 3,000 criminal customers is a page one story.' Blum pointed out that the BCCI was not a bank which made an adequate return on investment through lending out depositors' funds like other banks, but a 'Ponzi scheme', which used new depositors' funds to pay current expenses and to repay early depositors, creating a pyramid of mounting obligations that sooner or later would collapse. 'BCCI people', he explained, 'would go out and bribe central bank officials and high government officials to get them to deposit their country's foreign exchange at BCCI, and in exchange for whatever amount of money, suddenly the foreign exchange reserves of a country would be put there and put to use.'[6]

One of Blum's 3,000 would undoubtedly have been Munther Bilbeisi, described as 'a portly and flamboyant Jordanian merchant'. Bilbeisi was one of BCCI's best customers. He smuggled coffee between 1982 and 1986 and used BCCI to avoid export taxes, fees and taxes in South America and to avoid US coffee-import quotas and sanitation inspections. An internal report from Lloyd's of London, the insurance institution, revealed that BCCI provided a 'flexible system of payments to foreign associates in Central America'. Bilbeisi and his associates needed unquestioning acceptance of their import and shipping documents to ensure safe payment to associates in Central America because these documents were defective. BCCI officials obliged.[7]

Bilbeisi went beyond coffee smuggling and insurance fraud, also trafficking in weapons to many of the world's trouble spots in Africa, Asia and South and Central America. His illegal deals involved machine guns, tanks, helicopter gunships, fighter planes, and even, apparently, 2,000 lb of enriched uranium that might be used in the production of nuclear weapons. 'Without BCCI Bilbeisi would have had a really difficult time organizing and financing his deals,' said one investigator. 'With BCCI, they were a snap.'[8]

Arms dealers and drug traffickers are overwhelmingly non-ideological; they simply want the money. BCCI's support of ideological criminals, that is, terrorists, developed out of several factors, according to the Kerry Report.

First, as a principal financial institution for a number of Gulf sheikhdoms, with branches all over the world, it was a logical choice for terrorist organizations, who received payment at BCCI-London and other branches directly from Gulf-state patrons, and then transferred those funds whenever they wished without apparent scrutiny. Secondly, BCCI's flexibility regarding the falsification of documentation was helpful for such activities.

Finally, to the extent that pragmatic considerations were not sufficient of themselves to recommend BCCI, the bank's pan third-world and pro-Islam ideology would have recommended it to Arab terrorists groups.[9]

The Palestinian Abu Nidal was the terrorist most associated with BCCI. His organization, according to the US State Department, carried out terrorist attacks in 20 countries, killing or injuring almost 900 people, including American, British, French, Israelis and moderate Palestinians.[10] Nidal's commercial network consisted of several businesses with the long-term goal of establishing legitimate trading enterprises in various countries. The association with BCCI helped Nidal's group in this as well as in procuring arms.[11] BCCI also aided Nidal in what amounted to a protection racket on a scale far beyond that practised by any gangster. In 1984, Sheikh Zayed bin Sultan al-Nahyan was just one of many Arab officials who agreed to pay up. He paid $17 million to Abu Nidal, part of which was through BCCI bank accounts in London.[12]

Although in this case BCCI was helping the terrorist enemies of the United States, it was not above, however, helping terrorists who were friends of the United States. BCCI played an important part in the Iran–Contra scandal of the mid-1980s, in the course of which it was revealed that the bank was complicit in the covert American effort to support the Nicaraguan Contras who were using terrorist methods in their effort to defeat the left-wing Sandinista government. After the Boland Amendment that banned aid to the Contras was passed in 1982, the Reagan administration sought to continue its crusade against communism in Central America by enlisting the support of foreign political leaders and business interests. At this time terrorist groups associated with Iran were also holding American citizens hostage in Lebanon. US officials therefore chose to pursue the complicated machiavellian policy of secretly selling arms to Iran, then involved in a war with Saddam Hussein's Iraq, through Israeli intermediaries. Reagan's men then diverted the profits generated by these transactions to the Contras. Criminals, in and out of governments, were naturally drawn into the intrigues that accompanied this privatization of foreign policy.

BCCI's connection to Iran–Contra is summarized by Nikos Passas, a specialist in the study of financial crime:

Key actors in this affair, such as Col. Oliver North, Saudi businessman Adnan Khashoggi and Iranian arms dealer Manuchar Ghorbanifar, maintained accounts at a number of BCCI branches (including Paris, Monte Carlo and Grand Cayman). These accounts handled millions of dollars from sales of missiles to Iran. As all parties were willing to deliver but were not prepared to take financial risks, Khashoggi was the middle-man who would make the initial payment and then collect from the Iranians. Khashoggi turned to BCCI for financing, while indicating that he was acting with the approval of the governments of the USA, Iran and Israel. BCCI offered revolving credit at very favorable terms. Bank records and other evidence suggest that BCCI facilitated a number of Iran–Contra operations, including an unpaid loan to Khashoggi, the transfer of profits to a Saudi Arabian branch and payment to Contra leader Adolfo Calero.[13]

Calero's organization, the FDN, regularly kidnapped and killed agrarian-reform workers and civilians, and Contra terrorism was admitted by former CIA Director Stansfield Turner in 1985 when he told a con-gressional committee, 'I believe it is irrefutable that a number of the Contras' actions have to be characterized as terrorism, as State-supported terrorism.'[14]

It was not, however, BCCI's connections with arms dealers and crim-inals in government that brought it down but its connections with drug traffickers. The bank had shown its most impressive growth in South America particularly in Colombia and two of its most successful branches were in Medellin, the city then most associated with the cocaine trade. BCCI, according to one American investigator, 'absolutely and specifi-cally sought out narco money' and one of its most favoured clients was José Gonzalo Rodríguez Gacha, a leading trafficker.[15] Given that US law-enforcement agencies had begun to focus on money laundering in their efforts against the drug trade, it was inevitable that BCCI would come under scrutiny.

In 1986 US Customs began an undercover investigation of drug-money laundering by American banks. Agent Robert Mazur posed as a business-man who was prepared to help drug dealers in getting their street earnings out of the United States and safe from investigation. Mazur realized that BCCI kept coming up as the dealers' favourite bank and, eventually, the bank itself became the target of the investigation. By 1988, Mazur had laundered around $14 million through BCCI branches. Towards the end of the year, Mazur staged a party in Tampa, Florida, to celebrate his impending fictitious marriage and invited several of his friends from the BCCI–drug world. Eleven of these were duly arrested while government agents raided BCCI offices throughout the United States to collect evid-ence and prepare for an indictment.[16] The Bank of England, in co-ordination with regulators around the world, finally closed the bank down on 5 July 1991. The following year, New York District Attorney Robert Morgenthau announced two indictments that shocked many. These charged six individuals, including Clark Clifford and Robert Altman, two of the most powerful and respected Washington lawyers, for criminal conduct arising out of the operation of BCCI. Morgenthau put it bluntly,

> This indictment spells out the largest bank fraud in world history. BCCI was operated as a corrupt and criminal organization throughout its entire 19 year history. It systematically falsified its records. It knowingly allowed itself to be used to launder the illegal income of drug sellers and other criminals. And it paid bribes and kickbacks to public officials.[17]

Most serious analysts agree that the BCCI fraud did not happen in a vacuum. It happened above all because of regulatory failure and the negligence or complicity of auditors. European, American and other countries' government agencies and professionals, responsible for preventing and detecting criminal activities such as those practised routinely by BCCI, all failed. The banking agencies, the accountants, the prosecutors all failed to protect the depositors.[18] After the bank's collapse the liquidators reported that up to $9 billion was unaccounted for. Most of the lost money was to developing governments and individuals.[19] Over the following years, most of the money rescued from the collapse has gone to American government agencies. This prompted a spokesman for the BCCI Depositors' Protection Association to comment, 'Having been robbed in the first place largely as the result of the failure of regulators worldwide . . . that money is going to profit the very regulators that failed to protect us.'[20]

Although *Time Magazine* called the bank 'the $20 billion rogue empire',[21] BCCI was no aberration in the otherwise respectable world of international banking. The affair in fact left a lot of unanswered questions. As Christopher Whalen put it in the *Journal of Commerce*, BCCI was 'a small fish in the vast ocean of offshore money' and stressed that it should be assumed that big banks do dirty deals. The questions for Whalen were not whether they did dirty deals but 'how often, where, and under what degree of foreknowledge and acquiescence by responsible politicians and regulators'.[22] Nikos Passas also questioned the common assumption that BCCI was the most criminal bank in history. Was it, he wondered, 'simply the most investigated bank'? Passas preferred to describe BCCI as 'a mirror of global evils reflecting structural sources of social problems, international crime, and regulatory failures'.[23]

16

Evasion, Flight and Fraud in McWorld

The trend towards the globalization of financial markets over recent decades has been accompanied by the rapid growth of three kinds of illicit financial activity. While the US has tried to crack down on one of these – money laundering – it has done little to promote more effective control of tax evasion and capital flight, which are much more pernicious.

Tax evasion, as explained by the economic historian Eric Helleiner, involves funds that were legally earned but that have become illicit because they are placed in such a way as to evade tax authorities. Technological developments, particularly those facilitating the instant movement of funds, and the elimination of capital controls by many countries, have made tax evasion much simpler and apparently almost obligatory amongst the wealthy.[1] The US Internal Revenue Service, for example, estimated in 2002 that between one and two million Americans evaded taxes by secretly depositing money in tax havens like the Cayman Islands and then withdrawing it using American Express, MasterCard and Visa credit cards. These offshore accounts were more likely to be used by those amongst the top 1 per cent of taxpayers such as entertainers, business owners, investors and others who control what is reported to the IRS and use offshore accounts to hide fees, profits, dividends, interests and capital gains. Ordinary workers whose wages are reported to the IRS by their employers would have little to gain from similar offshore accounts. The IRS could do little to deter such activity given that Congress, in its desire to reduce the burdens of government, had sharply reduced its budget for tax enforcement.[2] The US federal government often in fact obstructed real efforts against tax evaders. Robert M. Morgenthau, Manhattan District Attorney, for example, complained that his office's efforts to pursue tax cheats had often been stymied not just by foreign governments but by the federal government, especially the Justice and State departments and the intelligence agencies.[3]

Of course, as we have seen, not all of the money that finds its way into offshore tax havens has been legally earned. As William Greider puts it in *One World*: 'Big money hides itself in the global economy. Respectable capital mingles alongside dirty money from illegal enterprise (drugs, gambling, illicit arms sales) because the offshore banking centers allow both to hide from the same things: national taxation and the surveillance of government regulators.'[4] Despite the almost universal acceptance that offshore havens were full of dirty money, in April 2001, US Treasury Secretary Paul O'Neill restated American opposition to European-led efforts to reform the offshore-banking system. This led journalist Lucy Komisar to comment that instead, the allegedly '"tough on crime" Republicans would stand shoulder to shoulder with the shady characters in Nauru, Aruba, Liechtenstein and elsewhere who offer state-of-the-art financial services for crooks'.[5]

While its wealthier citizens have been successfully hiding much of their income in offshore havens, the United States has been making it easier for wealthy foreigners to hide their money in US banks. From the 1970s the US has encouraged foreign tax-dodgers by not having a withholding tax on income from non-resident savings deposits in US banks. Latin American investors, in particular, took advantage of this loophole and evaded taxes on billions of dollars because their home governments were kept in the dark about this large source of mobile capital. Foreign tax-dodgers also took full advantage of a 1984 US government decision to abolish its 30 per cent withholding tax on interest payments to foreign holders of domestic bonds and by beginning to issue government bonds in bearer (i.e. anonymous) form to non-residents.[6] Commenting on this action, Professor Rudiger Dornbusch of the Massachusetts Institute of Technology made the criminal consequences of this move clear, 'The administration, in an effort to fund our own deficits at low cost, has promoted tax fraud on an unprecedented scale. The only purpose one can imagine for the elimination of the withholding tax on nonresident asset holdings in the United States is to make it possible for foreigners to use the U.S. financial system as a tax haven.'[7]

Of course not all tax dodging is illegal. When it is legal it is often achieved by multinational corporations through the technique discussed in Chapter 8 known as 'transfer pricing'. These corporations avoid taxes by deliberately overpricing imports and underpricing goods and services for export, allocating profits to various parts of the group in different countries. Prem Sikka, Professor of Accounting at the University of Essex, quotes the following overpriced imports by American corporations in the multinational profit shuffle: plastic buckets from the Czech Republic at $972.98 each, fenceposts from Canada at $1,853.50 each, a kilo of toilet paper from China for $4,121.80, a litre of apple juice from Israel for $2,052, a ballpoint pen from Trinidad for $8,500 and a pair of tweezers from Japan at $4,896. Underpriced imports include prefabricated buildings to Trinidad and Tobago at $1.20 each and missile and rocket launchers to Israel for $52.03!

The corporations use arcane language to justify these prices and are served by big accountancy firms who audit their accounts and then declare them to be 'true and fair'. Given that the world's largest 100 corporations control 20 per cent of global foreign assets and around 60 per cent of world trade is internal to multinational corporations, the opportunities for this kind of tax avoidance are plentiful. Sikka cites studies that have estimated that the US Treasury alone has lost around $175 billion of tax revenues during the three years between 2000 and 2003.[8]

Returning to more straightforwardly illicit financial activity, the second kind on the rise since the 1970s, according to Professor Helleiner, is 'capital flight'. This he describes as the cross-border movement of financial capital which evades national capital controls. Although most rich countries have eliminated capital controls and thus reduced the volume of capital flight because cross-border financial flows that were once illegal are now legal, many poor, developing countries retain capital controls as a way of building up their economies. The poor countries have been the losers as opportunities for the evasion of these controls have proliferated as the global financial market place has opened up.[9] While the adherents of financial liberalization claimed that opening up financial markets would result in capital flowing from where it is plentiful to where it is scarce and thus help the development of poor countries, in reality capital flight has ensured that the reverse has happened. In 2002 the US current-account deficit was around a staggering $392 billion. *Financial Times* journalist Martin Wolf has estimated that one of the most likely sources of much of the unrecorded funding for this deficit is capital flight from poor countries.[10] In such ways it seems that the poor are being robbed to sustain the living standards of the rich.

The huge US deficit thus helps to explain why combating tax evasion and capital flight are much lower down the list of US crime-control priorities than money laundering. The 1984 decisions to issue bearer bonds and eliminate the withholding tax made international tax evasion easier and attracted vast amounts of much desired foreign capital. The same concerns, according to Helleiner, contributed to an almost complete lack of US interest in international regulatory or information-sharing initiatives to combat capital flight.[11] Lobbyists for American financial institutions have of course kept up the pressure against any regulatory efforts to curb the very profitable enterprise in handling hot money.

The American state has therefore nurtured a boom in private banking that continued even after the debt crises of the late 1980s onwards cut down on opportunities to lend to Third World governments. The closing of one source of opportunity led to the opening of another as Western banks began to pursue wealthy individuals in the Third World to encourage them to place their wealth in private bank accounts, and the biggest beneficiaries have been US banks. Raymond Baker, a financial specialist at the Brookings Institute, noted that the US's lax or inadequate oversight has led to the US becoming 'the largest repository of ill-gotten gains in the world'. A 1999 US Senate investigation revealed that 350 of Citibank's clients were senior government officials or their relatives including these natural successors to Suharto, Marcos and Mobutu:

> President Omar Bongo of Gabon, who transferred $100 million through personal accounts in Citibank's New York branches. Bongo had two private accounts in the name of shell corporations as well as a special account to receive payments from oil companies ... Citibank made more than $1 million a year net from Bongo's accounts.

> Asif Ali Zardari, the husband of former Pakistan prime minister, Benazir Bhutto, who transferred some $40 million through Citibank accounts, of which $10 million is believed to be from kickbacks on a gold importing contract.

> The three sons of Nigeria's General Sani Abacha, who held some $110 million in Citibank accounts, including some in the name of shell corporations set up by Citibank. The bank lent two sons $39 million to deposit in another bank account in Switzerland after the new Nigerian government began investigations into corruption in 1998.

> Raul Salinas, the brother of former Mexican President Carlos Salinas, who transferred $80 to $100 million in alleged drug money out of Mexico between 1992 and 1994 through Citibank accounts.[12]

All this is clearly a reversal of Robin Hood's alleged policy of robbing the rich to feed the poor.

★

Not only banks and corrupt politicians have benefited from the criminal opportunities made possible by globalization, as Robert Tillman, in his *Global Pirates: Fraud in the Offshore Insurance Industry* (2002), makes clear.

Tillman has tracked the careers of Alan Teale and other offshore-insurance fraudsters. These have proliferated in today's deregulated financial environment where crimes are increasingly being committed 'in a legal no-man's-land where geography has lost its relevance'. Teale was a British national, described as 'the archetypal pin-striped grey man', whose career was unblemished until he found a host of opportunities in America's changing insurance market of the 1980s. By 1984 Teale had made enough contacts to create an elaborate network of insurance companies, reinsurance companies and brokerage houses that would be used to cheat individuals and companies out of millions of dollars. An essential part of this network of con men was that many of the companies were formed in foreign countries such as Belgium, the Turks and Caicos Islands, the Republic of Ireland and the Bahamas to avoid the licensing and auditing procedures required of American insurance companies. These companies were run on the 'Ponzi' principle of keeping early customers happy in order to attract more customers to defraud. The dollars paid by policyholders in insurance premiums were channelled through a series of brokers, insurance companies and offshore-reinsurance companies. Each of these siphoned off significant proportions of the original premium dollars and in the end, when claims were submitted, there were no funds left to pay claims and all of the people involved in the insurance chain pointed their fingers at each other claiming they, too, were being victimized. If state insurance regulators shut down any of the companies, Teale and his co-conspirators would simply set up new ones under different names and continue operating.[13] As we saw in Chapter 1, variations of Teale's schemes persist in the American insurance industry.

Teale and the host of con artists who developed variations on the same scams were able to hide their activities from US authorities by locating their companies in foreign countries that asked few questions before handing out charters. Tillman describes how a new generation of offshore criminals has taken this logic one step further by simply creating their own countries. Once created, either on disputed areas of terra firma or platforms in the ocean or completely in cyberspace, these 'countries', Tillman writes, 'can not only issue charters for insurance companies but also license banks, issue bonds, sell passports, and even declare war'.[14] One of these, the Dominion of Melchizedek (DOM), was based on two rocks, 400 miles off the coast of Colombia and set up in 1990. An American official described DOM's illicit activities as follows:

> Promoting a phony sovereign country provides diversified opportunities to engage in fraudulent activities. One's imagination of the various types of fraud possible has become a reality with DOM. A phony government consisting of fraudsters creates phony citizenships, ambassadorships, embassy and legation offices, issues diplomatic passports, registers financial aid, grants business licenses, creates a stock exchange etc. etc. – all phony. However, each facet of this operation is a source which generate substantial illegal income.[15]

In these and other ways, deregulated markets create opportunities for crime only limited by the imagination of criminals.

17

Toxic Capitalism

In many ways multinational corporations are in the business of escape. Apart from seeking to escape from tax, as we have seen, they also seek to escape from environmental-protection laws and laws which protect the health and welfare of workers and consumers. The tendency of manufacturing multinationals over the past three decades, for example, has been to escape from the heavily unionized and protected workforces of North America and Europe to where regulations concerning safety, health and pollution were less severe or less likely to be vigorously enforced.[1]

The inadequacy of health and safety protection in many developing countries has meant, for example, that pesticides found to be too dangerous for the American consumer are widely sold in other countries, particularly in poorer parts of the world. In these countries, a lack of protective equipment, unsafe application and storage practices and inadequate training of pesticide applicators increase the health dangers of already unsafe products. The United States remains a major producer and exporter of pesticides and at least 21 million lb of pesticides that are forbidden in the US were exported in 1995 and 1996 alone. Banned products that were exported in these years included monocrotophos (504 tons), which is highly toxic to humans. Ingesting just 120 milligrams of monocrotophos can be fatal. The largest amounts of this compound were shipped under the trade name Azodrin to Mexico. Use of such substances poisons the soil and therefore the food chain, as well as having more direct victims. However, although the dangers of dust-cropping planes spraying pesticides indiscriminately on fields, field hands, and homes have been known for decades, efforts to stop the export trade in such poison have been slow and inadequate.[2]

In 2004 a large-scale study found evidence that children living in regions of intensive pesticide use in India may be at risk for impaired mental development, reinforcing similar evidence found in Mexico. Greenpeace, India, tested a total of 899 children in Indian states where pesticides, including monocrotophos, were used intensively for growing cotton and compared the results to children in areas where pesticide use was small. Taking income and social-status factors into account, the study found that in more than two thirds of the tests, children living in the areas affected by pesticides performed significantly worse. Those involved in the study noted that it captured the 'more insidious effects of pesticides' that took away 'the very basic right to healthy development'.[3]

Poor countries also hold out the prospect of looser enforcement of environmental regulations and therefore greater corporate profits. This fact partly explains the explosive growth of *maquiladoras* or assembly plants in the free-trade zone on the Mexican side of the US–Mexico border since 1980. That year there were 620 *maquiladora* plants employing 119,550 workers. Twelve years later there were 2,200 factories employing more than 500,000 Mexican workers for many giant US companies including General Electric, Ford, General Motors and Westinghouse, located there to take advantage of the low production costs. Studies have shown evidence of massive toxic dumpings in the *maquiladora* zones, polluting rivers, ground water and soils and causing severe health problems amongst workers and deformities amongst babies born to young women working in the zone.[4]

The industrial disaster that to date dwarfs all others, with the possible exception of Chernobyl, was caused by a leak at an American transnational plant making pesticides in the Indian city of Bhopal. This plant, operated by Union Carbide of India Limited, a subsidiary of Union Carbide Corporation, used highly toxic chemicals including methyl isocyanate (MIC) in its production processes. On the night of 2 December 1984, as a result of a leak from the plant, a white cloud of toxic fumes killed, maimed or injured around half the city's population. As many as 8,000 people may have died as an immediate result of the tragedy, and up to 30,000 have died prematurely in the longer term. No agreed figure exists as to the number of deaths caused by the poison leak partly because of the initial reaction of the authorities. 'Truck drivers have come forward to talk about how they saw hundreds of bodies dumped in the forests,' according to Satinath Sarangi, the director of a clinic that treats Bhopal victims.[5]

Dominique Lapierre and Javier Moro's investigative account *Five Past Midnight in Bhopal* (2003) captures the horror and human impact of the slaughter more powerfully than bare statistics: 'The two geysers of gas had merged to form an enormous cloud about a hundred yards wide. Twice as heavy as air, the MIC made up the base of the gaseous ball that was formed by the chemical reaction in tank 610 . . . Above it, in several successive layers, were other gases, among them . . . hydrocyanide acid and monoethylamine with its suffocating smell of ammonia.' The account then focused on the impact of these poisonous gases on the guests at the wedding of a young couple:

> Bablubhai bent over to grab his child, A gust of vapour caught him there. It paralysed the dairyman's breathing instantaneously and he was struck down in a faint, over the body of his lifeless baby.
>
> Similar respiratory paralysis overtook several of the other guests in mid-flight. Another small greenish cloud laden with hydrocyanide acid drifted into old Prema Bai's hut. It killed the midwife outright, as she lay on her *charpoy*. She and many of the other guests had sought refuge in their homes . . . Of all the gases making up the toxic mass, hydrocyanide acid was one of the deadliest. It blocked the action of the enzymes carrying oxygen from the blood to the brain, causing immediate brain death.[6]

Study of the causes of the tragedy has revealed that Union Carbide safety procedures were negligent and the company was responsible for the slaughter. Warnings made prior to the leakage were not heeded. In 1982, for example, reports pointed out safety deficiencies at the plant in instrumentation and safety valves, lax maintenance procedures, and a high turnover of both operational and managerial staffs. Although the plant stored a large quantity of MIC in tanks, which should have been refrigerated, the refrigeration unit had been turned off in order to save $50 per week.[7]

Frank Pearce and Steve Tombs, in *Toxic Capitalism* (1999), have also pointed out problems in the plant design itself:

> Plant instrumentation was inadequate to monitor normal plant processes . . . The refrigeration plant at Bhopal, even when working, was not powerful enough to cool all of the MIC stored there, and the vent gas scrubber and flare tower were only designed to deal with single phase . . . emissions.

They conclude that far fewer people would have died if:

> the plant had not been sited near shanty towns; there had been adequate risk assessment, modeling and monitoring of discharges and emergency planning and management; the plant personnel, local medical services and the state and national government had known more about the nature and effects of the deadly gaseous emissions.[8]

Five years after the disaster, Union Carbide and the Indian government, reached a settlement of $470 million to compensate the 20,000-plus people seriously injured by the toxic fumes and the families of those who died. Once divided up, individual payments were paltry and not even enough to cover medical expenses.[9] The settlement would have probably been far greater had the case been tried in the United States. The legal representatives of the Bhopal victims and the Indian government had argued that the case should be tried in the US, partly because the relevant documents and personnel were to be found there and partly because discovery procedures were inadequate in India. Their arguments were ignored and the case was settled in India.[10]

The Indian government is still at the time of writing continuing to pursue criminal charges against the former Union Carbide chairman Warren Anderson, who has since retired. In 1999 Union Carbide was taken over at a cost of over $9 billion by the Dow Chemical group, which of course makes continued legal action against the perpetrators of one of the greatest industrial disasters more difficult. As Dow's president, Frank Popoff, put it when questioned about Dow's legal responsibility for the charges against Carbide, 'It is not in my power to take responsibility for an event which happened fifteen years ago, with a product we never developed, at a location where we never operated.' Residents of Bhopal still suffer severe health problems as a result of the poison gas leak and the polluted site of the abandoned factory is still poisoning local ground water. Despite this continuing tragedy, there appears to be no corporation responsible.[11]

Another major cost that manufacturing companies have sought to reduce is that of disposing of toxic waste. This greatly increased in rich industrialized countries as anti-pollution laws came into force from the 1970s. At the same time, global liberalization of trade has made it easier to ship toxic waste around the world. Therefore many waste-generating firms decided that exporting their toxic wastes to countries with less strict environmental regulations and lower dumping fees was a cost-effective practice. In the 1980s, for example, the disposal cost per ton of toxic waste was between $100 and $2,000 in Europe or the United States, while the disposal cost in Africa was less than $50 and in some cases as low as $2.50. Multinational firms began finding clandestine ways to take advantage of this discrepancy with the help of 'toxic commodity brokers' who operated discreetly from a number of sites including Gibraltar, the Isle of Man and Liechtenstein. These commodity brokers arranged for ships to load the waste, which was then identified as something harmless like fertilizer and taken to destinations that were often undisclosed. Bribing local officials or paying local tribespeople ensured that finding a dump site rarely proved much of an obstacle. One notorious case of dumping was discovered in Koko, Nigeria, in 1987. Around 8,000 leaking barrels of poisonous chemical waste were dumped on the land of a village chief who had been convinced that the waste was harmless. The toxicity of the waste, however, caused the deaths of a number of local people, including the chief and his wife. Despite the criminality involved in such practices and the damaging long-term health consequences, there is little evidence that the international community has come close to addressing this problem in any meaningful way.[12]

In the last decade millions of tons of electronic 'e-waste' such as broken computer monitors and redundant mobile phones have been added to the poisons being exported, mainly by sea, to poorer countries, mostly going to China, west Africa, Pakistan and India. Workers taking apart the old machines in these countries are handling toxic chemicals that can pose serious health problems. In Guiyu, a town 200 miles north-east of Hong Kong, for example, there were found to be around 100,000 migrant labourers breaking up and reprocessing obsolete computers from around the world. Apart from the damage to the health of these workers, the well water in Guiyu became so polluted as to be undrinkable. According to one environmental group, 'They call this recycling, but it's really dumping by another name. Yet to our horror, we discovered that rather than banning it, governments are actually encouraging this ugly trade in order to avoid finding real solutions to the massive tide of obsolete computer waste generated.'[13]

The unofficial attitude of the global financial community to dumping in poor countries was perhaps expressed best by Laurence Summers in 1991, while chief economist at the World Bank. In an internal memo he wrote the following to a colleague:

> Just between you and me, shouldn't the World Bank be encouraging more migration of the dirty industries to the LDCs (Less Developed Countries) . . . I think the economic logic behind dumping a load of toxic waste in the lowest wage country is impeccable and we should face up to that . . . I've always thought that under-populated countries in Africa are vastly under-polluted.[14]

The trade in contraband toxic waste at sea is so large for the same reasons that contraband trade at sea in general is so large. The laws, treaties, conventions and organizations that are meant to regulate the sea are hopelessly inadequate and leave countless loopholes for criminals to exploit. Of an estimated 143,000 ships around the globe, most sail under 'flags of convenience' registered in such obscure places as Tuvalu in the Pacific. Many are dangerously and poorly maintained, undermanned and with poorly paid crews. The owners of these vessels are hidden behind multiple fronts and shell companies, and therefore difficult to trace and thus unaccountable for any crimes or disasters that might happen. There now exists an International Law of the Sea but its effectiveness is

severely restricted by the failure of the US, the world's largest trading
nation, to ratify it. Thus the potential for successful, illegal, trading
practices remains large and the situation will probably remain poorly
addressed until a disaster on the scale of 11 September 2001 provokes a
concerted governmental response.[15]

★

There is also evidence that the interests of some corporations have been
served by violence and intimidation. Enron stands out amongst American
corporations guilty of such practices. The harassment, arbitrary arrest and
ill-treatment of Indians protesting against the construction of a power
plant by the Dabhol Power Company (DPC) in the Ranagiri district of
Maharashtra has been well documented. The DPC was a joint venture of
three US-based multinational corporations, including General Electric and
Bechtel Corporation but led by Enron with an 80 per cent share. Opposition to the project was based partly on allegations of corruption surrounding the setting up of the project: politicians were accused of being bought
off with bribes running into millions of dollars. There were also concerns
about the procedures used for the granting of official clearance for the
project, including the lack of consultation of affected people and the
inadequate environmental-impact assessment. Essentially the project was
ill conceived and vastly expensive.

After affected villagers and environmental activists took part in protests against the project, DPC employed private security guards and
reportedly requested the state government to provide police protection.
According to the Amnesty International Report, following this request,
the DPC allegedly entered into a contractual security arrangement with
the Government of Maharashtra, which involved the services of 100
State Reserve Police (SRP). This SRP 'battalion' and local police were
then involved in a series of incidents involving harassment, violence,
and arbitrary arrest and detention. One of these incidents involved
Sugandha Vasudev Bhalekar, the wife of one of the leaders of the
protests. Detailing the circumstances of her arrest on 3 June 1997, she
testified as follows:

[a]t around 5 in the morning when I was in the bathroom, several male
police with batons in their hands forcibly entered the house and started
beating members of (my) family who were asleep . . . Being terrified, I told
them from inside the bathroom that I was taking a bath and that I would
come out after wearing my clothes. I asked them to call for women police
in the meantime and to ask them to wait near the door. But without paying
any attention to my requests, the policemen forcibly opened the door and
dragged me out of the house into the police van parked on the road. [While

dragging me] the police kept beating me with batons. The humiliation meted out to the other members of the family was similar to the way I was humiliated . . . my one and half year old daughter held on to me but the police kicked her away.

Another incident involved Adiath Kaljunkar, a leader of another protest group. On the evening of 27 February 1997, four *goondas* (ruffians) came to his house and threatened to murder him if he continued to oppose the Enron project, as they had taken on-site contracts and would suffer losses. The local police refused to record Kaljunkar's complaint.[16]

Opponents of the Dabhol project eventually prevailed, however, as it became clear that the power plant had been a complete failure. DPC began supplying electricity to Maharashtra in 1999 at a price seven times higher than other electricity costs in India and the state decided not to pay. Two years later the plant was forced to close down, adding the cost of thousands of jobs to the millions of dollars that India had already put into the wasteful project.[17]

It is worth emphasizing that India had traditionally used its own technology and capital to build its infrastructure and its nationalized electricity sector had been seen as one of the country's success stories. However, partly as a result of pressure from the World Bank and the IMF, India decided in the 1990s to undertake structural adjustments to make its economy more attractive to foreign investors. As a result the government made its first step towards 'liberalization' by opening up the country's electricity industry to foreign investment in 1992. Ironically, the Dabhol project was once seen as a symbol of the country's commitment to globalization and economic reforms and given as evidence by the international financial community that 'India was moving in the right direction'.[18]

The writer Arundhati Roy took part in the struggle against Enron and later commented on the negative impacts of privatization on the mass of the population in poor countries. 'Essentially', she concluded,

it is the transfer of productive public assets from the state to private companies. Productive assets include natural resources. Earth, forest, water, air. These are assets that the state holds in trust for the people it represents. In a country like India, seventy percent of the population live in rural areas. That's seven hundred million people. Their lives depend directly on access to natural resources. To snatch these away and sell them as stock to private companies is a process of barbaric dispossession on a scale that has no parallel in history.[19]

Despite the well-publicized criminal activity of those associated with Enron in pushing through the Dabhol project, the administration of

George W. Bush and Vice-President Dick Cheney, in particular, pushed hard to collect millions of dollars' worth of debts incurred in the Enron misadventure.[20]

Enron's complicity in the Maharashtra human rights violations is not an exception to the rule of multinational corporate responsibility. In recent years dozens of corporations have been implicated in abuses that have often been more severe than those already detailed. American corporations are not of course the only offenders. Many commercial institutions elsewhere in the West have committed serious crimes in poorer countries. Britain, whose organized criminality and empire building have long and closely related histories, has been home to many, particularly ruthless offenders.

The most significant recent development, however, involves Unocal, an oil and gas firm headquartered in El Segundo, California. Unocal, in association with a French corporation, Total, began to build a pipeline in Burma (Myanmar) in the early 1990s. Villagers in the region where the pipeline was built alleged that they were forced into slave labour by the Myanmar army, and that they suffered torture, assault, rape, loss of homes and property, and other violations in the process. With the help of human rights activist organizations, the villagers sued Unocal on the grounds that they had 'aided and abetted' gross violations of their human rights, claiming that when Unocal asked the army for help in building the pipeline, the corporation knew that the army would be prepared to violate their human rights. In 1997, a US federal-district court in Los Angeles concluded that corporations and their executive officers can be held legally responsible under the Alien Tort Claims Act (ATCA) for violations of human rights norms in foreign countries and that the US courts have the authority to adjudicate such claims. In December 2004, Unocal announced that, in principle, it had agreed to settle this suit.

Although this and other developments might suggest that multinational corporations might be brought to account for human rights violations in which they are complicit, legal experts Celia Wells and Juanita Elias warn that 'Many corporations, like states, have the resources and power both to perpetuate and to escape responsibility for abuse.' They are particularly good 'at being one step ahead of the game'.[21]

18

Smuggling, Violence and Corruption in the International Arms Bazaar

The ending of the Cold War, the debt crisis and the globalization of trade have all had a pernicious influence on the extent and organization of the global arms trade, which in turn has fuelled violent conflict across the globe.

The Cold War, as the historian Eric Hobsbawm has pointed out, flooded the world with its capacity for producing arms. While there were no actual wars between the United States and the Soviet Union, the armaments industries of the two superpowers and their allies were working at full capacity. At the end of the Cold War much of this vast arsenal became available in most parts of the world.[1]

The collapse of the Soviet Union meant that the 'greatest stock of military surplus was suddenly dumped on the market'. Although some of this vast supply of weaponry stayed in Russia and fell into the hands of ethnic insurgent forces, private security firms and the criminal gangs mentioned earlier, much of it poured onto the world market, according to economist R.T. Naylor. Compounding the problem was the Russian government's decision to encourage its arms manufacturers to seek foreign sales. This put Russia in the unique position of having flows of new material from its factories competing directly with stocks sold by its military. The result, Naylor concluded, was 'top-of-the-line material at unbeatable prices . . . An AK-47 that used to cost about US$125 factory fresh in the Soviet Union can now be picked up for US$30–$40 on the Russian flea market. In Uganda its price is about the same as that of a chicken, while in Angola and Mozambique it will exchange for the equivalent of a bag of maize.'[2]

The American arms industry continues to feed the needs of paramilitaries, guerrillas and drug traffickers in South and Central America, as well as armed groups in Africa, Asia and Europe. The curious logic of

America's war on drugs has even meant that the United States now arms both sides in its Mexican neighbour's own war on drugs. Because of loose gun sale and gun ownership laws, as opposed to strict gun control laws in Mexico, the United States became an open arms bazaar for Mexican drug traffickers and other criminals during the 1990s. They equipped themselves with the latest weaponry north of the border and were often able to outgun Mexican drug agents, killing more than 200 Mexican police in 1996 alone. Instead of taking on the powerful anti-gun control lobby in the United States, the Clinton administration decided to step up aid to the Mexican military and provide them with firepower capable of taking on the drug traffickers. Amongst other forms of aid, the administration asked Congress for $9 million in military aid for Mexico for the fiscal year 1998 for the purchase of new weapons from American arms manufacturers.[3] Mexico's violent and profitable drug trade continues, of course.

There is also every reason to be pessimistic on the impact of globalization and free trade on the arms trade. Deregulation and free trade have been a gift for the arms industry. 'It is able', Gideon Burrows writes in *The No-Nonsense Guide to the Arms Trade* (2002), 'to reap the benefits of international agreements to break down trade barriers, drawn up by the World Trade Organization (WTO) and similar bodies, while being subject to few of the restrictions they impose and the standards they demand.' Just as companies manufacturing sports equipment, toys and other goods have done, arms manufacturers now locate 'their production lines to open up new markets, and wherever labor and tax is cheapest, environmental requirements are non-existent, employment regulations are weakest and regulations for the export of armaments most easily obtained'.[4]

Arms companies are no longer state-controlled and supervised companies. The simple concepts of the arms trade and arms companies have disappeared into a labyrinth of licensed production, joint ventures, conglomerates, strategic partnerships and Cooperative Armaments Programs in our new globalized world. Weapons 'systems' may be designed in one country, manufactured piecemeal in several others and sold both to the collaborating states and to others. In our world without borders, arms companies are only nominally subject to the legal, tax and moral obligations of their host countries yet they are still treasured as national assets by the countries from which they sprang, receiving special treatment, political and financial support.[5]

The arms companies compete aggressively to supply the market for killing and much of the trade in their products is illegal. In theory most major arms-producing countries attempt to regulate the sale of weapons but, in practice, smuggling and evasion are easy.[6] Arms are part of a massive global black market economy that consists of a series of arm's-length commercial relationships. A modern, covert, arms deal is likely to take place within a matrix of black market transactions, involving cash or sometimes hostages, specialist middlemen, shell companies situated in offshore havens, ships sailing under flags of convenience, and alliances amongst groups as varied as career smugglers, legal arms manufacturers, political party bagmen, gangsters, insurgent armies and intelligence service agents.

Victor Bout was one of many to profit in the global black market. According to the International Consortium of Investigative Journalists, he was 'the most notorious gunrunner of the post-Cold War period'. Bout was born in Tajikistan, trained in Moscow's Military Institute of Foreign Languages and made his first fortune when his air force regiment was disbanded in Afghanistan during the breakup of the former Soviet Union. Bout took the opportunity to exploit the great expansion of the private market in arms that followed the end of the Cold War. He developed the capacity to deliver not only small arms but also major weapons systems almost anywhere in the world. His associates ranged from former US and Russian military officials and African heads of state to African rebel leaders and well-connected gangsters. His maze of companies employed around 300 people and owned and operated 40 to 60 aircraft but was organized in such a way as to make it almost impossible to trace his activities. He leased aircraft to other individuals and companies so that he was not directly tied to illegal activities.

Bout, according to the consortium of journalists, was

> among the major arms suppliers to combatants in Africa and Afghanistan, often in violation of international embargoes. His planes carried weapons to war zones, and left loaded with diamonds and other valuable resources, such as the mineral coltan, used in the electronics industry. Bout's international shipping business operated through a maze of companies registered around the world, and he was expert at maneuvering through the labyrinth of brokers, transportation companies, financiers and transshipment points. Shuttling through Africa, Russia, Europe, the Persian Gulf and Central Asia, Bout left few, if any trails.[7]

Bout's successful career owes much to the 'flags of convenience' system. A flag of convenience can be defined as a legal identity for a ship or a plane registered easily for a fee in a jurisdiction where it is not ultimately owned, for the purposes of commercial or tax advantages. Bout and countless others have used this system to evade regulation. If, as happens on occasion, ships and planes are de-registered by one suspicious jurisdiction, it makes little difference, since it takes only a matter of hours to take the whole company and register it in another country that will not investigate its activities so closely. Ships and planes do not even have to be physically present in the new jurisdiction to be registered.[8]

Those like Bout and others who exploit the lack of effective control over the global trade in arms supply a market for the means to kill that is always buoyant in the world's most troubled areas. Although some African governments and elites are little more than criminal syndicates, the consortium of journalists concluded, in another study of the arms trade, they need foreign partners to sell the precious resources of their countries, such as diamonds, timber and oil on the world market. 'The people doing the extracting, the bribing, the arms dealing, and the deal-making are South African, Belgian, American, Israeli, French, Ukrainian, Lebanese, Canadian, British, Russian, Malaysian, and Syrian. They are a class of entrepreneur that operates beyond borders.'[9]

19

The Traffic in Exploitable People

The globalization process of recent years has made possible the growing mobility of goods, finances and, because air transportation in particular has become less expensive, businesspeople and vacationers. However, while such increased mobility is granted to goods, finances and relatively privileged people, governments of richer nations have strictly denied it to the less privileged poor wanting to improve their condition. In a world that has become less equal, there is only one logical decision for millions of people today: to leave poor countries and feed the demand for cheap labour in rich countries, particularly in the United States. Most migrants, of course, earn better money than they could in their homelands, even in low-wage, long-hour jobs in farms, abattoirs, restaurants and domestic service, but large numbers are trapped into conditions equivalent to debt or sometimes even sex slavery.

People have been moving between countries to better their condition for centuries but the key development in recent years has been an unprecedented and international investment in suppression of the illicit movement of people across international boundaries. Essentially, this investment in suppression has had the counter-productive effect of changing illegal border crossing from a low-cost to a high-cost undertaking and therefore attracting both professional criminal organizations and more complex networks of both legal and illegal actors.

Until the 1980s, for example, crossing the Mexico–United States border illegally was relatively simple and cheap. If a migrant happened to be caught by the poorly funded Immigration and Naturalization Service (INS), he or she would be returned to Mexico, probably only until they were ready to make another attempt. The US policy response to illegal immigration was, however, significantly toughened up in 1986 when the Immigration Reform and Control Act (IRCA) was passed. This Act was followed in the 1990s by a big boost to the INS budget, making it the fastest-growing federal agency at a time when the budgets of most other federal agencies were being cut or at least frozen. The new technologically enhanced methods of the INS, aided by the supporting role of the US military, were successful in cutting off the more obvious border-crossing points but no more successful in stopping the flow of illegal immigrants. People now relied on the services of professional smugglers whereas before these had been no more than a convenience. The fees smugglers charged increased dramatically.[1]

'The most consequential impact of higher prices', writes Peter Andreas in a study of migrant smuggling, 'has been to enhance the wealth and power of smuggling groups ... Beefed-up policing has removed some smugglers but simply increased the market position of others. Moreover, many of those arrested are the lowest-level and most expendable members of migrant smuggling organizations – the border guides and drivers who are the "foot soldiers" of the business.'[2]

Beefed-up enforcement and greater profits for smugglers has also led to increased corruption both sides of the border. In 1995, for example, US Customs inspector Guy Henry Kmett was arrested for helping a smuggling ring move migrants from Central America through his inspection lane. Kmett had paid cash for such things as a swimming pool, computers and televisions during the previous year. On the other side of the border, the following year, Mexican officials in Tijuana were found to be taking bribes of around $40,000 a month to permit the operation of safe houses where migrants could stay before attempting to cross into the United States.[3]

While large criminal networks undoubtedly participate in people trafficking, the business has never been monopolized by such groups. Ko-lin Chin's study of Chinese people smuggling, for example, found that most people smugglers are not gang or tong members, although some gang or tong members are involved. Small, loosely knit groups were the norm in this business. Moreover, there are three main stages in the people trade – the recruitment of illegal migrants; the shipping to transit points and countries of destination; the establishment and control of immigrants in their country of destination – and different groups are likely to be involved in each of these stages. Ostensibly legitimate agencies, organizations and professionals can also be involved in any of the stages. For the first of the stages, agencies in the home countries may specialize in the recruitment of men and women, register them for fees, then turn the next stage over to professional smuggling groups.[4] The transit stage itself may not necessarily be organized by professional criminals. In April 2004, for example, the Golden State Transportation Company, a bus company that operated from Arizona and other southern states, pleaded guilty to charges involving the smuggling of 42,000 illegal immigrants and laundering the money it took in as a result. As part of its plea, the company was ordered to forfeit its bus terminal in Phoenix, valued at about $2 million.[5]

An example of a professional being involved in the final stage, establishing illegal immigrants in their country of destination, is provided by Robert Porges. Porges was the head of one of the US's largest immigration-asylum law firms, which was based in New York. In 2002 he pleaded guilty to faking asylum applications to help more than 1,000 immigrants stay in the United States. 'I was aware that many of the stories submitted by the aliens were either false, inaccurate or exaggerations,' he admitted. 'I deliberately did not investigate.' As part of the plea, Porges, whose wife was also convicted, agreed to forfeit $6 million, again as in the case involving Golden State, indicating the scale of profits to be made trafficking in people. Their lawyer did make the point, however, that they were being singled out for a practice that was so common that advertisements in Chinese newspapers coaxed prospective immigrants to contact law firms to perfect their asylum applications.[6]

It is therefore more usual for networks to consist of otherwise legitimate professionals and businesspeople, despite the usual 'snakehead' imagery used in the media. Chinese smuggling rings do use more traditional gangsters to enforce debt repayment in the receiving country if necessary, but these may be just hired hands and easily replaceable if caught by the authorities.[7]

As well as rising costs, dangers have substantially increased for would-be immigrants since anti-smuggling efforts have been stepped up. Organized Chinese people smuggling, for example, first attracted attention in the modern era in 1993 when the freighter Golden Venture ran aground near New York with 260 undocumented Chinese aboard; 10 passengers drowned while attempting to swim ashore.[8] The deadliest recorded smuggling event to date in the United States, however, came in 2003, when 19 Mexicans, Dominicans and Hondurans died in an abandoned truck from suffocation and heat stroke near Victoria, Texas.[9] An even greater loss had occurred three years earlier in Dover, England in 2000, when 58 Chinese immigrants died in a refrigerated truck.[10] The deadliest smuggling event of all to date, however, occurred in the Mediterranean between Malta and Sicily when a boat able to hold about 100 people sunk as 300 tried to board it from a larger ship. Most of the 300 died as a result.[11] Individual deaths of immigrants in transit are, of course, much more common and therefore scarcely noticed by the media, but many have died in the Mexican-American border deserts, for example, after being abandoned by guides or by drowning when crawling through storm drains.[12]

When they arrive in the promised lands of the United States, Western Europe, or Japan the experience shared by most migrants is exploitation – sometimes criminal but always severe. Some of this exploitation is sexual. Numbers are impossible to estimate but in the United States, for example, there are known cases in which young women from Mexico, Russia, Eastern Europe, and other countries have been lured away with promises of jobs or marriage, and were forced into prostitution and robbed of their earnings. One case involved four Mexican teenagers being held captive as prostitutes at a brothel in Plainfield, New Jersey. Two Mexican women were sentenced to 210 months in prison for the offence.[13] Many migrant women are, however, aware of the type of job they will do in the rich world and 'choose' a period of time as prostitutes to improve their own or their families' life prospects.

The availability of so many illegal migrants has helped to revive sweatshop production, a type of manufacturing production that had been virtually eliminated by New Deal reforms of the 1930s. Mainly associated with garment manufacturing, every American city that had significant garment manufacturing had sweatshop labour by the 1980s. A study of Philadelphia's new sweatshops, for example, showed that they were unlicensed, illegal, off-the-books operations paying 'no minimum wages, unemployment insurance or health benefits'. They ignored child-labour laws and overtime-pay regulations and forced mainly Asian females to work up to 17 hours a day, every day of the week. Many were forced to stay on the premises night and day and to sign agreements to have their room-and-board costs deducted from their wages, if indeed they got any wages. The study concluded that the workers were 'little more than indentured servants'.[14]

By the late 1990s there were more than 100,000 garment workers in the Los Angeles area alone, most undocumented. The worst case of exploitation came to light in a nearby city, El Monte. Eighty illegal Thai immigrants and almost as many from South and Central America lived in slave conditions for between three and seven years. They slept on mattresses, 25 to a small room and worked for up to 18 hours a day in a compound that was surrounded by both barbed and razor wire. Eventually, in 1996, the sweatshop's owners pleaded guilty to charges of harbouring illegal aliens and involuntary servitude.[15]

The cases mentioned so far have of course been extreme examples of exploitation. However, as migration specialists David Kyle and John Dale point out, even when free to find employment on their own terms, 'illegal immigrants with large usurious loans make an especially docile and hard-working labor force – a point not overlooked by employers or states in receiving countries.'[16]

Illegal workers are playing an increasingly significant role in the American economy. Apart from garment manufacturing, several other major American industries also encourage the employment of illegal immigrants, including construction companies, nurseries, fruit growers, meat and poultry companies. There are also of course hundreds of thousands of illegal-immigrant domestic nannies and maids making life easy for America's richest 20 per cent. However, the most significant cases involve the giant retailing concern, Wal-Mart. In October 2003, federal agents raided 60 Wal-Mart stores across the nation and arrested more than 250 illegal immigrants, mainly from Russia, Lithuania and Poland, who worked as janitors in Wal-Mart stores. Their conditions of work were harsh, being forced to work seven days a week and not paid overtime. They were not employed directly by Wal-Mart but by con-tractors and subcontractors. These, according to industry experts inter-viewed by the *New York Times*, appeared to play a shell game, continually closing down, filing for bankruptcy and reincorporating under different names. Some regularly cheated workers by closing down without paying workers their last month's pay. At the time of writing a grand jury is still investigating Wal-Mart's possible complicity in these schemes but one government official told the *New York Times* that the government believed that company officials were aware of the widespread use of illegal immigrants at its stores.[17]

It is unlikely that Wal-Mart will suffer much from any action that emerges from the investigation, however. Enforcement of sanctions against employers has been as inadequate in the United States as in other receiving states. From 1994 to 1996, for example, only 3,765 of the 15,039 US employers charged with knowingly employing illegal immi-grants received fines; these totalled $34 million, but only $14 million were collected, hardly amounting to a deterrent.[18]

Vincenzo Ruggiero concluded in an article on global markets and crime that

> the increase in flexible and casual work in most Western countries has created a situation where workers who display low social and economic expectations are highly desirable . . . Among these workers, illegal migrants seen to have a formidable advantage, because as soon as their expectations become higher employers may always report them to the police as illegal . . . Strict immigration policies, in this context, do not limit the flow of people seeking relocation in rich countries, but only contribute to lowering the expectations and demands of those who migrate. Paying a fee to traffickers is part and parcel of this strategy, as migrants are taught that it is a privilege to enter an advanced country and that, once there, they had better not blow such a unique opportunity by demanding too much.[19]

Certainly there is little evidence that American and other efforts to tighten border controls have been successful in stopping the smuggling of people across borders. Neither have these efforts done much to reduce the debt bondage, forced prostitution and relentless exploitation that many of those who are smuggled endure once they arrive in their receiving country.

20

SAPs, Slums and the New Slavery

In 2003 the United Nations Human Settlements Programme (UN-Habitat) released the findings of its hugely significant study, *The Challenge of the Slums*. Around 924 million people now live in slums and the study documents the massive population shifts in recent years from rural to urban areas that accounts for this rapidly increasing number. It demonstrates the rapidly deteriorating condition of the urban poor and offers an authoritative explanation for such a vast and massively destabilising global trend. Armed conflict in Asia, Africa, Latin America and parts of the former communist world has of course displaced millions of people in the period since the end of the Cold War; neo-liberalism, however, has already displaced and continues to displace many millions more.

The report's conclusions are worth quoting at length:

> Much of the economic and political environment in which globalization has accelerated over the last 20 years has been instituted under the guiding hand of a major change in the economic paradigm – that is, neo-liberalism. Globally, these policies have re-established a rather similar international regime to that which existed in the mercantilist period of the 19th century when economic booms and busts followed each other with monotonous regularity, when slums were at their worst in Western cities, and colonialism held global sway. Nationally, neo-liberalism has found its major expression through Structural Adjustment Programmes (SAPs), which have tended to weaken the economic role of cities throughout most of the developing world and placed emphasis on agricultural exports, thus working against the primary demographic direction moving all of the new workers to towns and cities. These policies, as much as anything else, have led to the rapid expansion of the informal sector in cities, in the face of shrinking formal urban employment opportunities.[1]

The study makes the case that the primary direction of both national and international interventions during the last 20 years has actually increased urban poverty and slums and increased exclusion and inequality.

The urban historian Mike Davis has estimated that there may be more than quarter of a million slums on earth. The five great metropolises of

South Asia (Karachi, Mumbai, Delhi, Kolkata and Dhaka) alone contain about 15,000 distinct slum communities with a total population of more than 20 million. The building blocks of this slum planet, he writes, 'are both utterly interchangeable and spontaneously unique', from the *chawls* of Mumbai, the *kampungs* of Jakarta, and the *iskwaters* of Manila to the *favelas* of Brazil and the, appropriately termed, *villas miserias* of Argentina. Most slum settlement, however, has tended to involve large-scale corruption and organized crime, 'national and local political machines', he continues,

> usually acquiesce in informal settlement (and illegal private speculation) as long as they can control the political complexion of the slums and extract a regular flow of bribes or rents. Without formal land titles or home ownership, slum dwellers are forced into quasi-feudal dependencies upon local officials and party bigshots. Disloyalty can mean eviction or even the razing of an entire district.[2]

The urban poor, the UN-Habitat report contends, are trapped in an informal and 'illegal' world:

> in slums that are not reflected on maps, where waste is not collected, where taxes are not paid and where public services are not provided. Slum dwellers mostly exist outside of the law. If they come into contact with government at all they are more likely to be hindered in their attempts to provide the fundamentals of life – shelter and livelihood – rather than helped. They live in a state of permanent insecurity and illegality and business crooks and gangsters move into these ungoverned vacuums.[3]

In Rio de Janeiro, for example, drug traffickers have moved to a position of total dominance over other community institutions in many *favelas* and violence is as much a way of life in reality as the award-winning film *City of God* depicted in fiction. In 2003, for example, Rio's police killed 1,000 people during operations and homicide is now the chief cause of death for the city's young men, with an annual rate of 205 murders per 100,000 people. As one community activist put it, 'tyrannical young men now settle the most basic disputes on a whim and a gunshot.'[4]

The world's worst city for gang violence is not Rio, however, nor Los Angeles, Moscow nor any likely to spring immediately to mind. According to a survey by the Economist Intelligence Unit, Port Moresby, capital of Papua New Guinea, is the worst place to live amongst 130 world capitals as a result of its poverty, crime, poor healthcare and a particularly vicious 'raskol' gang culture. Gangs of young men have been known to rob banks with machine guns, car drivers with machetes, and to take part in gang-rapes. The houses of the wealthy in the city are heavily protected behind walls, wires and guided by armed private police. Visitors are warned not to walk many of the city's streets even by day for fear of violent attack. Police brutality seems to be the only serious governmental response to 'raskol' violence and there seems little prospect of improvement while the island remains mired in poverty.[5]

The market-driven globalization process has led to rapid and uncontrolled economic change across the developing world. This in turn has bred corruption and violence in many countries that had before been relatively stable, with traditions, customs and rules that served to some extent to protect the most vulnerable in the population. These traditions, customs and rules have now broken down in many places to be replaced by many and varied forms of collective brutality and exploitation.[6]

For every one thief or exploiter in the slums, there are dozens of exploited, and most of these are children. The World Health Organization estimates that there are 10 to 30 million street children in the world today. Apart from the large numbers in Latin America and Asia, there are growing numbers of street children in eastern Europe, especially in Moscow. More than one million of these become prostitutes each year, according to the charity Free the Children. They help feed the demand from men in affluent countries for sex tourism – the business of making arrangements to travel to other countries to have sex with children. Children are usually 13 to 17 years old, but can be as young as five.

When parents cannot pay off debts to landlords themselves, children are also forced into bonded labour. In New Delhi, for example, the problem is so severe that an organization exists to work for the liberation of slave children and child labourers. The South Asian Coalition on Child Servitude (SACCS) physically rescues such children, who are taken from their parents, often forced to work 18 hours a day and are sometimes beaten and sexually abused. SACCS chairperson, Kailash Satyarthi, reports that,

> You will also see children working in most of the street restaurants or street hovels. If you visit a middle class Indian home, you will see children working as domestic labor. A young girl will be cleaning house and serving tea. Children work in retail industries, in plastics and metal industries . . . You will find child labor in all automobile workshops . . . You will also see a large number of children begging in the streets of Delhi, but few are begging for themselves. The money does not go into their pockets . . . gangsters force children to do this.[7]

Child labour under conditions akin to slavery does not simply affect local economies. In the carpet industries of India, Pakistan, Nepal and

Morocco, for example, it helps supply a global market, according to reports and studies by charities such as the Anti-Slavery Society. The Society claims that sources for child labour might be local but can also be obtained from areas that are even poorer 'by purchasing or coercing children from Bihar in north-east India to Uttar Pradesh; or from small villages in Nepal to Kathmandu; or from outlying villages to small towns in Pakistan; and even children trafficked from other countries, such as children imported from west Nepal to Uttar Pradesh'. The low cost of many carpets in the West can thus be explained by the widespread use of 'unfree' and illegal labour. 'Ever growing populations and seemingly never growing economies give enormous impetus to mass migration, economic asylum seekers and the return of the slave trade as unscrupulous groups traffic in human beings,' concluded Robert Stern, a former US State Department counter-terrorist officer.[8]

Structural Adjustment Programmes, explosive population growth and unprecedented mass migration have thus created huge concentrations of people leading to problems or potential problems even beyond those mentioned in this account. 'How long,' warns Stern,

> will the third world be content to watch us live high on the hog (satellite television and the internet assure they know how we live) while their children starve? . . . Increasingly the world is divided between haves and have-nots and the have-nots are not going to be content to stay that way . . . If we are unable to see that our future and our children's future is directly tied to lowering world population growth and improving opportunity across-the-board, then we are asking to be overwhelmed.[9]

One need not share Stern's Malthusian influences to recognize that he raises questions that need to be addressed before we descend further into barbarism.

Sadly, Stern's former bosses in the George W. Bush White House and their corporate-media cheerleaders project global problems in much simpler good versus evil terms. At the time of writing, many of the world's problems boil down to Al Qaida, presented as a ubiquitous, well-organized terror network run by an evil mastermind, Osama Bin Laden. This is as far removed from the messier reality of terrorism as the notion of a few Mafia-type organizations running organized crime in America and elsewhere once was. All such simple-minded notions distract attention away from the need to address more fundamental faults in the international political economy if a safer, saner world is to emerge. If these faults are not addressed then criminally inclined corporations, warlords, gangsters and entrepreneurs will continue to prosper.

Epilogue

The Alternatives

Reforms that will move societies away from the tendency towards gangster capitalism will be opposed by special interests but they are possible. They involve many more people around the world and in the US itself challenging the post-Cold War orthodoxy that US-style neo-liberal democracy and market capitalism is the only way forward. Many more people both inside and outside of the business communities need to push for changes in both national and international financial and legal architectures that reduce the opportunities for any organized criminals, be they corporate, professional or gangster.

On corporate crime control, criminologists and legal scholars such as Harry Glasbeek, Russell Mokhiber, Laureen Snider, Frank Pearce and Steve Tombs have made many pragmatic recommendations for reforms that, if implemented, would lead to more accountable and less damaging corporate behaviour. Joel Bakan's *The Corporation: The Pathological Pursuit of Profit and Power* (2004) crystallizes much of the wisdom from these sources and offers the following necessary prescriptions: government regulation should be rethought to bring corporations under democratic control and to ensure that they respect the interests of citizens, communities and the environment.

Enforcement agencies need to be made more effective with realistic staffing levels and penalties that have a clear deterrent effect. Penalties could include the suspension of the charters of corporations that flagrantly and persistently violate the public interest. As New York Attorney General Eliot Spitzer put it, if 'a corporation is convicted of repeated felonies that harm or endanger the lives of human beings or destroy our environment, the corporation should be put to death, its corporate existence ended, and its assets taken and sold at public auction'. The regulatory system should be reformed to improve accountability and avoid both 'agency capture' and the centralized and bureaucratic tendencies of current and past regimes.

211

The roles of trade unions and other workers' associations in monitoring and regulating the behaviour of corporations should be protected and enhanced, as should those of environmental, consumer, human rights, and other organizations that represent interests and constituencies affected by what corporations do.[1]

On the need for transparency and the development of effective efforts to control both offshore and onshore financial crime, scholars and investigators such as Michael Levi, Nikos Passas, R.T. Naylor and Jack Blum have much to offer. Nikos Passas, for example, has explained how secrecy and anonymity in international financial transactions hinder investigators by covering the tracks of the 'global offender'.

> Illegal financial transactions and losses that must be reported can be conducted and hidden through offshore entities of global enterprises. Secrecy jurisdictions serve as a 'black box' through all manner of illegal activities can be shielded against prosecution and punishment. In a sense, this sort of black box makes serious crime disappear. Many crimes are so well organized and concealed that they are nowhere recorded. Few, if any, outsiders know that they have been committed.[2]

The offshore system, as Blum points out, has also given 'rich individuals and international business the ability to opt out of national tax systems. That ability enables them to profit from societies without contributing to them. The revenue loss is serious enough to undermine essential services and undercut the power of the state . . . A financial system that operates outside of regulatory control places the entire world economy at risk,' he goes on to warn. 'The possibilities for fraud and abuse in this complex system are so significant that there can be no assurance that all the central banks could save the system if a real crash ever got started. There is no international criminal system to track down the fraud or to deter it. There is no international bankruptcy system to deal with the wreckage when a major failure occurs.'[3]

It is if anything even more important to combat abuses in the onshore system with greater accountability, transparency and vigilance. P.G. Crook of the Guernsey Financial Services Commission has pointed out that, 'All finance centres are attractive to fraudsters and other economic criminals.' The 'amount of economic crime that occurs in the major, onshore financial centres is acknowledged by the fair-minded to be many times that which goes through reputable offshore centres. When the profits of fraud end up offshore it has virtually always entered the financial system in one of the major onshore centres.'[4] In recent years progress has been made in making both offshore and onshore private banking less private but as Michael Levi points out, 'Less progress has been made to curb the

use of corporations, trusts or other devices as secrecy vehicles ...
Realistic guidelines for banking staff and others to counter money laundering', he continues, 'will need to anticipate new countermeasures by
those seeking to place corrupt funds.'[5]

Michael Jacobs, Adam Lent and Kevin Watkins, in a pamphlet entitled
Progressive Globalisation (2003), have made constructive recommendations to address the failure to rebuild the global financial architecture after
Nixon's expedient dismantling of the old Bretton Woods system in the
early 1970s. These include the establishment of a World Financial
Authority to undertake the proper supervision of international markets
and flows. Such an Authority could set common standards, in particular,
for transparency and the provision of information.[6] BCCI and other
banking scandals could not have happened in such a transparent system.
Essentially Jacobs and his colleagues hope to internationalize the
response of Franklin Roosevelt and other Americans who wished to check
the flaws and abuses of unfettered capitalism that allowed crooks to
prosper in the 1920s. 'Let us turn on the light,' Roosevelt had demanded.
'Publicity is the enemy of crookedness.'[7] In general, better informed and
more sophisticated business and financial regulation at both national and
international levels is of course essential to combat many forms of
organized criminal activity.

Reasonably effective responses to at least two more areas of significant
transnational, organized, criminal activity – drug trafficking and people
trafficking – will also require radical changes of direction from the
current policies of both national governments and international organizations.

Historically efforts to prohibit drugs have only succeeded in keeping
prices high for goods that are easy to grow or manufacture. Gainers have
been traffickers, corrupt government officials and those private professionals, such as lawyers and accountants, that facilitate the illegal
trade, plus, of course, the hundreds of thousands of police and increasingly military professionals who take part in unwinnable wars on drugs.
These wars had racist origins more than a century ago as Americans
reacted against the opium-smoking of some Chinese immigrants by
criminalizing the habit and thus driving it underground.

Laws prohibited opium, heroin, cocaine, cannabis and a multitude of
synthetic, manufactured drugs but crucially could not end the demand for
these drugs and a massive illegal industry emerged. Attacking the supply
of these drugs has taken American police and military into the homes of
many of its citizens and into the growing fields of many countries abroad.
The results of these efforts have often been devastating but have never
achieved more than to shift areas of production, change smuggling routes

or disrupt trafficking networks. The demand has always been met and a vast amount of policing effort has been wasted. The only possibly effective response to the trade in illegal drugs is to work out ways to reduce prices and profits. This could involve states outbidding traffickers for opium and coca crops in Asia and South America. It could also involve doctors in the rich consuming countries supplying heroin addicts with their drugs on prescription as was the case in Britain before the 1970s. Governments have a duty to inform citizens of the dangers involved in the use of certain kinds of drug, just as they do with the dangers of alcohol and tobacco. There are also useful contributions that governments can make to reduce the damage that all these substances do, such as the recent tendency towards banning smoking in public spaces, which will reduce the dangers of passive smoking.

However, governments should also find more effective ways of reducing the damage that drugs do to society than the current approach. Experience in many countries shows that today's prohibition-based policies generally increase the damage that drugs do to society. All government drug warriors, especially those responsible for the implementation of UN narcotic conventions, should be required to answer the question set by Representative John Coffee to Congress in 1938. 'Why', he asked, 'should persons in authority wish to keep the dope peddler in business and the illicit-drug racket in possession of its billion dollar income?'[8]

In such a disordered, violent and dishonest world, governments should not continue to distort statistics and discourse so that more fruitless efforts to save people from themselves can continue. Again in Roosevelt's words, we 'must abolish useless offices' and we 'must eliminate unnecessary functions of government'. He was not referring to those offices and functions that regulate business but to the Prohibition Bureau and the enforcement of alcohol prohibition. His point stands for drug prohibition. The use of drugs in ways that do not put other adults or children at risk has to be legalized. Half-way solutions are always going to be inadequate and frequently counter-productive. Many well-meaning people advocate decriminalization of drug use and possession but this will always fail since it leaves the trade and therefore the profits in the hands of criminals.

A huge global traffic in people mainly exists because many from poor countries wish to escape an intolerable existence. They pay traffickers exorbitant fees for the chance of a difficult but tolerable existence in rich countries, often working illegally for employers who want their cheap labour. Those states primarily affected, notably in North America and Europe, have initiated campaigns to combat people trafficking, involving increased efforts by the police and immigration officials and moves towards greater international co-operation aimed against smuggling. Few of these efforts have made a significant impact, however, and the number of those smuggled continues to expand. The objective of most states is to tighten their border controls. However, as the political scientist Rey Koslowski points out, 'since tighter border controls often yield the unintended consequences of more customers for smugglers and more people entering the smuggling business, the prospects that recent anti-smuggling initiatives will be very effective remain quite dim.'[9] Even if the significant obstacles to genuine international police co-operation based on issues of state sovereignty are overcome, the demand from people in poor countries for better and more secure lives and therefore the impetus to pay traffickers will persist. Governments could begin to make an impact on the extent of trafficking by overcoming the opposition and evasion of those employers who gain from cheap and illegal labour but a more fundamental solution must involve powerful nations allowing poor nations the opportunity to improve the conditions of their citizens themselves. To achieve this there has to be a move towards the progressive globalization advocated and elaborated by Jacobs and his colleagues. They describe a positive way forward by calling for a new system of global governance based on four pillars.

The first of these pillars would be a requirement that trade amongst developed and less developed countries be based on fair and equitable trade principles rather than the inequities of the neo-liberal free-trade agenda. Instead of forcing less developed countries to reduce and eliminate trade barriers which help protect sectors of their domestic economies, the global community needs to develop a series of rules and conditions which define how far protection is justified, how far it can benefit the poor and how it can be controlled and phased out as development occurs. These rules also need to confront the blatant protectionism of sectors of the economies of developed industrialized countries. Bangladesh, for example, must pay the United States $314 million a year for the privilege of selling its garments in that country. Rich nations impose, on average, tariffs four times higher on goods from poor nations than on goods from other rich nations, because the other rich nations can fight back.[10]

The second pillar would be the regulation of global economic activity in ways that promote economic stability, and protect employees, consumers and the environment. Legislation should, for example, be passed in the home countries of transnational corporations forbidding them from breaking codes of practice, on employees, consumer and environmental protection in foreign countries. To provide for more comprehensive financial regulation, a World Financial Authority needs to be established properly to supervise international financial markets and flows.[11] This authority could set common standards for transparency and the provision of information and curb the proliferation of 'black box' secrecy jurisdictions that have so clearly facilitated transnational criminal activity in recent decades.

The third pillar would be the establishment of global mechanisms for the redistribution of income and wealth from rich nations and actors to poorer ones. As Jacobs and his colleagues point out, the greatest contribution of social democrats during the twentieth century was that they alone pushed for robust state intervention and this ensured that the tendency of the unfettered market to create great chasms of inequality in wealth, education, housing, health and opportunity was checked by redistributive welfare systems.[12] Unless there is an equivalent redistribution of income and wealth at the global level, the crime-breeding mega-slums discussed in the last chapter will continue to grow and the pockets of people traffickers and other parasites will continue to be filled.

The final pillar would be the introduction of democratic legitimacy into the system of global governance, involving a stronger role for the United Nations, the establishment of the principle of one member, one vote in all major international economic institutions and tougher scrutiny of institutions of global governance by national and regional parliaments. Most importantly, international law needs to be expanded to allow national sovereignty to be overridden in cases of severe abuse of human rights, such as genocide.[13]

In sum, there needs to be a reversal of many of the inequitable and crime-breeding global trends of recent years. Governments and citizens should heed the warnings of Karl Polanyi in 1944 and never again allow the market to be the sole director of the fate of human beings.

A serious effort to reduce the conditions that favour the businesses of drug traffickers, people traffickers, gangsters, corporate criminals and a host of criminal opportunists involves much more than the American-led emphasis on the police and military targeting of groups and individuals. Chris Braiden, a retired Canadian police superintendent, was speaking from experience when he observed that 'The criminal species will survive the hunt; it will not survive the loss of its habitat.'[14]

The only real alternative to a system of gangster capitalism is to attack the habitat and move towards a more progressive, democratic and socially just world. Millions of people around the world have been coming to conclusions not far out of line with many of the above prescriptions for genuine international and national organized-crime control. Indeed, some powerful interests inside the global business and financial community accept the need for at least some of these reforms, if only to prevent the

whole capitalist edifice from crumbling down just as it did once before –
in the 1930s.

Increasingly we face a choice between a return to the principles and
high ideals of progressive reform on the one hand and the destruction of
democracy and freedom in the name of 'free markets' on the other. It is
time to decide whether Franklin D. Roosevelt or George W. Bush best
represents our global future – a future of endless war and increasingly
shameless fraud or of hope and real if incomplete respite for the wretched
of the world.

Notes

Foreword

1   Antonio Maria Costa, Executive Director, United Nations Office on Drugs and Crime (UNODC) quoted in United Nations Press Release, UNIS/CP/439, 7 July 2003, at http://www.unodc/en/press_release_2003-07-07.

2   United Nations, United Nations General Assembly, Ninth United Nations Congress on the Prevention of Crime and the Treatment of Offenders, Discussion Guide, A/CONF.169/PM.1, 27 July 1993, 9.

3   For a convincing interpretation of the limits of gangster power see Letizia Paoli's 'The Paradoxes of Organized Crime', *Crime, Law and Social Change* 37: 2002, 51–97.

4   Gene Mustain and Jerry Capeci, *Mob Star: The Story of John Gotti* (New York: Alpha Books, 2002; first published 1988) 1; Bonnie Angelo, 'Organized Crime – Wanted a New Godfather Teflon Don', *Time*, 13 April 1992; Jocelyn Targett, 'Boss of the USA', *Guardian Weekend*, 10–11 August 1991, 4–7, 35.

5   Rod Nordland, 'Goodbye, Don', *Newsweek*, 13 April 1992; *The Gotti Tapes: Including the Testimony of Salvatore (Sammy the Bull) Gravano* (London: Arrow, 1992) 9–10, 108.

6   Gould quoted on the Texas State Library and Archives Commission website at http://www.tsl.state.tx.us/exhibits/railroad/intro.html. Early uses of the phrase 'organized crime' are discussed in Michael Woodiwiss, *Organized Crime and American Power: A History* (Toronto: University of Toronto Press, 2001) 176–83.

7   Huntington quoted in John Hutchinson, *The Imperfect Union: A History of Corruption in American Trade Unions* (New York: E.P. Dutton, 1972) 20.

8   K. Austin Kerr (ed.), *The Politics of Moral Behaviour: Prohibition and Drug Abuse* (Reading, Masschusetts: Addison-Wesley, 1977) 73, 96, 154; John J. Rumbarger, *Profits, Power and Prohibition: Alcohol Reform and the Industrializing of America, 1800–1930* (Albany: State University of New York Press, 1989) 175–83.

9   *Manchester Guardian* quoted by Walter Lippmann, 'The Underworld as Servant', in Gus Tyler (ed.), *Organized Crime in America* (Ann Arbor: University of Michigan Press, 1967) 63.

10 Leo Katcher, *The Big Bankroll* (New York: Harper, 1958).

11 Bruce J. Schulman, *The Seventies: The Great Shift in American Culture, Society and Politics* (New York: The Free Press, 2000) 48.

12 See Frank Costigan, 'White Collar Crime: Reflections on the 80's and Lessons to be Learned for the 1990s', at http://www.justice.net.au/publications/mc_book/white.pdf.

13 *Detroit Free Press*, 30 March 1972: *New York Times*, 18 February 1983, 7 October 1984.
14 Study by Malcolm W. Klein of the University of Southern California cited in *Narcotics Control Digest*, 26 February 1992.
15 Mike Davis, *City of Quartz* (London: Vintage, 1990) 287; Matt Lait and Scott Glover, 'Ex-officer Admits to Robberies', *Los Angeles Times*, 20 October 2004.
16 See Douglas Valentine, *The Strength of the Wolf: The Secret History of America's War on Drugs* (London: Verso, 2004) for a recent but not always reliable history of the Federal Bureau of Narcotics.
17 Alan Travis, 'British Top Euro League of Cocaine Abusers', *Guardian*, 26 November 2004.
18 For an account of changes in the British drug-control system see Michael Woodiwiss, *Crime, Crusades and Corruption: Prohibitions in the United States, 1900–1987* (London: Pinter, 1988) 220–2.
19 Susan Strange, *Casino Capitalism* (Manchester: Manchester University Press, 1997) 171.
20 These issues are discussed in Anthony Woodiwiss, *Making Human Rights Work Globally* (London: Glasshouse, 2003); Saskia Sassen, *Globalization and Its Discontents* (New York: New Press, 1998); and Robert Tillman, *Global Pirates: Fraud in the Offshore Insurance Industry* (Boston: Northeastern University Press, 2002).
21 Journalists Peter Truell and Larry Gurwin name some of those who were associated with both the World Bank and BCCI in *False Profits: The Inside Story of BCCI, the World's Most Corrupt Financial Empire* (Boston: Houghton Mifflin, 1992) 97–8.
22 See James S. Henry, *The Blood Bankers: Tales from the Global Underground Economy* (New York: Four Walls Eight Windows, 2003) 52, for this point applied to the Marcos regime in particular.
23 Conal Walsh and Oliver Morgan, 'Parmalat: Could it Happen Here?', *Observer*, Business, 11 January 2004; Sophie Arie, 'Parmalat Admits Real Debt is £14 Billion', *Guardian*, 27 January 2004.
24 See UN-Habitat, *The Challenge of the Slums: Global Report on Human Settlements* (London: United Nations, 2003) and Mike Davis' discussion of the report in 'Planet of Slums', *New Left Review*, vol. 26, March/April 2004, 5–34.
25 Alan Block, 'Bad Business: A Commentary on the Criminology of Organized Crime in the United States', in Tom Farer (ed.), *Transnational Crime in the Americas* (London: Routledge, 1999) 230–1.
26 Roosevelt's nomination address, Franklin and Eleanor Roosevelt Institute website at http://www.feri.org/archives/speeches/jul0232.cfm.

Part 1   The United States and Gangster Capitalism: Introduction to

1 For a longer discussion on the evolution of organized crime definitions see Michael Woodiwiss, *Organized Crime and American Power: A History* (Toronto: University of Toronto Press, 2001) 227–311.
2 G.L. Hostetter and T.Q. Beesley, 'Twentieth Century Crime', in Gus Tyler (ed.) *Organized Crime in America* (Ann Arbor: University of Michigan Press, 1967) 49–57.

3 Edward A. Ross, *Sin and Society: An Analysis of Latter-Day Iniquity* (Boston: Houghton Mifflin, 1907) 29–30.

4 Ibid., 26.

5 Walter Lippmann, 'The Underworld as Servant', *Forum*, January and February 1931, excerpted in Tyler (ed.), *Organized Crime in America*, 58–69.

6 Poem quoted in Frederick Lewis Allen, *Only Yesterday* (New York: Bantam, 1929) 182.

7 Donald C. Stone, 'Reorganization for Police Protection', *Law and Contemporary Problems*, vol. 1, no. 1, December 1934, 452.

8 Roosevelt speech quoted in Arthur M. Schlesinger Jr, *A Life in the Twentieth Century: Innocent Beginnings, 1917–1950* (Boston: Houghton Mifflin, 2000) 123.

9 Ed Reid, *Mafia* (New York: Random House, 1952), 1.

1 Cradle to Crematorium, Womb to Cadaver Lab

1 Jules Bonavolonta and Brian Duffy, *The Good Guys: How We Turned the FBI Round and Finally Broke the Mob* (New York: Pocket Books, 1997); Ernest Volkman, *Gangbusters: The Destruction of America's Last Great Mafia Dynasty* (New York: Avon Books, 1999); Joe Griffin and Don Denevi, *Mob Nemesis: How the FBI Crippled Organized Crime* (Amherst: Prometheus Books, 2002). For an example of an article on the same theme see David E. Kaplan, 'Getting it Right: The FBI and the Mob', *U.S. News and World Report*, 18 June 2001.

2 Stephen M. Rosoff, Henry N. Pontell and Robert H. Tillman, *Profit Without Honor: White Collar Crime and the Looting of America* (New York: Prentice-Hall, 2003) 403–4; *U.S. News and World Report*, 16 March 1992.

3 Rosoff et al., *Profit Without Honor*, 405–6; Alejandro N. Mayorkas, United States Attorney, Central District of California, 'Fugitive Fertility Doctor Arrested in South America on Federal Fraud Charges', 19 January 2001; see also US Department of Justice website at http://www.usdoj.gov/usao/cac/pr2001/015.html.

4 Andy Schneider, 'Reducing Medicare and Medicaid Fraud by Drug Manufacturers: The Role of the False Claims Act', prepared for Taxpayers Against Fraud Education Fund, Washington, DC, November 2003, at http://www.taf.org/publications%5 CPDF%5Cdrug%20report.pdf, 12.

5 Paul Jesilow, Henry N. Pontell and Gilbert Geis, *Prescription for Profit: How Doctors Defraud Medicaid* (Berkeley: University of California Press, 1992) 19.

6 Kurt Eichenwald, 'Tenet Healthcare Paying $54 Million in Fraud Settlement', *New York Times*, 7 August 2003.

7 Barbara Starfield, 'Is US Health Care the Best in the World?', *Journal of American Medical Association*, 284, 26 July 2000, 483–5.

8 Eichenwald, 'Tenet Healthcare Paying $54 Million in Fraud Settlement'.

9 Christine Hanley, 'Clinics Find Surgery Scam Pays', *Los Angeles Times*, 20 June 2004.

10 Walter Hamilton and Kathy M. Kristof, 'Insurance Broker Scandal Alleged', *Los Angeles Times*, 15 October 2004.

11 Samuel Maull, 'Marsh Broker Pleads Guilty in Fraud', *Washington Post*, 7 January 2005.

12 Michelle Andrews, 'An Illusion of Health Insurance', *New York Times*, 19 October 2003.

13 Clifford J. Levy, 'Panel Urges Changes in New York Homes for the Mentally Ill', *New York Times*, 24 September 2002.

14 Benita L. Weddle, New York State Archives, *Mental Health in New York State, 1945–1998*, at http://www.archives.nysed.gov/a/researchroom/rr_health_mh_hist. shtml, 39.

15 Clifford J. Levy, 'Here, Life is Squalor and Chaos', *New York Times*, 29 April 2002.

16 Clifford J. Levy, 'Voiceless, Defenseless and a Source of Cash', *New York Times*, 30 April 2002.

17 'Operator of Queens Adult Home Pleads Guilty and Pays $1.65 Million in Restitution', Press Releases, Office of New York State Attorney General Eliot Spitzer, 19 July 2004, at http://www.oag.state.ny.us/press/2004/jul/jul20a_04.html.

18 Clifford J. Levy, 'U.S. Indicts Doctor in Fraud and State Homes for Mentally Ill', *New York Times*, 7 January 2003.

19 Department of Justice, *Crime in the United States, 2002*, at http://www.fbi.gov/ucr/ cius_02/html/web/specialreport/05-SRbankrobbery.html.

20 Schneider, 'Reducing Medicare and Medicaid Fraud by Drug Manufacturers', 6–11.

21 US Food and Drug Administration website at http://www.fda.gov/; Foster Klug, 'Researchers, Government Scramble to Fight Drug Counterfeiters', *USA Today*, 12 April 2004.

22 David Lawrence, 'HealthSouth Fraud Impacts Millions', *People's Weekly World*, 22 November 2003, at http://www.pww.org/article/articleview/4433/0/; Katherine Vogt, 'HealthSouth Fraud Figures Higher than Thought', *AMNews*, 9 February 2004, at http://www.ama-assn.org/amednews/2004/02/09/bisc0209.htm.

23 Bob Williams, 'Phone Fund for Schools, Libraries Riddled with Fraud', The Center for Public Integrity, at http://www.publicint...org/printer-friendly.aspx?aid = 99.

24 Federal Communications Commission Washington, DC, Office of Inspector General, Memorandum, *Semiannual Report*, 31 October 2002, at http://www.fcc.gov/oig/ sar902.pdf.

25 Paul Davidson, Greg Toppo and Jayne O'Donnell, 'Cries for Reform Swell for FCC's E-Rate Program', *USA Today*, 9 June 2004.

26 Estimates from ECPAT (End Child Prostitution, Child Pornography and Trafficking in Children for Sexual Purposes) International website at http://ecpat.net/eng/ index.asp.

27 'US Breaks Child Porn Ring', *BBC News*, 8 August 2001, at http://news.bbc.co.uk/ 1/hi/world/americas/1481253.stm; 'Operation Avalanche: Tracking Child Porn', *BBC News*, 11 November 2002, at http://news.bbc.co.uk/1/hi/uk/2445065.stm.

28 James William Coleman, *The Criminal Elite: The Sociology of White Collar Crime* (New York: St Martin's Press, 1989) 33.

29 C. Calhoun and H. Hiller, 'Coping with Insidious Injuries: The Case of Johns-Manville Corporation and Asbestos Exposure', in *Social Problems*, vol. 35, no. 2, April 1988, 165; David Kotelchuck, 'Asbestos: "The Funeral Dress of Kings" and Others', in David Rosner and Gerald Markowitz (eds), *Dying for Work: Workers' Safety and Health in Twentieth Century America* (Bloomington: Indiana University Press, 1989), 170–85; Joan Lowy, 'Study: 10,000 a Year Will Die of Asbestos Exposure', *Medline Plus*, 3 March 2004, at http://www.nlm.nih.gov/medlineplus/ news/fullstory_16394.htlm.

30 Michael Bowker, *Fatal Deception: The Terrifying True Story of How Asbestos is Killing America* (New York: Touchstone, 2003) 145–9.

31 Lowy, 'Study: 10,000 a Year Will Die of Asbestos Exposure', *Scripps Howard News Service*, 28 February 2005.

32 Coleman, *The Criminal Elite*, 39.

33 Rosoff et al., *Profit Without Honor*, 98–117.

34 Richard Kluger, *Ashes to Ashes: America's Hundred-Year Cigarette War, the Public Health, and the Unabashed Triumph of Philip Morris* (New York: Vintage, 1997) 231–3.

35 Quoted in Myron Levin, 'Long-Secret Documents Now Hurting Tobacco', *Los Angeles Times*, 5 October 1998, at http://www.no-smoking.org/may98/05-10-98-1.html.

36 Rosoff et al., *Profit Without Honor*, 91–2.

37 'Smoking-Attributable Mortality and Years of Potential Life Lost', *Morbidity and Mortality Weekly Report* (Atlanta, Georgia: Centers for Disease Control), 23 May 1997, vol. 46, no. 20, 449.

38 Tobacco Information and Prevention Source, 'Annual Deaths Attributable to Cigarette Smoking – United States, 1995–1999', at http://www.cdc.gov/tobacco/overview/attrdths.htm.

39 Rosoff et al., *Profit Without Honor*, 97.

40 Eric Schlosser, *Fast Food Nation* (London: Penguin, 2002) 153–4.

41 Ibid., 172.

42 David Barstow, 'U.S. Rarely Seeks Charges for Deaths in the Workplace', *New York Times*, 22 December 2003.

43 Melody Peterson and Christopher Drew, 'New Safety Rules Fail to Stop Tainted Meat', *New York Times*, 10 October 2003.

44 Schlosser, *Fast Food Nation*, 196–7.

45 Coleman, *The Criminal Elite*, 28.

46 Rosoff et al., *Profit Without Honor*, 63.

47 Kurt Eichenwald, *The Informant* (New York: Broadway Books, 2001) 14.

48 Ibid., 217.

49 Rosoff et al., *Profit Without Honor*, 64–5.

50 Adam Smith, *An Inquiry into the Nature and Causes of the Wealth of Nations, Volume 1* (Oxford: Clarendon Press, 1880) 135.

51 Gretchen Morgenson, 'Mutual Fund Accused of Fraud in Rapid Trading by Managers', *New York Times*, 29 October 2003.

52 Frank Partnoy, *Infectious Greed: How Deceit and Risk Corrupted the Financial Markets* (London: Profile Books, 2004) 421–2.

53 David Teather, 'Spitzer – The Improbable Missionary', *Guardian*, 8 September 2003; Landon Thomas Jr and Riva D. Atlas, 'Merrill Fires Three Brokers Over Trading', *New York Times*, 4 October 2003; Riva D. Atlas, 'S.E.C. Examining Funds Trading at Another Firm', *New York Times*, 14 October 2003; Brooke A. Masters, 'Fund Probers Target Firm for Shutdown', *Washington Post*, 6 November 2003.

54 Rosoff et al., *Profit Without Honor*, 408.

55 Ibid., 406–9.

56 'Crematory Grounds Could Yield 200-plus Bodies', *CNN.com*, 18 February 2002, at http://cnn.usnews.pr...86011574&partnerID=2004&expire=_1; Robert D. McFadden, 'Scores of Bodies Strewn at Site of Crematory', *New York Times*, 17 February

2002; Elliot C. McLaughlin, 'Settlements Reached in Class-action Suit', *Online Athens – Athens Banner-Herald*, 11 March 2004, at http://216.116.224.17...ries/031204/new_20040312045.shtml.

57   John F. Wasik, 'Special Report: Fraud in the Funeral Industry', *Consumer Digest*, September/October 1995, vol. 34, issue 5; Jon Burstein, 'Judge Signals Approval of Settlement Against Two Menorah Gardens Cemeteries', *Sun-Sentinel.com*, 18 March 2004, at http://www.sun-senti...nt.story?coll=sfla-home-headlines.

58   John Broder, 'In Science's Name: Lucrative Trade in Body Parts', *New York Times*, 12 March 2004; Nicholas Riccardi, 'Companies That Purchased Body Parts Are Sued', *Los Angeles Times*, 17 March 2004.

2   Barons, Crusaders and the Land of Criminal Opportunity

1   Matthew Josephson, *The Robber Barons: The Great American Capitalists, 1861–1901* (New York: Harcourt, Brace & World, 1962, first published 1934) v.

2   Gustavus Myers, *History of Great American Fortunes* (New York: The Modern Library, 1936) 380–4.

3   Gabriel Kolko, *Main Currents in Modern American History* (New York: Harper & Row, 1976) 93.

4   David Rosner and Gerald Markowitz (eds), *Dying for Work: Workers' Safety and Health in Twentieth Century America* (Bloomington: Indiana University Press, 1989) xi.

5   Joseph A. Page and Mary-Win O'Brien, *Bitter Wages* (New York: Grossman, 1973) 52–3.

6   Drew quoted in Bouck White, *The Book of Daniel Drew* (New York: Arno Press, 1973, first published 1910) 278. Although there is some doubt about the authenticity of this book there is little doubt that these observations reflect late nineteenth-century business culture accurately.

7   Quoted in Josephson, *The Robber Barons*, 15.

8   Herbert Spencer, *Social Statistics* (London: Williams and Norgate, 1868), p. 354.

9   Andrew Carnegie, 'Wealth', *North American Review*, 148, no. 391 (June 1889) 653, 657–62.

10   Andrew Sinclair, *Prohibition: The Era of Excess* (London: Faber and Faber, 1962) 117–23.

11   Quoted in John Helmer, *Drugs and Minority Oppression* (New York: The Seabury Press, 1975) 12.

12   Francisco E. Thoumi, *Illegal Drugs, Economy, and Society in the Andes* (London; The Johns Hopkins University Press, 2003) 20.

13   Alan A. Block and William Chambliss, *Organizing Crime* (New York: Elsevier, 1981) 53.

14   Rufus King, *The Drug Hang-Up: America's Fifty Year Folly* (New York: W.W. Norton, 1972) 25.

15   David Bewley-Taylor, *The United States and International Drug Control, 1909–1997* (London: Pinter, 1999) 36.

16   Quoted in Paul Sann, *The Lawless Decade* (New York: Bonanza Books, 1957) 214.

3 The Racket-ridden Twenties and the Origins of the Great Depression

1 Daniel Yergin, *The Prize: The Epic Quest for Oil, Money and Power* (London: Simon & Schuster, 1991) 212–15.
2 An excellent account of power-industry corruption during the twentieth century and into the twenty-first is provided by Sharon Beder in *Power Play: The Fight to Control the World's Electricity* (New York: The New Press, 2003). See pp. 32–5 for detail on stock-watering during the 1920s.
3 Arthur M. Schlesinger Jr, *The Crisis of the Old Order* (London: Heinemann, 1957) 160.
4 W.A. Swanberg, *Citizen Hearst* (New York: Bantam, 1971) 322–6.
5 Stan Nettleton, 'Newspapering in 1930's Chicago – Part One', *HistoryBuff.com* at http://www.historybuff.com/library/refchicago1.html.
6 Frank Tannenbaum, *Crime and the Community* (Boston: Ginn and Company, 1938) 40–2.
7 Keith Sward, *The Legend of Henry Ford* (New York: Russell and Russell, 1968) 398–9.
8 *People's Press*, 7 December 1935, available on the *History Matters* website at http://historymatters.gmu.edu/d/5089/.
9 Joseph A. Page and Mary-Win O'Brien, *Bitter Wages* (New York: Grossman, 1973) 63.
10 Joseph A. Page and Mary-Win O'Brien, *Bitter Wages* (New York: Grossman, 1973) 59–63.
11 Dominique Lapierre and Javier Moro, *Five Past Midnight in Bhopal* (London: Scribner, 2003) 33.
12 Alan A. Block and William Chambliss, *Organizing Crime* (New York: Elsevier, 1981) 65; G.L Hostetter and T.Q. Beesley, 'Twentieth Century Crime', in Gus Tyler (ed.), *Organized Crime in America* (Ann Arbor: University of Michigan Press, 1967) 49–58.
13 Hostetter and Beesley, 'Twentieth Century Crime', 49.
14 Adams quoted in Tannenbaum, *Crime and the Community*, 161–2.
15 See Michael Woodiwiss, *Crime, Crusades and Corruption: Prohibitions in the United States, 1900–1987* (London: Pinter, 1988) 9–39, for more detail on the problems involved in attempting to enforce Prohibition.
16 Craig Thompson and Raymond Allen, *Gang Rule in New York* (New York: Dial Press, 1940) 100; Eisen quoted in F.D. Pasley, *Al Capone: The Biography of a Self-made Man* (London: Faber and Faber, 1966) 292.
17 Mabel Willebrandt, *The Inside of Prohibition* (Indianapolis: Bobbs-Merrill, 1929) 200.
18 Quoted in Charles R. Geisst, *Wall Street: A History – From its Beginnings to the Fall of Enron* (New York: Oxford University Press, 2004) 172.
19 Frederick Lewis Allen, *Since Yesterday: The 1930s in America* (New York: Harper & Row, 1972) 52–5. Bruno Richard Hauptmann was electrocuted for the crime in 1936. Doubts remain as to his guilt.
20 Quoted in Richard Gid Powers, *G-Men: Hoover's FBI in American Popular Culture* (Carbondale and Edwardsville: Southern Illinois University Press, 1983) 9.
21 Quoted in Tyler (ed.), *Organized Crime in America*, 5.
22 Hugh Brogan, *The Penguin History of the USA* (London: Penguin, 2001) 507.

23 Raymond B. Vickers, *Panic in Paradise: Florida's Banking Crash of 1926* (Tuscaloosa: University of Alabama Press, 1998) 1–13.

24 Allen, *Since Yesterday: The 1930s in America*, 136.

25 John Kenneth Galbraith, *The Great Crash: 1929* (London: Hamish Hamilton, 1972) 183.

26 Robert S. McElvaine, *The Great Depression: America, 1929–1941* (New York: Times Books, 1981) 50.

27 David M. Kennedy, *Freedom from Fear: The American People in Depression and War, 1929–1945* (Oxford: Oxford University Press, 1999) 43.

28 Walter la Feber, Richard Polenberg and Nancy Woloch, *The American Century: A History of the United States from the 1890s* (New York: McGraw-Hill, 1992), p. 176.

29 Ibid.

4 The New Deal and Organized Crime

1 Franklin D. Roosevelt, The Forgotten Man Speech, 7 April 1932, accessed on the *New Deal Network* website at http://newdeal.feri.org/speeches/1932c.htm.

2 Adolph A. Berle and Gardiner C. Means, *The Modern Corporation and Private Property* (New York: Harcourt, Brace & World, 1932); Alan Brinkley, *The End of Reform: New Deal Liberalism in Recession and War* (New York: Vintage, 1995) 37–8, 266.

3 Charles A. Beard, 'The Myth of Rugged American Individualism', in Howard Zinn (ed.), *New Deal Thought* (Indianapolis: Bobbs-Merrill, 1967) 10.

4 Walter Lippmann, 'The Underworld as Servant', in Gus Tyler (ed.), *Organized Crime in America* (Ann Arbor: University of Michigan Press, 1967) 61.

5 Murray Gurfein, 'The Racket Defined', in Tyler (ed.), *Organized Crime in America*, 181–8.

6 Franklin D. Roosevelt, 'Portland Speech: Public Utilities Hydro-Electric Power', 21 September 1932, http://newdeal.feri.org/speeches/1932a.htm. *New Deal Network*, http://newdeal.feri.org.

7 Franklin D. Roosevelt, Nomination Address, 2 July 1932, accessed on Franklin and Eleanor Roosevelt Institute webpage at http://www.feri.org/archives/speeches/ju10232.cfm.

8 The Oglethorpe speech is available on the *New Deal Network* website at http://newdeal.feri.org/.

9 Brinkley, *End of Reform*, 5.

10 Franklin D. Roosevelt, Nomination Address, 2 July 1932, accessed on Franklin and Eleanor Roosevelt Institute webpage at http://www.feri.org/archives/speeches/ju10232.cfm.

11 Senator Robert F. Wagner of New York, speech made in the Senate of the United States, 17 February 1931, reprinted in USA Constitutional Documents, *Repeal the Eighteenth Amendment*, Washington, DC, 1931.

12 David E. Kyvig, *Repealing National Prohibition* (Chicago: University of Chicago Press, 1979) 178, 186.

13 V.O. Key, *Southern Politics* (New York: Vintage, 1949) 235.

14 Mark Haller, 'Bootleggers as Businessmen: From City Slums to City Builders', in David E. Kyvig (ed.), *Law, Alcohol and Order: Perspectives on National Prohibition* (Washington, DC: Greenwood Press, 1985) 143–5; James H. Grey, *Booze: The*

Impact of Whisky on the Prairie West (Toronto: Macmillan of Canada, 1972) 138–9.

15 Franklin D. Roosevelt, Nomination Address, 2 July 1932, accessed on Franklin and Eleanor Roosevelt Institute webpage at http://www.feri.org/archives/speeches/ju10232.cfm.

16 Franklin D. Roosevelt, Inaugural Speech, Washington, DC, 4 March 1933, *The Literature Page* website at http://www.literaturepage.com/read/fdr_inaugural_speech-1.html.

17 Ronald Edsforth, *The New Deal* (Oxford: Blackwell, 2000) 190–1.

18 Joseph G. Rayback, *A History of American Labor* (New York: The Free Press, 1966) 342–6.

19 Daniel Bell, *The End of Ideology: On the Exhaustion of Political Ideas in the Fifties* (New York: The Free Press, 1962) 131.

20 Dewey's career as prosecutor and governor of New York is detailed in Michael Woodiwiss, *Crime, Crusades and Corruption: Prohibitions in the United States, 1900–1987* (London: Pinter, 1988) 47–72.

21 Schultz quoted in Hank Messick and Burt Goldblatt, *The Mobs and the Mafia* (London: Spring, 1972) 138.

22 Cummings quoted in Kenneth O'Reilly, 'A New Deal for the FBI: The Roosevelt Administration, Crime Control and National Security', *Journal of American History*, vol. 69, no. 3, December 1982, 643.

23 Frederick Lewis Allen, *Since Yesterday: The 1930s in America* (New York: Harper & Row, 1972) 146–7.

24 O'Reilly, 'A New Deal for the FBI', 643; Robert Sherrill, *The Saturday Night Special* (New York: Penguin, 1973) 63–5.

25 Sharon Beder, *Power Play: The Fight to Control the World's Electricity* (New York: The New Press, 2003) 64–6; see also Richard Rudolph and Scott Ridley, *Power Struggle: The Hundred Year War over Electricity* (New York: Harper & Row, 1986) 214–9.

26 Edsforth, *The New Deal*, 192–3.

27 Alan Dawley, *Struggles for Justice: Social Responsibility and the Liberal State* (London: Belknap Press, 1991) 348.

28 David Kennedy, *Freedom from Fear: The American People in Depression and War, 1929–45* (Oxford: Oxford University Press, 1999) 366–7.

29 Edsforth, *The New Deal*, 194; Arthur M. Schlesinger, *Age of Roosevelt: The Coming of the New Deal* (Boston: Houghton Mifflin, 1959) 426.

30 See Susan P. Shapiro, *Wayward Capitalists: Targets of the Securities and Exchange Commission* (New Haven: Yale University Press, 1987) for a history of the SEC's enforcement policies.

31 Roosevelt quoted in Joel Bakan, *The Corporation: The Pathological Pursuit of Profit and Power* (London: Constable, 2004) 86.

5 States of Denial and Mafia Distractions

1 Elizabeth A. Fones-Wolf, *Selling Free Enterprise: The Business Assault on Labor and Liberalism, 1945–60* (Urbana: University of Illinois Press, 1994) 2–7.

2 Otto Friedrich, *City of Nets: A Portrait of Hollywood in the 1940s* (London: Headline, 1986) 401–2.

3 Francis Stoner Saunders, *Who Paid the Piper: The CIA and the Cultural Cold War* (London: Granta, 1999) 294–5, demonstrates that the Central Intelligence Agency was responsible for these and other changes from the book to the film.

4 For an analysis of the move towards 'compensatory' liberalism see Alan Brinkley, *Liberalism and Its Discontents* (Cambridge, Massachusetts: Harvard University Press, 1998); Ira Katznelson, 'Was the Great Society a Lost Opportunity?', in Robert Griffiths and Paula Baker (eds), *Major Problems in American History Since 1945* (Boston: Houghton Mifflin, 2001) 235.

5 See, for example, Frank Pearce, *Crimes of the Powerful* (London: Pluto Press, 1976) and the work of criminologists contributing to Frank Pearce and Laureen Snider (eds), *Corporate Crime: Contemporary Debates* (Toronto: University of Toronto Press, 1995).

6 Laureen Snider, 'Researching Corporate Crime', in Steve Tombs and Dave Whyte (eds), *Unmasking the Crimes of the Powerful: Scrutinizing States and Corporations* (Oxford: Peter Lang Publishing, 2003) 63.

7 Michael Bowker, *Fatal Deception: The Terrifying True Story of How Asbestos is Killing America* (New York: Simon & Schuster, 2003) 88–90.

8 President's Commission on Law Enforcement and the Administration of Justice, *The Challenge of Crime in a Free Society* (Washington, DC: Government Printing Office, 1967) 187–209.

9 Gus Russo, *The Outfit: The Role of Chicago's Underworld in the Shaping of Modern America* (New York: Bloomsbury, 2003) 497–8.

10 Frederic T. Martens and Michele Cunningham-Niederer, 'Media Magic, Mafia Mania', *Federal Probation*, June 1985, 61.

11 Jack Lait and Lee Mortimer, *USA Confidential* (New York: Crown, 1952) 15.

12 See Michael Woodiwiss, *Organized Crime and American Power: A History* (Toronto: University of Toronto Press, 2001) 227–65 for an analysis of this process.

13 Hoover quoted in *New York Times*, 30 January 1960. See Lee Bernstein, *The Greatest Menace: Organized Crime in Cold War America* (Boston: University of Massachusetts Press, 2002) 5.

14 Anthony Summers, *Official and Confidential: The Secret Life of J. Edgar Hoover* (London: Victor Gollancz, 1993) 237–59.

15 President's Commission on Law Enforcement and the Administration of Justice, *The Challenge of Crime in a Free Society*, 187–209.

16 For a good account of the Teamsters' association with mobsters see James Neff, *Mobbed-Up: Jackie Presser's High Wire Life in the Teamsters, the Mafia and the FBI* (New York: Dell, 1989).

17 Arthur M. Schlesinger, in *Robert Kennedy and His Times* (London: Futura, 1979) 519–22, gives a credible account of these machinations. He writes that with 'Giancana shot seven times in the throat and mouth as he was frying sausages in his Chicago kitchen in June 1975, with Rosselli hacked up, stuffed into an oil drum and dumped into the sea near Miami in July 1976, it is impossible to know how they viewed their CIA mission'. Schlesinger's study of these episodes gave him the strong impression 'that the hoods, if they did not regard the whole thing as a big joke, at most only went through the motions of carrying out their assignment'.

18 See, for example, Joseph L. Albini, *The American Mafia: Genesis of a Legend* (New York: Appleton-Century-Crofts, 1971) and Dwight Smith, *The Mafia Mystique* (London: Hutchinson, 1975).

19   This is an edited version of the argument of Chapter 5 of Woodiwiss, *Organized Crime and American Power*.

20   Joseph L. Albini, *The American Mafia*, 328.

21   All quotes taken from Executive Office of the President, President's Advisory Council on Executive Organization, *Organized Crime Strike Force Report*, Washington, DC, 19 November 1969, folder: Sourcebook, Organized Crime, Egil Krogh Files: Box 50, WHCF (PACEO), Nixon Presidential Materials Staff, National Archives.

22   *Wall Street Journal*, 16 March 1982.

23   Ehrlichman testimony in *Federal Drug Enforcement*. Hearings before the Permanent Subcommittee on Investigations of the Committee on Government Operations, US Senate, 94th Congress, Second Session, 27, 28, 29 July 1976, Part 4 (Washington, DC: Government Printing Office, 1976) 794.

24   Arnold Trebach, *The Heroin Solution* (New Haven, Connecticut: Yale University Press, 1982) 237; Rufus King, *The Drug Hang-Up: America's Fifty Year Folly* (New York: W.W. Norton, 1972) 307–22.

25   John Finlator, *The Drugged Nation* (New York: Simon & Schuster, 1973) 322–3; August Bequai, *Organized Crime* (Lexington, Massachusetts: Lexington Books, 1979) 146; King, *The Drug Hang-Up*, 319.

26   Ehrlichman testimony in *Federal Drug Enforcement*, 804.

27   James B. Jacobs and Lauryn P. Gouldin, 'Cosa Nostra – The Final Chapter', in Michael Tonry (ed.), *Crime and Justice: A Review of Research, Volume 25* (Chicago: University of Chicago Press, 1999) 175–6.

28   Selwyn Raab, 'Officials Say Mob is Shifting Crimes to New Industries', *New York Times*, 10 February 1997.

29   Prepared statement of Mr Richard H. Walker, Director Division of Enforcement, Securities and Exchange Commission to the Oversight Hearing before the House Subcommittee on Finance and Hazardous Materials, Committee on Commerce, 13 September 2000, available on the US Securities and Exchange Commission website at http://www.sec.gov/news/testimony/ts142000.htm.

30   William K. Rashbaum, 'Officials Say Mob Stole $200 Million Using Phone Bills', *New York Times*, 11 February 2004.

31   Gary W. Potter, *Criminal Organizations: Vice, Racketeering, and Politics in an American City* (Prospect Heights, Illinois: Waveland Press, 1994) 7.

32   Benjamin Strolberg, 'Thomas E. Dewey: Self-Made Myth', *American Mercury*, June 1940, 140–7.

33   Melanie Nayer, 'FBI Documents Acknowledge Barboza's Guilt and Association with Deegan Murder', *New Bedford Standard-Times*, March 2002, at http://www.bu.edu/com/jo/washjocenter/S...2002_Stories/newswire_nayer_fbi0302.htm; Gato quote from Hearing before the Committee on Government Reform, House of Representatives, One Hundred Seventh Congress, First Session, 3 May 2001, Serial No. 107–25, *The FBI's Controversial Handling of Organized Crime Investigations in Boston: The Case of Joseph Salvati* (Washington, DC: US Government Printing Office, 2001) 29–30.

34   Pete Earley and Gerald Shur, *WITSEC: Inside the Federal Witness Protection Program* (New York: Bantam, 2002) 153–5.

35   Thomas Powers, 'Secrets of September 11', *New York Review of Books*, 10 October 2002, 47–8.

36 Associated Press, 'Ex-Agents: FBI Enlist Violent Informants', *New York Times*, 2 March 2003.

37 *Pittsburg Press*, 14 August 1991.

38 R.T. Naylor, *The Wages of Crime: Black Markets, Illegal Finance, and the Underworld Economy* (Ithaca: Cornell University Press, 2002) 263.

39 Eric Blumenson and Eva Nilsen, 'The Drug War's Hidden Economic Agenda', *The Nation*, 9 March 1998.

40 Jack Biggs, 'Forfeiture!', *Los Angeles Reader*, 18 December 1992, 11–12.

41 Brant Hadaway, 'Executive Privateers: A Discussion on Why the Civil Asset Forfeiture Reform Act Will Not Significantly Reform the Practice of Forfeiture', *University of Miami Law Review*, vol. 55, no. 1, October 2000, 81–121, available at the FEAR website at http://www.fear.org/hadaway.html. For a longer account of asset forfeiture see Woodiwiss, *Organized Crime and American Power*, 354–60.

6 Capital Corruption

1 Joseph A. Page and Mary Win-O'Brien, *Bitter Wages* (New York: Grossman, 1973) 191–2. See also Frank Pearce and Steve Tombs, *Toxic Capitalism: Corporate Crime and the Chemical Industry* (Toronto: Canadian Scholars' Press, 1999) 266–8.

2 Richard Milhouse Nixon, Second Inaugural Address, 20 January 1973, available at http://www.bartleby.com/124/pres59.html.

3 Bruce J. Schulman, *The Seventies: The Great Shift in American Culture, Society, and Politics* (New York: The Free Press, 2000) 41–2.

4 Eric Hobsbawm, *Age of Extremes: The Short Twentieth Century* (London: Abacus, 1994) 271.

5 Alan Greenspan, 'The Assault on Integrity', in Ayn Rand (ed.), *Capitalism: The Unknown Ideal* (New York: The New American Library, 1966) 116.

6 Richard Campbell and Jimmie L. Reeves, *Cracked Coverage: Television News, The Anti-Cocaine Crusade, and the Reagan Legacy* (Durham, North Carolina: Duke University Press, 1994) 76–7; Jerome L. Himmelstein, *To the Right: The Transformation of American Conservatism* (Berkeley: University of California Press, 1990) 130.

7 M.J. Heale, *Twentieth Century America: Politics and Power in the United States, 1900–2000* (London: Arnold, 2004) 292.

8 Quoted in Mary Beth Norton et al., *A People and A Nation: A History of the United States* (Boston: Houghton Mifflin, 1994) 1034.

9 Marshall B. Clinard, *Corporate Corruption: The Abuse of Power* (New York: Praeger, 1990) 115; *Newsweek*, 7 March 1983, 24–31; Adam Raphael, *Ultimate Risk: The Inside Story of the Lloyd's Catastrophe* (London: Transworld, 1994) 162.

10 Russell Mokhiber, 'Top 100 Corporate Criminals of the Decade', available at http://www.informationclearinghouse.info/article3676.htm.

11 Gary W. Potter and Karen S. Miller, 'Thinking about White Collar Crime', in Gary W. Potter, *Controversies in White Collar Crime* (Conklin, NY: Matthew Bender, 1992) 18–20.

12 David Burnham, *Above the Law: Secret Deals, Political Fixes, and Other Misadventures of the U.S. Department of Justice* (New York: Scribner, 1996) 246.

13 Rosoff et al., *Profit Without Honor*, 138.

14 Browner and Clapp quoted in Martin Engel, 'Road to Ruin: America Eats Itself', *Guardian*, 24 October 2003, 8.

15 Paul Z. Pilzer and Robert Deitz, *Other People's Money: The Inside Story of the S & L Mess* (New York: Simon & Schuster, 1989) 100–1; Rosoff et al., *Profit Without Honor*, 278.

16 Kitty Calavita and Henry Pontell, 'Savings-and-Loan Fraud as Organized Crime: Towards a Conceptual Typology of Corporate Illegality', *Criminology*, vol. 31, no. 4, 1993, 519–48.

17 Stephen Pizzo, Mary Ricker and Paul Muolo, *Inside Job: The Looting of America's Savings and Loan* (New York: McGraw-Hill, 1989) 209, 193; Frank Hagan and Peter Benekos, 'What Charles Keating and "Murph the Surf" Have in Common: A Symbiosis of Professional and Occupational and Corporate Crime', *Criminal Organizations* (International Association for the Study of Organized Crime) vol. 7, no. 1 (1992) 24.

18 Kitty Calavita and Henry Pontell, '"Other People's Money" Revisited: Collective Embezzlement in the Savings and Loan and Insurance Industries', *Social Problems*, vol. 38, no. 1, February 1991, 99.

19 Quoted in James Ring Adams, *The Big Fix: Inside the S & L Scandal* (New York: John Wiley, 1990) 274.

20 Timothy Curry and Lynn Shibut, 'The Cost of the Savings and Loan Crisis: Truth and Consequence', *FDIC Banking Review*, December 2000, at http://www.fdic.gov/bank/analytical/banking/2000dec/brv13n2_2pdf.

21 Calavita and Pontell, 'Other People's Money', 94; John Kenneth Galbraith, *The Culture of Contentment* (Harmondsworth: Penguin, 1992) 61.

22 Robert Bryce, *Pipe Dreams: Greed, Ego, and the Death of Enron* (Oxford: Public Affairs, 2002) 87.

23 Clinton quoted in Frank Partnoy, *Infectious Greed: How Deceit and Risk Corrupted the Financial Markets* (London: Profile Books, 2004) 145.

24 Ibid., 163.

25 Richard W. Stevenson and Allison Mitchell, 'Parties Maneuver Over Risks in Growing Business Scandal', *New York Times*, 28 June 2002.

26 Partnoy, *Infectious Greed*, 173–216.

27 Roger Lowenstein, *Origins of the Crash: The Great Bubble and its Undoing* (New York: Penguin, 2004) 44–5.

28 Joseph E. Stiglitz, *The Roaring Nineties: A New History of the World's Most Prosperous Decade* (New York: W.W. Norton, 2003) 126.

29 Quoted in Will Hutton, *The World We're In* (London: Little, Brown, 2002) 204.

30 Molly Ivins, 'Gingrich and Gramm, Enablers of Corrupt Corporations', *Star-Telegram*, 4 August 2002, at http://www.dfw.com/mld/startelg.

31 Thomas Frank, *One Market Under God: Extreme Capitalism, Market Populism and the End of Economic Democracy* (London: Secker & Warburg, 2000) x.

32 Robert Bremner, 'Towards the Precipice', *London Review of Books*, 6 February 2003, 20.

33 PBS Homepage, *Frontline*, 'The Long Demise of Glass-Steagall', 8 May 2003, at http://www.pbs.org/wgbh/pages/frontline/shows/wallstreet/weill/demise.html.

34 See *Understanding How Glass-Steagall Act Impacts Investment Banking and the Role of Commercial Banks* at http://www.cftech.com/BrainBank/SPECIAL REPORTS/GlassSteagall.html for a useful explanation.

35 Stiglitz, *The Roaring Nineties*, 160–1.

36 Partnoy, *Infectious Greed*, 402.

37 Bryce, *Pipe Dreams*, 37–42; Lowenstein, *Origins of the Crash*, 128–9.

38 Partnoy, *Infectious Greed*, 348.
39 Campaign contribution figures available from Steven Weiss, 'The Fall of A Giant: Enron's Campaign Contributions and Lobbying', *Money in Politics Alert*, 9 November 2001, vol. 6, no. 31, at http://www.opensecrets.org/alerts/v6/alertv6_31.asp.
40 The Associated Press, 'Tapes: Enron Traders Discussed Manipulation', *USA Today*, 3 June 2004.
41 Lowenstein, *Origins of the Crash*, 143.
42 Jeff Madrick, 'Enron: Seduction and Betrayal', *New York Review of Books*, 14 March 2002, 21.
43 Partnoy, *Infectious Greed*, 350–1.
44 Lynne W. Jeter, *Disconnected: Deceit and Betrayal at WorldCom* (Hoboken, New Jersey: John Wiley, 2004) xx–xxi; Keith Brody and Sancha Dunstan, *The Great Telecoms Swindle* (London: Capstone, 2003) xxi–xxii, 13–15.
45 Statement of Richard Thornburgh, Bankruptcy Examiner, Kirkpatrick and Lockhart, LLP, Washington, DC, to the Hearing before the Committee on the Judiciary, United States Senate, *The WorldCom Case: Looking at Bankruptcy and Competition Issues*, 108th Congress, First Session, 22 July 2003, Serial No. J.-108-26 (Washington, DC: Government Printing Office, 2004) 5.
46 Statement of William P. Barr, General Counsel of Verizon Communications, Washington, DC, to the Hearing before the Committee on the Judiciary, United States Senate, *The WorldCom Case: Looking at Bankruptcy and Competition Issues*, 108th Congress, First Session, 22 July 2003, Serial No. J.-108-26 (Washington, DC: Government Printing Office, 2004) 10.
47 Bremner, 'Towards the Precipice', 22.
48 Justin O'Brien, 'Conflicts of Interest on Wall Street: Corrupted Actors or System?', paper presented at the XI International Anti-Corruption Conference in Seoul. Dr O'Brien has written widely on the subject of financial-market fraud, including *Wall Street on Trial, A Corrupted State?* (Chichester: John Wiley, 2003).
49 Kurt Eichenwald, 'Reform Effort at Businesses Feels Pressure', *New York Times*, 14 January 2005.
50 Christopher S. Stewart, 'After Serving Time, Executives Now Serve up Advice', *New York Times*, 1 June 2004, 1, 8.
51 Eichenwald, 'Reform Effort at Businesses Feels Pressure'.
52 'It's Time to Punish WorldCom/MCI', 17 June 2003, on the *US Labor Against the War* website at http://www.uslaboragainstwar.org/article.php?id = 4499.
53 David Cay Johnston, 'Tax Inquiries Fall as Cheating Increases', *New York Times*, 14 April 2003; David Cay Johnston, 'Crackdown on Tax Cheats Not Working', *New York Times*, 20 October 2003.
54 Statistics taken from Joel Friedman, 'The Decline of Corporate Income Tax Revenues', *Center on Budget and Policy Priorities*, 24 October 2003, at http://www.cbpp.org/10-16-03tax.htm. Friedman's research was based on US government sources.
55 An interview with Jared Bernstein, 'The Hierarchy: Income Inequality in the United States', *Multinational Monitor*, May 2003, vol. 24, no. 5.
56 David Cay Johnston, *Perfectly Legal: The Covert Campaign to Rig Our Tax System to Benefit the Super Rich – and Cheat Everybody Else* (New York: Portfolio, 2003).
57 John Gray, *False Dawn: The Delusions of Global Capitalism* (London: Granta, 2002) 108.

7 Zero Tolerance and the Rise of the Gangs

1   Jonathan Simon, 'Governing Through Crime', in Lawrence M. Friedman and George Fisher (eds), *The Crime Conundrum: Essays on Criminal Justice* (Boulder, Colorado: Westview Press, 1996) 173–4.

2   David Garland, *The Culture of Control: Crime and Social Order in Contemporary Society* (Oxford: Oxford University Press, 2001) 98–100.

3   Arnold S. Trebach, *The Heroin Solution* (London: Yale University Press, 1982) 227.

4   Mike Davis, *City of Quartz: Excavating the Future in Los Angeles* (London: Vintage, 1990) 270, 314.

5   *Los Angeles Times*, 17 May 1988, quoted in Davis, *City of Quartz*, 314.

6   Figures taken from government publications and reproduced in *Drug War Facts 2004*, available at http://www.drugwarfacts.org. The figures are updated annually.

7   Bruce Bullington, 'America's Drug War: Fact or Fiction', in Ross Coomber (ed.), *The Control of Drugs and Drug Users: Reason Or Reaction* (Amsterdam: Harwood Academic Press, 1998) 113.

8   Steven R. Donziger (ed.), *The Real War on Crime: The Report of the National Criminal Justice Commission* (New York: Harper Perennial, 1996) 15; see also *Drug War Facts* website at http://www.drugwarfacts.org/crime.htm.

9   Francis A.J. Ianni, *Black Mafia: Ethnic Succession in Organized Crime* (London: New English Library, 1976) 157–8.

10 Geoffrey Hunt et al., 'Changes in Prison Culture: Prison Gangs and the Case of the Pepsi Generation', *Social Problems*, vol. 40, no. 3, August 1993, 404.

11 Anti-Defamation League (1999), *From the Prisons to the Streets: The Nazi Low Riders Emerge in California*, http://www.adl.org/issue-combating-hate/nazi-low-riders.html.

12 Christian Parenti, *Lockdown America: Police and Prisons in the Age of Crisis* (London: Verso, 2000) 197.

13 Hunt et al., 'Changes in Prison Culture', 400–1.

14 Parenti, *Lockdown America*, 205–6.

15 Ibid., 209.

16 See M.W. Klein, *The American Street Gang: Its Nature, Prevalence and Control* (New York: Oxford University Press, 1995) for a sophisticated analysis of the problem; Allen L. Hixon, 'Preventing Street Gang Violence', *American Family Physician*, 15 April 1999, at http://www.aafp.org/afp/990415ap/medicine.html.

17 Fox Butterfield, 'Rise in Killings Spurs New Steps to Fight Gangs', *New York Times*, 17 January 2004.

18 Steven R. Wiley, 'Violent Street Gangs in America', Statement before the Senate Committee on the Judiciary, Washington, DC, 23 April 1997, at http://www.hi-ho.ne.jp/taku77/refer/gang.htm.

19 Fox Butterfield, 'Gun Industry Ex-Official Describes Bond of Silence', *New York Times*, 4 February 2003.

20 'Illicit Flow of Guns from Ohio to New Jersey Using College Students', *Global Crime Update*, no. 67, January 2004, 2.

21 Boyle quoted in Burhan Wazir, 'Lost Angeles', *Observer Magazine*, 7 July 2002, 31.

22 Randall Richard, '500,000 Deportees from U.S. Wreaking Havoc', azcentral.com, 26 October 2003, at http://www.azcentral..../news/articles/1026exports26.html.

23 Rupert Widdicombe and Duncan Campbell, 'Poor Neighbours Fall Prey to US Gang Culture', *Guardian*, 27 May 2003, 12.

24 Sandra Jordan, 'El Salvador's Teenage Beauty Queens Live and Die by Gang Law', *Observer*, 10 November 2002, at http://www.observer.co.uk/Print/0,3858, 4543400,00.html.

25 Fen Montaigne, 'Deporting America's Gang Culture', *Mother Jones Magazine*, July/ August 1999, at http://www.altenativemuseum.org/...ntheline/decesare/decesare_ 2.html.

8 The Broken Promise of Roosevelt's Global Freedoms

1 Speech in *Congressional Record* (Washington, DC: Government Printing Office, 1941), vol. 87, pt 1.

2 W.A. Swanberg, *Luce and His Empire* (New York: Dell, 1973) 259–60.

3 Wallace quoted in John C. Culver, 'Seeds and Science: Henry A. Wallace on Agriculture and Human Progress', Inaugural Lecture, March 1996, Henry A. Wallace Center for Agricultural and Environmental Policy, Winrock International at http:/ /www.winrock.org/wallacecenter/puborderform.cfm.

4 Alan Brinkley, *The End of Reform: New Deal Liberalism in Recession and War* (New York: Vintage, 1995) 150–3.

5 Eric Helleiner, *States and the Reemergence of Global Finance: From Bretton Woods to the 1990s* (Ithaca: Cornell University Press, 1995) 31–5.

6 Ibid., 27–8; James M. Boughton, 'The Case against Harry Dexter White: Still Not Proven', *IMF Working Paper*, August 2000, WP/00/149 (International Monetary Fund, 2000) 18.

7 President Roosevelt's Message to Congress on Bretton Woods Money and Banking Proposals, 12 February 1945, see http://oll.temple.edu/hist249/cou...ent_roosevelt. on_Bretton_woods.htm.

8 Morgenhau quoted in Armand Van Dormael, *The Bretton Woods Conference: Birth of a Monetary System* (London: Macmillan, 1978), excerpted on the Hoover Institution website at http://www.imfsite.org/origins/confer4.html.

9 Polanyi quoted in Susan George, 'A Short History of Neoliberalism', *Conference on Economic Sovereignty in a Globalising World*, 24–6 March 1999, available on the *Global Policy Forum* website at http://www.globalpolicy.org/globaliz/econ/ histneol.htm.

10 Richard J. Barnett and Ronald E. Muller, *Global Reach: The Power of Multinational Corporations* (London: Jonathan Cape, 1975) 67. British prime minister Harold Macmillan quoted in Eric Hobsbawm, *Age of Extremes: The Short Twentieth Century, 1914–1991* (London: Abacus, 1995) 257.

11 Ha-Joon Chang, 'Kicking Away the Ladder: Infant Industry Promotion in Historical Perspective', *Oxford Development Studies*, vol. 31, no. 1, 2003, 1–32; Scott Newton, *The Global Economy: 1944–2000: The Limits of Ideology* (London: Arnold, 2004) 111.

12 Hugh Brogan, *The Penguin History of the United States* (London: Penguin, 1999) 577.

13 Tony Judt, 'The Way We Live Now', *New York Review of Books*, 27 February 2003.

14 *Public Papers of the Presidents of the United States: Harry S. Truman, 1945–53* (Washington, DC: Government Printing Office, 1963) 17–18.

15 H.W. Brands, *The Wages of Globalism: Lyndon Johnson and the Limits of American Power* (Oxford: Oxford University Press, 1997) 256, 262.

16 George Kennan, memorandum, 'Review of Current Trends, U.S. Foreign Policy', PPS/23, Top Secret. Included in *Foreign Relations of the United States, 1948* (Washington, DC: Government Printing Office, 1976) vol. 1, pt 2, 509–29. Quoted in Raymond Bonner, *Waltzing with a Dictator: The Marcoses and the Making of American Policy* (New York: Times Books, 1987) 33.

17 William Blum, *The CIA: A Forgotten History* (London: Zed Books, 1986) 68.

18 Daniel Yergin, *The Prize: The Epic Quest for Oil, Money and Power* (London: Simon & Schuster, 1991) 470.

19 For accounts of Operation Ajax see also John Ranelagh, *The Agency: The Rise and Decline of the CIA* (London: Sceptre, 1988) 261–4; James William Coleman, *The Criminal Elite: The Sociology of White Collar Crime* (New York: St Martin's Press, 1989) 69–70.

20 Lytle quoted in Walter La Feber, *The American Age: American Foreign Policy at Home and Abroad from 1750 to the Present* (London: W.W. Norton, 1994) 546.

21 Thomas McCann, former United Fruit executive, quoted in Stephen Schlesinger and Stephen Kinzer, *Bitter Fruit: The Untold Story of the American Coup in Guatemala* (Garden City, New York: Doubleday, 1982) 73.

22 Nick Cullather and Piero Gleijeses, *The CIA's Classified Account of its Operations in Guatemala, 1952–1954* (Palo Alto, California: Stanford University Press, 1999) 8–15.

23 Schlesinger and Kinzer, *Bitter Fruit*, 26.

24 Ibid. and Blum, *The CIA*, 77–89; Ranelagh, *The Agency*, 264–8; Cullather and Gleijeses, *The CIA's Classified Account*, xxv–xxvi.

25 Ranelagh, *The Agency*, 437–40; Rhodri Jeffreys-Jones, *Cloak and Dollar: A History of American Secret Intelligence* (New Haven, Connecticut: Yale University Press, 2002) 203.

26 Andrew Carnegie, 'Wealth', *North American Review*, 148, no. 391 (June 1889) 653, 657–62.

27 Barnett and Muller, *Global Reach*, 146–60.

28 'The Baby Food Tragedy', *New Internationalist*, 006, August 1973; Mike Muller, *The Baby Killer* (London: War on Want, 1974), available on the War on Want website at http://www.waronwant.org/.

9 Nixon and the New World Economic Disorder

1 Allen J. Matusow, *Nixon's Economy* (Lawrence: University Press of Kansas, 1998) 4–5.

2 Irving Bernstein, *Guns or Butter: The Presidency of Lyndon Johnson* (New York: Oxford University Press, 1996) 533.

3 Robert Gilpin, *Global Political Economy: Understanding the International Economic Order* (Princeton: Princeton University Press, 2001) 238; Walter La Feber, *The American Age: American Foreign Policy at Home and Abroad from 1750 to the Present* (New York: W.W. Norton, 1995) 645.

4 La Feber, *American Age*, 645–6.

5 Quoted in Matusow, *Nixon's Economy*, 117.

6 Matusow, *Nixon's Economy*, 149–81: Matusow's account drawn from the diaries and recollections of Nixon's White House Chief of Staff, Bob Haldeman, and other participants in the meetings.

7 Matusow, *Nixon's Economy*, 154

8 Gilpin, *Global Political Economy*, 239.

9 David Burnham, *Above the Law: Secret Deals, Political Fixes, and Other Misadventures of the U.S. Department of Justice* (New York: Scribner, 1996) 222.

10 James William Coleman, *The Criminal Elite: The Sociology of White Collar Crime* (New York: St Martin's Press, 1989) 71.

11 Morton Halperin, Jerry Berman, Robert Borosage and Christine Marwick, *The Lawless State: The Crimes of the U.S. Intelligence Agencies* (Harmondsworth: Penguin, 1976) 15–29; John Ranelagh, *The Agency: The Rise and Decline of the CIA* (London: Sceptre, 1988) 514–20; Anthony Sampson, *The Sovereign State: The Secret History of ITT* (London: Coronet, 1974) 242–56; Coleman, *The Criminal Elite*, 70–2; William Blum, *The CIA: A Forgotten History* (London: Zed Books, 1986) 232–43.

12 Eric Hobsbawm, *Age of Extremes: The Short Twentieth Century, 1914–1991* (London: Abacus, 1995) 442.

13 Susan George, 'How to Win the War of Ideas: Lessons from the Gramscian Right', *Dissent*, Summer 1997, vol. 44, no. 3.

14 On transfer pricing see Ingo Walter in *Secret Money* (London: Unwin, 1988) 16.

15 United Nations, *Fifth United Nations Congress on the Prevention of Crime and the Treatment of Offenders, Report Prepared by the Secretariat* (Geneva, 1–2 September 1975) 10–11.

16 Information on UNCTC from: Human Rights Sub-Commission 2000, *Relations between the United Nations and Transnational Corporations*, at http://www.cetim.ch/20000/00FS04W4.htm; Gerald Piel, 'Globalopolies', *The Nation*, 18 May 1992, at http://www.globalpolicy.org/reform/gpiel.htm; Friends of the Earth – International Forum of Globalization, *Towards a Progressive International Economy: A History of Attempts to Control the Activities of Transnational Corporations: What Lessons Can Be Learned?*, at http://www.foe.org/progressive-economy/history.html.

17 Ian Williams, 'Why the Right Loves the U.N.', *The Nation*, 13 April 1993, at http://www.globalpolicy.org/reforms/williams.htm.

10 The War on Drugs and the Rise of International Drug Traffic

1 Egil Krogh, 'Meeting on Drugs with Top Administration Officials and Military Chiefs', Memo for: The President, 2 June 1971; 'Summary, Narcotic Meeting, State Dining Room, 3 June 1971', Egil Krogh Files: Box 4, WHCF, - 1971, Nixon Presidential Materials Staff, National Archives.

2 Henry Kissinger, 'Study of Means to Stop International Traffic in Heroin', Memo for: The Secretary of State, the Attorney General, 29 September 1969, Egil Krogh Files: Box 30, WHCF, Folder: Heroin/Turkey - 1969, Nixon Presidential Materials Staff, National Archives.

3 Quotes from contemporary newspapers and magazines in Lawrence A. Gooberman, *Operation Intercept: The Multiple Consequences of Public Policy* (New York: Pergamon Press, 1974) available on the website of the Schaffer Library of Drug Policy at http://www.druglibrary.org/schaffer/history/e1960/intercept/chapter1.htm.

4   Albert Goldman, *Grass Roots* (New York: Harper & Row, 1979) 100; Richard C. Schroeder, *The Politics of Drugs* (Washington, DC: Congressional Quarterly Inc., 1980) 123.

5   The Drug Abuse Council, *The Facts about 'Drug Abuse'* (New York: The Free Press, 1980) 38; Schroeder, *The Politics of Drugs*, 130; David Musto, *The American Disease: Origins of Narcotic Control* (New York: Oxford University Press, 1987) 256–7.

6   John E. Ingersoll, 'Delegation Report of the Second Special Session of the U.N. Commission on Narcotic Drugs', Memo to Egil Krogh, 2 November 1970, Egil Krogh Files, Box 31, Folder: International Trafficking – UN Commission, Box 31, WHCF, - 1970, Nixon Presidential Materials Staff, National Archives.

7   Commission on Narcotic Drugs, Special Session, Geneva, 25 September – 3 October 1970, *Preliminary US Proposals*, Talking Paper, Egil Krogh Files, Box 31, Folder: International Trafficking – UN Commission, Box 31, WHCF, - 1970, Nixon Presidential Materials Staff, National Archives.

8   For an account of the scandal that led to the abolition of the Federal Bureau of Narcotics see Michael Woodiwiss, *Organized Crime and American Power: A History* (Toronto: University of Toronto Press, 2001) 256–7; see also Douglas Valentine, *The Strength of the Wolf: The Secret History of America's War on Drugs* (London: Verso, 2004).

9   David R. Bewley-Taylor, *The United States and International Drug Control: 1909–1997* (London: Pinter, 1999) 167.

10 Egil Krogh, 'Meeting on Drugs with Top State Department Officials, Top Administration Officials, CIA Officials and Ambassadors to South Vietnam, France, Turkey, Thailand and Luxembourg, 14 June 1971', Memo for: The President, 11 June 1971; 'Meeting with Ambassadors and State Department Officials on International Narcotics Trafficking, 14 June 1971', Memo for: The President's File, 26 July 1971, Egil Krogh Files: Box 4, WHCF, - 1971, Nixon Presidential Materials Staff, National Archives.

11 Ethan A. Nadelmann, *Cops Across Borders: The Internationalization of U.S. Criminal Law Enforcement* (University Park, Pennsylvania: The Pennsylvania State University Press, 1993) 141.

12 Ibid., 14. For DEA staffing and budget figures see the DEA website at http://www.usdoj.gov/dea/agency/staffing.htm.

13 National Commission on Law Observance and Enforcement, *Final Report* (Washington, DC: Government Printing Office, 1931) 51.

14 For a detailed description of Khun Sa's role in international drug trafficking see Alfred W. McCoy's *The Politics of Heroin: CIA Complicity in the Global Drug Trade* (New York: Lawrence Hill Books, 1991) 423–35.

15 Frontline, PBS television documentary *The Opium Kings,* interview with Donald Ferraone, DEA agent in Burma in the 1980s, Chief DEA officer in Bangkok, 1993–5, in February 1996. Transcript available at http://www.pbs.org/wgbh/pages/frontline/shows/heroin/interviews/ferraone.html.

16 Alfred W. McCoy, 'Requiem for a Drug Lord: State and Commodity in the Career of Khun Sa', in Josiah McC. Heyman, *States and Illegal Practices* (Oxford: Berg, 1999) 150–61.

17 McCoy, *The Politics of Heroin*, 445–60.

18 *BBC News*, 'Profile: Gulbuddin Hekmatyar', 28 January 2003; Gary Leupp, 'Meet Mr. Blowback: Gulbuddin Hekmatyar, CIA Op and Homicidal Thug', *Counter-Punch*, 14 February 2003, at http://www.counterpunch.org/leupp02142003.html.

19 Carlotta Gall, 'Afghan Poppy Growing Reaches Record Level, U.N. Says', *New York Times*, 19 November 2004.

20 Letizia Paoli, *Mafia Brotherhoods: Organized Crime, Italian Style* (Oxford: Oxford University Press, 2003) 148–9.

21 John Dickie, *Cosa Nostra: A History of the Sicilian Mafia* (London: Hodder & Stoughton, 2004) 384–5.

22 Schroeder, *The Politics of Drugs*, 121.

23 Clare Hargreaves, *Snowfields: The War on Cocaine in the Andes* (London: Zed Books, 1992) 71–83; M. Linklater, I. Hilton and N. Ascherson, *The Fourth Reich: Klaus Barbie and the Neo-Fascist Connection* (London: Hodder & Stoughton, 1984) 16–19, 215–319; Noam Chomsky, *Turning the Tide: US Intervention in Central America and the Struggle for Peace* (London: Pluto Press, 1985) 198–207; Francisco E. Thoumi, *Illegal Drugs, Economy, and Society in the Andes* (Baltimore: The Johns Hopkins University Press, 2003) 120–1.

24 Thoumi, *Illegal Drugs*, 6.

25 Ibid., 204–5.

26 Mark Bowden, *Killing Pablo* (London: Atlantic, 2001) 80.

27 Thoumi, *Illegal Drugs*, 210–11.

28 Ron Chepesiuk, *The Bullet or the Bribe: Taking Down Colombia's Cali Drug Cartel* (Westport, Connecticut: Praeger, 2003) 175–6.

29 Ibid., 261.

30 Thoumi, *Illegal Drugs*, 80.

31 Robin Kirk, *More Terrible than Death: Violence, Drugs, and America's War in Colombia* (New York: Public Affairs, 2003) 241–2.

11 Dumbing the International Response to Drugs and Organized Crime

1 Information on the Bureau for International and Law Enforcement Affairs taken from the State Department's website at http://www.state.gov/www/publications/statemag_dec99/bom.html, accessed on 15 November 2003.

2 Sherman Hinson, 'Bureau of the Month: On the Front Lines: International Narcotics and Law Enforcement Affairs', *State Magazine: Bureau of the Month*, May 1997, at http://www.state.gov/www/publications/statemag_may/bom.html.

3 Ethan Nadelmann, *Cops Across Borders: The Internationalization of U.S. Criminal Law Enforcement* (University Park, Pennsylvania: Pennsylvania State University Press, 1993) 470.

4 David Mansfield and Colin Sage, 'Drug Crop Producing Countries: A Development Perspective', in Ross Coomber, *The Control of Drugs and Drug Users: Reason or Reaction?* (Amsterdam: Harwood Academic Publishers, 1998) 163.

5 Francis E. Thoumi, *Illegal Drugs, Economy and Society in the Andes* (Baltimore: The Johns Hopkins University Press, 2003) 169–70.

6 Juan Forero, 'Hide-and-Seek Among the Coca Leaves', *New York Times*, 9 June 2004.

7   Michael Woodiwiss, *Crime, Crusades and Corruption: Prohibitions in the United States, 1900–1987* (London: Pinter, 1988) 216.
8   Richard Hartnoll in Coomber, *The Control of Drugs and Drug Users*, 235–6.
9   UN statistics available from http://www.undcp.org.
10 For Sterling's connection with the CIA see John Ranelagh, *The Agency: The Rise and Decline of the CIA* (London, Sceptre, 1988) 697–8. See also Sterling's three books: *The Terror Network: The Secret War of International Terrorism* (New York: Henry Holt, 1981); *Octopus: The Long Reach of the International Sicilian Mafia* (New York: Simon & Schuster, 1990); and *Thieves' World: The Threat of the New Global Network of Organized Crime* (New York: Simon & Schuster, 1994).
11 Linnea P. Raine and Frank J. Cilluffo, *Global Organized Crime: The New Empire of Evil* (Washington, DC: Center for Strategic and International Studies, 1994) 106.
12 Ibid., ix.
13 Joel M. Ostow, review of Andrei Shleifer and Daniel Triesman, *Without a Map: Political Tactics and Economic Reform in Russia* (Cambridge, Massachusetts: MIT Press, 2001) in *Comparative Political Studies*, vol. 36, no. 3, April 2003, 345–51.
14 Adam Edwards and Peter Gill (eds), *Transnational Organised Crime: Perspectives on Global Security* (London: Routledge, 2003) 8–9. Martin Elvins' contribution to this volume, 'Europe's Response to Transnational Organised Crime', 28–41, is particularly relevant.
15 United Nations Background Release, *World Ministerial Conference on Organised Transnational Crime to be Held in Naples, Italy, from 21 to 23 November*, 17 November 1994.
16 United Nations Background Release, *Statement by the Secretary-General on the Occasion of the World Ministerial Conference on Organised Transnational Crime*, Naples, 21 November 1994.
17 All quotes taken from United Nations Background Release, *Proposed Formulation of Global Convention Against Organised Crime Discussed at World Ministerial Conference*, 22 November 1994.
18 All quotes taken from United Nations Background Release, *Proposed Formulation of Global Convention Against Organised Crime Discussed at World Ministerial Conference*, 22 November 1994.
19 United Nations Economic and Social Council, *Appropriate Modalities and Guidelines for the Prevention and Control of Organised Transnational Crime at the Regional and International Levels, Background Document*, E/CONF.88/5, 19 September 1994.
20 United Nations Crime Prevention and Criminal Justice Newsletter, *The World Ministerial Conference on Organized Transnational Crime, Naples, Italy, 21–23 November 1994*, nos 26/27, November 1995, 23–8.
21 The UN Convention against Transnational Organized Crime (Document A/55/383) is available on http://www.odccp.org/palermo/theconvention.html.
22 Other crimes in the list included: traffic in persons, counterfeiting currency, stealing of cultural objects, stealing of nuclear materials, terrorism, the illicit manufacturing of firearms, the illicit traffic in motor vehicles and corruption of public officials and officers of private institutions. United Nations, General Assembly, Ad Hoc Committee on the Elaboration of a Convention against Transnational Organized Crime, *Revised draft United Nations Convention against Transnational Organized Crime* (A/AC.254/4/Rev4) 19 July 1999, 52–3. These crimes are not specified in the final version of the convention.

23 US Department of State, 'Crime Convention will soon advance to U.S. Senate', *International Information Programs* [online] at http://usinfo.state./gov/topical/global/traffic/01021401.htm, February 2001.

24 Recent estimates quoted in Mark Tran, 'Drug War Just an Exercise in Futility', *Guardian*, 11 June 1998, 19; United Nations Office for Drug Control and Crime Prevention, *Global Illicit Drug Trends 2003* (Austria: United Nations Publications, 2003) reproduced on the *Drug War Facts* website at http://www.drugwarfacts.org/druguse.htm.

Part 3 A World of Criminal Opportunity, 1965–
   Introduction to

1 Eric Helleiner, 'From Bretton Woods to Global Finance: A World Turned Upside Down', in Richard Stubbs and Geoffrey R.D. Underhill (eds), *Political Economy and the Changing Global Order* (Oxford: Oxford University Press, 2000) 163–70.

2 Susan George, 'Several Pounds of Flesh', *New Internationalist*, 189, November 1988, at http://www.newint.org/issue189/flesh.htm.

3 Scott Newton, *The Global Economy, 1944–2000: The Limits of Ideology* (London: Arnold, 2004) 145.

4 Figures taken from *Working for Justice* website, 'A Brief History of the Debt', at http://www.columban.com/debthist.htm.

5 Newton, *The Global Economy*, 146.

6 See Jonathan Friedman, 'Neoliberal Globalization', *The University of Michigan Journal of International Affairs*, Issue 4, March 2004, at http://www.umich.edu/ ~ ias/mjia/issue4/jfriedman.htm for a useful summary.

7 Newton, *The Global Economy*, 149; *Working for Justice* website, 'A Brief History of the Debt'.

8 Joseph Stiglitz, *Globalization and its Discontents* (London: Penguin, 2002) 140.

9 Eric Hobsbawm, *Age of Extremes: The Short Twentieth Century, 1914–1991* (London: Abacus, 1995) 564.

10 Stiglitz, *Globalization and its Discontents*, 58.

11 UN-Habitat, *The Challenge of the Slums: Global Report on Human Settlements, 2003* (London: United Nations Human Settlement Programme, 2003) 44.

12 Newton, *The Global Economy*, 179.

12 Suharto and the Looting of Indonesia

1 Frances Stoner Saunders, *Who Paid the Piper: The CIA and the Cultural Cold War* (London: Granta, 1999) 141.

2 Susan George, *How the Other Half Dies: The Real Reason for World Hunger* (Harmondsworth: Penguin, 1980) 56.

3 Seth S. King, 'Purge in Indonesia', *New York Times*, 8 May 1966.

4 US Central Intelligence Agency, *Research Study: Indonesia – The Coup that Back-fired*, 1968.

5 George, *How the Other Half Dies*, 56–9.

6 William Blum, *The CIA: A Forgotten History* (London: Zed Books, 1986) 221.

7 Jonathan Kwitny, *Endless Enemies: The Making of an Unfriendly World* (New York: Penguin, 1986) 283.

8   Ibid., 284–5.
9   *BBC News*, 'Suharto Tops Corruption Rankings', 25 March 2004, at http://newsvote.
    bbc.co.uk/mpapps/...c.co.uk/2/hi/buisness/3567745.stm.
10 Kwitny, *Endless Enemies*, 285.

13   Marcos Takes the Philippines

1   For a history of Marcos and the Phillippines see Stanley Karnow, *In Our Image:
    America's Empire in the Philippines* (New York: Ballantine, 1990).
2   R.T. Naylor, *Hot Money and the Politics of Debt* (London: Unwin, 1987) 334.
3   See Sam Gwynne, 'Confessions of a Loan Shark', *New Internationalist*, 189, Novem-
    ber 1988, at http://www.newint.org/issue189/shark.htm, for an account of the experi-
    ences of one of these young corporate bankers.
4   Karnow, *In Our Image*, 5.
5   Naylor, *Hot Money and the Politics of Debt*, 335; *Working for Justice* website, 'A Brief
    History of the Debt', at http://www/columban.com/debthist.htm.
6   Naylor, *Hot Money and the Politics of Debt*, 335–6.

14   Mobutu and Debt in Africa

1   Jonathan Kwitny, *Endless Enemies: The Making of an Unfriendly World* (New York:
    Penguin, 1986) 49–62; R.T. Naylor, *Hot Money and the Politics of Debt* (London:
    Unwin, 1987) 238.
2   John Ranelagh, *The Agency: The Rise and Decline of the CIA* (London: Sceptre, 1988)
    338–41.
3   Steve Askin and Carole Collins, 'Kick-backs and Kleptocracy', *New Internationalist*,
    259, September 1994, at http://www.newint.org/issue259/contents.htm; John Stock-
    well, *In Search of Enemies: A CIA Story* (New York: W.W. Norton, 1978) 203–12.
4   Askin and Collins, 'Kick-backs and Kleptocracy'; Naylor, *Hot Money and the Politics
    of Debt*, 239.
5   Kwitny, *Endless Enemies*, 90.
6   John Kay, *The Truth about Markets: Why Some Nations are Rich but Most Remain
    Poor* (London: Penguin, 2003) 273.
7   Steve Askin, 'Zaire's Den of Thieves', *New Internationalist*, 208, June 1990, at http:/
    /www.newint.org/issue208/den.htm.
8   Gideon Burrows, *The No-Nonsense Guide to the Arms Trade* (London: Verso, 2002)
    62–71.

15   Bankers and International Crime

1   Hussein's criminality of course continued long after the 1980s until he was deposed
    by the American-led invasion of Iraq in 2003. It involved war crimes, state crimes
    and organized financial crimes. Details of the 'oil-for-food' scam involving Saddam
    Hussein and those companies willing to do business with Iraq while it was under a
    UN-sanctions regime are beginning to emerge. US Senate investigators have charged
    that Hussein embezzled $21 billion by evading UN sanctions from 1997 to 2003.
    Although the focus in the US has been on the UN's complicity in this scandal it

should be noted that most of Hussein's illicit income came from oil smuggling, not kickbacks on UN contracts and that dealing with smuggling was mainly the job of the American Navy, not the UN. It would require an analysis of book length to do justice to the scale of both Hussein's organized criminality and that of many of the corporate interests involved in the invasion and occupation of his country. See Mark Gregory, 'Companies in 'oil-for-food scam', *BBC News*, 19 November 2004, and Judith Miller, 'Bribery inquiry needs at least a year, its chief says', *New York Times*, 10 August 2004.

2   Peter Truell and Larry Gurwin, *False Profits: The Inside Story of BCCI, the World's Most Corrupt Financial Empire* (Boston: Houghton Mifflin, 1992) 156–7.

3   Senator John Kerry and Senator Hank Brown, *The BCCI Affair: A Report to the Committee on Foreign Relations*, United States Senate, December 1992, 102nd Congress 2nd Session, Senate Print 102–140, available at http://www.fas.org/irp/congress/1992_rpt/bcci/, 1.

4   See Nick Kochran and Bob Whittington, *Bankrupt: The BCCI Fraud* (London: Victor Gollancz, 1991), for a view of the scandal from the perspective of British journalists and for Kochran's review of Truell and Gurwin, *False Profits*, see *Guardian*, 2 February 1993.

5   Kerry and Brown, *The BCCI Affair*, 1–2.

6   Blum quoted ibid., 2.

7   Kochran and Whittington, *Bankrupt*, 107.

8   Truell and Gurwin, *False Profits*, 178–82.

9   Kerry and Brown, *The BCCI Affair*, 13.

10 Abu Nidal Organization (ANO) for Terrorist Group Profiles, Dudley Knox Library, Naval Postgraduate School, at http://library.nps.navy.mil/home/tgp/abu.htm.

11 Kerry and Brown, *The BCCI Affair*, 13.

12 Truell and Gurwin, *False Profits*, 101.

13 Nikos Passas, 'Structural Sources of International Crime: Policy Lessons from the BCCI Affair', *Crime, Law and Social Change*, 20 (1993), 299.

14 Quoted in Holly Sklar, *Washington's War on Nicaragua* (Boston: South End Press, 1988) 177.

15 Truell and Gurwin, *False Profits*, 217.

16 Ethan B. Kapstein, *Governing the Global Economy: International Finance and the State* (Cambridge, Massachusetts: Harvard University Press, 1996) 165.

17 Quoted in Kochran and Whittington, *Bankrupt*, 14.

18 Henry H. Rossbacher and Tracy W. Young, 'BCCI: The Priority of Kings, or What's More Dangerous, the Cavalry or the Indians', *Journal of Financial Crime*, vol. 5, no. 4, 3, 365–6.

19 Nikos Passas, 'Globalization and Transnational Crime: Effects of Criminogenic Asymmetries', in Phil Williams and Dimitri Vlassis, *Combating Transnational Crime: Concepts, Activities and Responses* (London: Frank Cass, 2001) 39.

20 Rossbacher and Young, 'BCCI: The Priority of Kings', 367.

21 *Time Magazine*, 29 July 1991, at http://krigskronanikan.com.

22 Christopher Whalen, 'Good Guys are Hard to Find', *Journal of Commerce*, 28 October 1991, at http://www.rcwhelan.com/articles/joc_good_guys_are_hard_to_find.asp.

23 Nikos Passas, 'The Mirror of Global Evils: A Review Essay on the BCCI', *Justice Quarterly*, vol. 12, no. 2, June 1995, 382.

16 Evasion, Flight and Fraud in McWorld

1 Eric Helleiner, 'State Power and the Regulation of Illicit Activity in Global Finance', in H. Richard Friman and Peter Andreas (eds), *The Illicit Global Economy and State Power* (Lanham, Maryland: Rowman & Littlefield, 1999) 56.
2 David Cay Johnson, 'Treasury Chief: Tax Evasion is on the Rise', *New York Times*, 19 July 2001, accessed on the *Global Policy Forum* website at http://www.globalpolicy.org/.
3 David Cay Johnson, 'IRS Says Offshore Tax Evasion is Widespread', *New York Times*, 19 July 2001, accessed on the *Global Policy Forum* website at http://www.globalpolicy.org/.
4 William Greider, *One World, Ready or Not: The Manic Logic of Global Capitalism* (New York: Simon & Schuster, 1997) 33.
5 Lucy Komisar, 'After Dirty Air, Dirty Money', *The Nation*, 18 June 2001, at http://www.thenation.com.
6 Helleiner, 'State Power and the Regulation of Illicit Activity in Global Finance', 56.
7 Quoted in Karin Lissakers, *Banks, Borrowers and the Establishment: A Revisionist Account of the International Debt Crisis* (New York: Basic Books, 1991) 153.
8 Prem Sikka, 'Plastic Bucket: $972.98', *Guardian*, 30 June 2003.
9 Helleiner, 'State Power and the Regulation of Illicit Activity in Global Finance', 56–7.
10 Martin Wolf, 'An Unsustainable Black Hole', *Financial Times*, 26 February 2002.
11 Helleiner, 'State Power and the Regulation of Illicit Activity in Global Finance', 61.
12 Quote from Baker and details of 1999 Senate investigation come from Sue Hawley's incisive report, *Exporting Corruption: Privatisation, Multinationals and Bribery*, an issue paper briefing for the People's Health Assembly, 19 June 2000, accessed at http://phmovement.org/pdf/pubs/phm-pubs-hawley.pdf.
13 Robert Tillman, *Global Pirates: Fraud in the Offshore Insurance Industry* (Boston: Northeastern University Press, 2002) 21–60.
14 Ibid., 23.
15 Ibid., 113.

17 Toxic Capitalism

1 Tom Kemp, *The Climax of Capitalism: The US Economy in the Twentieth Century* (London: Longman, 1990) 201.
2 Marshall Clinard, *Corporate Corruption: The Abuse of Power* (New York: Praeger, 1990) 141–7; Carl Smith, 'Exporting Risk: Pesticide Exports from U.S. Ports', *Global Pesticide Campaigner*, vol. 8, no. 2, June 1998, available on the *Pesticide Action Network North America* website at http://www.panna.org/.
3 'Pesticides Affect Child Development in India', *Global Pesticide Campaigner*, vol. 14, no. 2, August 2004, available on the *Pesticide Action Network North America* website at http://www.panna.org/.
4 David C. Korten, *When Corporations Rule the World* (London: Earthscan, 1995) 129.
5 Frank Pearce and Steve Tombs, *Toxic Capitalism: Corporate Crime and the Chemical Industry* (Toronto: Canadian Scholars' Press, 1999) 197; Sarangi quoted in

Michael Sheridan, 'Poison Seeps into Bhopal, 20 Years On', *Sunday Times*, 21 November 2004.

6   Dominique Lapierre and Javier Moro, *Five Past Midnight in Bhopal* (London: Scribner, 2003) 296–7.

7   Clinard, *Corporate Corruption*, 140; Pearce and Tombs, *Toxic Capitalism*, 200.

8   Pearce and Tombs, *Toxic Capitalism*, 200.

9   Fred Pearce, 'Legacy of a Nightmare', *Guardian*, 13 August 1998, *Online*, 3.

10 Pearce and Tombs, *Toxic Capitalism*, 212.

11 Lapierre and Moro, *Five Past Midnight in Bhopal*, 379–84; Paul Brown, 'India Ordered to Pay Out Bhopal Fund', *Guardian*, 20 July 2004.

12 Cyril Mchenna Gwan, 'Toxic Wastes and Human Rights', *The Brown Journal of World Affairs*, Summer/Fall 2000, vol. VII, issue 2, 185–96.

13 John Vidal, 'Poisonous Detritus of the Electronic Revolution', *Guardian*, 21 September 2004.

14 Summers cited in Frank Pearce and Steve Tombs, 'States, Corporations, and the "New" World Order', in Gary Potter (ed.), *Controversies in White-Collar Crime* (Cincinnati, Ohio: Anderson, 2002) 189.

15 See Jonathan Raban's review of William Langewiesche's *The Outlaw Sea: A World of Freedom, Chaos and Crime* (New York: North Point Press, 2004) in the *New York Review of Books*, 12 August 2004, 23–5.

16 Amnesty International, *INDIA: The 'Enron Project' in Maharashtra: Protests Suppressed in the Name of Development*, July 1997.

17 James Hamilton, 'How Arundhati Roy Took Back the Power in India', *Sunday Herald*, 20 January 2002, at http://commondreams.org/headlines02/0120-03.htm.

18 Sharon Beder, *Power Play: The Fight to Control the World's Electricity* (New York: The New Press, 2003) 302–10.

19 Arundhati Roy, *Power Politics* (Boston: South End Press, 2001) 40.

20 Beder, *Power Play*, 310–12.

21 Celia Wells and Juanita Elias, 'Holding Multinational Corporations Accountable for Breaches of Human Rights', Discussion Paper, Cardiff Centre for Ethics, Law and Society, May 2003, at http://www.ccels.cardiff.ac.uk/pubs/wellspaper.html. See also Anthony J. Sebok, 'Unocal Announces It Will Settle a Human Rights Suit: What Is the Real Story Behind Its Decision?', *Findlaw's Legal Commentary*, 10 January 2005, at http://writ.news.findlaw.com/sebok/20050110.html.

18   Smuggling, Violence and Corruption in the International Arms Bazaar

1   Eric Hobsbawm, *The New Century* (London: Abacus, 2000) 12.

2   R.T. Naylor, 'The Rise of the Modern Arms Black Market and the Fall of Supply-Side Control', in Phil Williams and Dimitri Vlassis, *Combating Transnational Crime* (London: Frank Cass, 2001) 218–21.

3   Lora Lumpe, 'The US Arms Both Sides of Mexico's Drug War', *Covert Action Quarterly*, Summer 1997, no. 61, 39–46.

4   Gideon Burrows, *The No-Nonsense Guide to the Arms Trade* (London: Verso, 2002) 72.

5   Ibid., 13–22. Burrows cited Chris Wrigley's pamphlet *The Arms Industry*, March
    2001, available on the *Campaign Against the Arms Trade* website at http://www.
    caat.org.uk/information/publications/companies/arms-industry.php.
6   Naylor, 'The Rise of the Modern Arms Black Market', 17–18.
7   International Consortium of Investigative Journalists, 'The Merchant of Death', The
    Center for Public Integrity, 2002, at http://www.public-i.org.
8   For Victor Bout and the role of transport in the violations of sanctions see *United
    Nations Security Council Reports* accessible from the *Global Policy Forum* website at
    http://www.globalpolicy.org/intljustice/wanted/wntdindx.htm. Definition taken from
    Anthony B. van Fossen, *The International Political Economy of Pacific Islands Flags
    of Convenience*, Australia–Asia paper no. 66, December 1992.
9   International Consortium of Investigative Journalists, 'Making a Killing: The Business
    of War', The Center for Public Integrity, 2002, at http://www.public-i.org.

19   The Traffic in Exploitable People

1   Peter Andreas, 'The Transformation of Migrant Smuggling across the U.S.–Mexican
    Border', in David Kyle and Rey Koslowski (eds), *Global Human Smuggling* (Balti-
    more, Maryland: Johns Hopkins University Press, 2001) 111–16.
2   Ibid., 117.
3   Ibid., 121.
4   Vincenzo Ruggiero, 'Criminals and Service Providers: Cross-national Dirty Econom-
    ics', *Crime, Law and Social Change*, 28, 1997, 30–1. See also Ko-lin Chin, *Smuggled
    Chinese* (Philadelphia Temple University Press, 1995.)
5   Michael Marizco and Tim Steller, 'Bus Line Admits It Smuggled Entrants', *Arizona
    Daily Star*, 3 April 2004, at http://www.amren.com/news/news04/04/06/bus
    smugglers.html.
6   Courtroom Television Network, 'Lawyer, Wife Admit Chinese Smuggling Scheme',
    at http://www.courttv.com/archive/hr_block/newsb.html.
7   Rey Koslowski, 'Economic Globalization, Human Smuggling, and Global Govern-
    ance', in Kyle and Koslowski, *Global Human Smuggling*, 348.
8   Sheldon Zhang and Ko-lin Chin, 'Chinese Human Smuggling in the United States of
    America', *Forum on Crime and Society*, vol. 1, no. 2, December 2001, 31; for people
    trafficking into the United States and other aspects of the Chinese-American experi-
    ence at the beginning of the 20th century see Jeffrey Scott McIllwain, *Organizing
    Crime in Chinatown: Race and Racketeering in New York City* (Jefferson, North
    Carolina: McFarland, 2004).
9   Simon Romero, '3 New Arrests in Mass Deaths on Smugglers' Truck in Texas', *New
    York Times*, 20 May 2003.
10 Zhang and Chin, 'Chinese Human Smuggling in the United States of America',
    33.
11 Ruggiero, 'Criminals and Service Providers', 31.
12 Pauline Arrillaga, 'Human Cargo Gasps for Life', *Los Angeles Times*, 23 May
    2004.
13 For this case and other relevant cases see the United States Department of Justice
    website at http://www.usdoj.gov/trafficking.htm.
14 Alan A. Block, 'Bad Business: A Commentary on the Criminology of Organized
    Crime in the United States', in Tom Farer (ed.), *Transnational Crime in the Americas*
    (London: Routledge, 1999) 217–44. Block was referring to a study by Elizabeth

McLean Petras, later published as 'The Shirt on your Back: Immigrant Workers and the Reorganization of the Garment Industry', *Social Justice*, 19:1, Spring 1992, 76–114.

15 Block, 'Bad Business', 231.

16 David Kyle and John Dale, 'Smuggling the State Back In: Agents of Human Smuggling Reconsidered', in Kyle and Koslowski, *Global Human Smuggling*, 52.

17 Steven Greenhouse, 'Wal-Mart Raids by U.S. Aimed at Illegal Aliens', *New York Times*, 24 October 2003; Steven Greenhouse, 'Illegally in U.S., and Never a Day Off at Wal-Mart', *New York Times*, 5 November 2003.

18 Rey Koslowski, 'Economic Globalization, Human Smuggling, and Global Governance', in Kyle and Koslowski, *Global Human Smuggling*, 352.

19 Vincenzo Ruggiero, 'Global Markets and Crime', in Margaret Beare, *Critical Reflections on Transnational Organized Crime, Money Laundering, and Corruption* (Toronto: University of Toronto Press, 2003) 180.

20 SAPs, Slums and the New Slavery

1 United Nations Human Settlement Programme, *The Challenge of the Slums: Global Report on Human Settlements 2003* (London: Earthscan Publications, 2003) 6.

2 Mike Davis, 'Planet of Slums: Urban Involution and the Informal Proletariat', *New Left Review*, 26, March/April 2004, 14–16.

3 United Nations Human Settlement Programme, *The Challenge of the Slums*, 6–7.

4 Gareth Chetwynd, 'Deadly Setback for a Model Favela', *Guardian*, 17 April 2004.

5 David Fickling, *Guardian*, 22 September 2004.

6 For an analysis of processes that have led to millions of people being trapped in conditions akin to slavery see Kevin Bales, *Disposable People: New Slavery in the Global Economy* (Berkeley: University of California Press, 2004).

7 Camille Colatosi, 'Children in the Global City', *AGW – A Globe of Witnesses*, at http://thewitness.org/agw/colatosti.012502.html.

8 Robert H. Stern, 'The Demographic Bomb', *Crime and Justice International*, November/December 2003, 40.

9 Ibid.

Epilogue: The Alternatives

1 This is a paraphrased and edited version of Bakan's prescriptions taken from *The Corporation: The Pathological Pursuit of Profit and Power* (London: Constable, 2004) 157–63.

2 Nikos Passas, 'Globalization and Transnational Crime: Effects of Global Asymmetries', in Phil Williams and Dimitri Vlassis, *Combating Transnational Crime* (London: Frank Cass, 2001) 31.

3 Jack Blum, 'Offshore Money', in Tom Farer (ed.), *Transnational Crime in the Americas* (London: Routledge, 1999) 82–3.

4 P.G. Crook, 'Guernsey: Study of a Finance Centre and its Fight Against Fraud,' Guernsey Financial Services Commission, 17 September 1998, at http://www.gfsc.guernseyci.com/news/archive/pr170998.html.

5 Michael Levi, 'Money Laundering: Private Banking Becomes Less Private,' *Global Corruption Report*, 2001, at http://www.globalcorruptionreport.org/download/

gcr2001/gi_money_laundering.pdf. See also Levi's analysis, 'Liberalization and Transnational Financial Crime', in Mats Berdal and Monica Serrano (eds), *Transnational Organized Crime and International Security* (London: Lynne Rienner, 2002), 53–66. Levi emphasises the need 'to appreciate the subtlety, complexity, and depth of field of the organization of crime, both national and transnational' and therefore go beyond the shallow analysis of those who simply want to develop a moral panic to get more power and resources, 65.

6 Michael Jacobs, Adam Lent and Kevin Watkins, *Progressive Globalisation: Towards an International Social Democracy* (London: Fabian Society, 2003) 45–6.

7 Franklin Delano Roosevelt before the Democratic Convention accepting its nomination for President, Chicago, 7 July 1932. Available on *The American Presidency* website at http://www.geocities.com/presidentialspeeches/nomafdr32.htm?200514.

8 Coffee quoted in John C. McWilliams, *The Protectors: Harry J. Anslinger and the Federal Bureau of Narcotics, 1930-1962* ((Newark: University of Delaware Press, 1990) 92–3.

9 Rey Koslowski, 'Economic Globalization, Human Smuggling, and Global Governance', in David Kyle and Rey Koslowski (eds), *Global Human Smuggling* (Baltimore, Maryland: The Johns Hopkins University Press, 2001) 352–3.

10 George Monbiot, *The Age of Consent: A Manifesto for a New World Order* (London: Flamingo, 2003) 193.

11 Michael Jacobs, Adam Lent and Kevin Watkins, *Progressive Globalisation*, 33–47.

12 Ibid., 48–54.

13 Ibid., 55–62.

14 Braiden quoted in *Nathanson Centre Newsletter*, no. 5, Summer 2002, at http://www.yorku.ca/nathanson/default.htm.

Select Bibliography

Joseph L. Albini, *The American Mafia: Genesis of a Legend* (Appleton-Century–Crofts, 1971)

Joel Bakan, *The Corporation: The Pathological Pursuit of Profit and Power* (Constable, 2004)

Margaret E. Beare, *Critical Reflections on Transnational Organized Crime, Money Laundering, and Corruption* (University of Toronto Press, 2003)

Alan Brinkley, *The End of Reform: New Deal Liberalism in Recession and War* (Vintage, 1995)

David Caute, *The Great Fear: The Anti-Communist Purge Under Truman and Eisenhower* (London: Secker and Warburg, 1978).

Adam Edwards and Peter Gill (eds), *Transnational Organized Crime: Perspectives on Global Security* (Routledge, 2003)

Eric Helleiner, *States and the Re-emergence of Global Finance: From Bretton Woods to the 1990s* (Cornell University Press, 1995)

Michael Jacobs, Adam Lent and Kevin Watkins, *Progressive Globalization: Towards an International Social Democracy* (Fabian Society, 2003)

Matthew Josephson, *The Robber Barons: The Great American Capitalists, 1861–1901* (Harcourt, Brace & World, 1962)

Alfred W. McCoy, *The Politics of Heroin: CIA Complicity in the Global Drug Trade* (Lawrence Hill Books, 1991)

Allen J. Matusow, *Nixon's Economy: Booms, Busts, Dollars, and Votes* (University Press of Kansas, 1998)

Ethan A. Nadelmann, *Cops Across Borders: The Internationalization of US Criminal Law Enforcement* (Pennsylvania State University Press, 1993)

R.T. Naylor, *Wages of Crime: Black Markets, Illegal Finance, and the Underworld Economy* (Cornell University Press, 2002)

Letizia Paoli, *Mafia Brotherhoods: Organized Crime, Italian Style* (Oxford University Press, 2003)

Frank Pearce, *Crimes of the Powerful: Marxism, Crime, and Deviance* (Pluto, 1976)

Frank Pearce and Steve Tombs, *Toxic Capitalism: Corporate Crime and the Chemical Industry* (Canadian Scholars' Press, 1999)

Gary W. Potter, *Criminal Organizations: Vice, Racketeering and Politics in an American City* (Prospect, 1994)

Stephen M. Rosoff, Henry N. Pontell and Robert H. Tillman, *Profit Without Honor: White Collar Crime and the Looting of America* (Prentice-Hall, 2003)

Andrew Sinclair, *Prohibition: The Era of Excess* (Faber and Faber, 1962)

Joseph E. Stiglitz, *Globalization and its Discontents* (Allen Lane, 2002)

Edwin H. Sutherland, *White Collar Crime: The Uncut Version* (New Haven: Yale University Press, 1983).

Francisco E. Thoumi, *Illegal Drugs, Economy, and Society in the Andes* (The Johns Hopkins University Press, 2003)

Robert Tillman, *Global Pirates: Fraud in the Offshore Insurance Industry* (Northeastern University Press, 2002)

Index

Abacha, Sani   188
Abedi, Agha Hasan   179, 180
Abu Nidal   182
Ackerman, Harold   146
Adams, James Thurlow   51
Afghanistan   11, 142–3
Alabama Power Company   48
Albini, Joseph   77
Alien Tort Claims Act (ATCA)   197
Allende, Salvador   132–3
Alliance Capital Management   36
Altman, Robert   183–4
American Me   109
American Medical Association
   (AMA)   32
Amnesty International   195
Andreas, Dwayne   35
Angiulo, Gennaro   84
Anglo-Iranian Company   123
Animal Farm   70
Annan, Kofi   135
Anslinger, Harry J.   45–6
Anti-Saloon League   5
Anti-Slavery Society   210
Apalachin   74
Arbenz, Jacobo   124–5
Archer Daniels Midland (ADM)   35
Arizabaleta, Fanor   146
arms trade   13, 177–8, 198–201
Arthur Andersen   101
Aryan Brotherhood   109
asbestos   30–1, 71
asset forfeiture   2, 86, 87–8,
   152, 203
AstraZeneca   27
Atlantic Charter 1941   121–2
average wholesale price (AWP)   27
Azodrin   190

Bakan, Joel   211
Baker, Raymond   188
Bank of Credit and Commerce
   International (BCCI)   13,
   179–84, 213
bank robberies   53, 54, 63–4
Bankers Trust   97
banking   54–5, 65–6, 99–100, 179–84,
   212–13
Banzer, Hugo   144
Barbie, Klaus   144–5
Barboza, Joseph 'The Animal'   84–5
Barnett, Richard   126
Barstow, David   33
Bataan nuclear power plant   173
Beard, Charles   58
Bechtel Corporation   195
Beers, Rand   158
Beesley, T.Q.   19
Bell, Daniel   62
Berle, Adolph   57–8
Berlusconi, Silvio   156
Bernstein, Jared   106
Betancur, Belisario   145
Bhalekar, Sugandha Vasudev   195–6
Bhopal disaster   50, 191–3
Bilbeisi, Munther   181
Bitz, Irving   54
Black Guerillas   109
Block, Alan   44–5
Blum, Jack   181, 212
Board of Economic Warfare
   (BEW)   118
body parts, trade in   38–9
Boland Amendment   182
Bolivia   144–5
Bongo, Omar   188
Bonilla, Rodrigo Lara   145

bootleggers/bootlegging 6, 7, 8, 47, 51, 52, 61
Borchgrave, Arnaud de 154
Borget, Louis 100
Bout, Victor 200–1
Boutros-Ghali, Boutros 135, 155–6
Bowker, Michael 31
Boyle, Father Gregory 112
Braiden, Chris 216
Brands, H.W. 122
Bremner, Robert 103
Bretton Woods system 119–21, 129, 130–2, 163, 179, 213
Britain, drug control policies 11–12
British Petroleum 123
Broder, John 38
Brogan, Hugh 121
Brown, Lewis 71
Brown, Michael Francis 38
Browne Vintners 61
Browner, Carol 94
Buchalter, Lepke 63
Bulger, James 'Whitey' 85–6
Bureau of International Narcotic Matters (INM) 149, 150, 151, 152
Bureau of International Narcotics and Law Enforcement (INL) 149–50
Burns, Arthur 131
Burrows, Gideon 177, 199
Bush, George, Jr 31, 94, 100, 104, 108, 196–7, 217
Bush, George, Sr 31, 94, 97, 100, 108, 135, 173

Calderone, Antonio 143
Calero, Adolfo 183
Cali 144, 145–6
Campaign against Arms Trade 177
Campbell, Duncan 113
Canary Capital Partners 36
capital flight 187–8
Capone, Al 6, 46, 53
Carnegie, Andrew 4, 40, 42, 126
Carnegie Steel Works 41
Carter, Jimmy 92, 142
Casey, William 153
Castro, Fidel 75, 125
Caute, David 69
Central America, and US gang culture 112–13

Central Intelligence Agency (CIA) 70, 75, 132, 141, 142
  assassination attempts 125, 175
  operations 123–6
Centre for Disease Control and Prevention (CDC) 34
Chang, Ha-Joon 121
Chase Manhattan Bank 133, 164, 169
Chemical Bank 133
Cheney, Dick 196–7
Chepesiuk, Ron 146
child labour 209–10
child pornography 29–30
Chile 132–3, 134
Chin, Ko-lin 203
China, and capitalism 165
Church, Frank 175
Churchill, Winston 53
Citibank 164, 188
Clapp, Phil 94
Clifford, Clark 180, 183–4
Cline, Philip J. 111
Clinton, Bill 94, 97–8, 108, 199
Co-operative Armaments Programs 199
coal mines 41
cocaine 11, 44–5, 107, 108, 144, 183
Coffee, John 214
Cold War 7, 22, 67, 69, 122, 126, 198
Colombia 2, 10–11, 127, 144, 145–8, 153, 157, 183
Colorado Fuel and Iron Company 5
Columbine High School shooting 111
Comprehensive Drug Abuse Control Act 1970 79
ConAgra 35
Congo 126, 175–7
Connally, John 130–1
Connolly, John 85–6
consumers, and unsafe products 31–2, 34
containment 122–3
controlled delivery 158
Coppola, Francis Ford 8
Corallo, Anthony 'Tony Ducks' 80–1
Corporate Crime Task Force 104
Costello, 'Uncle' Frank 6, 73–4
crack cocaine 108, 111
'cramming' 82–3
Crook, P.G. 212
crop substitution programmes 151

Cullather, Nick 125
Cummings, Homer S. 63

Dabhol Power Company (DPC) 195–7
Dale, John 205
Dalla Chiesa, Carlo Alberto 144
dangerous substances 30–1, 71, 190
Davis, Mike 207–8
DeVito, Pete 49
Death of a Salesman 70
Debbi, Shaul 26–7
Delay, Tom 97
deregulation 8–9, 22, 92–3, 97, 104,
    106, 164
  and arms trade 199
  and environmental protection 94
  and savings and loans 95
  and telecommunications 99
Dewey, Thomas E. 62–3
Diamond, Jack 'Legs' 6
Dillard, James 112
Dillinger, John 53, 63
dioxin 93
Dirlove, Meyer 72
Dixon, Don 95
Doe, Samuel 179
Dominion of Melchizedek (DOM) 189
Dornbusch, Rudiger 186
Dosch, Arno 41
Dow Chemical group 32, 193
Drew, Daniel 41
Drug Enforcement Administration
    (DEA) 79–80, 87, 140, 146, 149
drug manufacturers 27–8
drug trafficking/traffickers 8, 9, 13, 72,
    152, 183, 208, 213
  see also illegal drugs; war on drugs
Dukakis, Michael 107
Dulles, Allen 125
Dulles, John Foster 124–5
Dynergy 102

Ebbers, Bernard 103
education system 28–9
Ehrlichman, John 80, 132
Eisenhower, Dwight D. 65, 175
El Paso energy company 102
El Salvador 113
Elias, Juanita 197

Enron 9, 36, 58, 96, 100–2, 104–5,
    113, 195–7
environmental protection 93–5, 190–7
Environmental Protection Agency
    (EPA) 30–1, 90, 94
Escobar, Pablo 13, 145–6, 148
Exxon Valdez oil spillage 93

Fairfield Camera and Instruments
    Company 94
Fall, Albert B. 47
Fastow, Andy 100, 101, 102
FDN (Nicaraguan Democratic
    Force) 183
Federal Bureau of Investigation
    (FBI) 7, 35, 63–4, 69, 74–5, 84–5
Federal Bureau of Narcotics (FBN) 45
Federal Power Commission 48
Federal Reserve 65
Federal Savings and Loan Insurance
    Corporation (FSLIC) 95, 96
Federal Trade Commission 66
fertility fraud 23–4
FGB/First American 180
Fiancés of Death 145
Financial Accounting Standards Board
    (FASB) 98
financial crime 95–7, 98, 99–100,
    185–7, 212
firearms industry 111–12
Flemmi, Stevie 'The Rifleman' 85–6
Floyd, Charles 'Pretty Boy' 53, 63
Fones-Wolf, Elizabeth 68
Food and Drug Administration
    (FDA) 27
food products 32–3, 72
Forbes, Genevieve 46
Ford Foundation 169
Ford, Gerald 92
Ford, Henry 49, 169
Ford Motor Company 49, 191
Ford Pintos 31
free market 8, 15, 91, 97, 106,
    133, 217
  see also neo-liberalism
Free the Children 209
Freeh, Louis 154, 155
Friedman, Milton 91
Fulton Fish Market 81, 82
funeral industry 37–8

Galbraith, John Kenneth   55
Gambino Crime Family   3, 82
gambling   8, 72, 78–9
gang wars   51–2, 61
Garn-St Germain Depository Institutions
    Decontrol Act 1982   95
Garo, Victor   84–5
Gauley Bridge tunnel disaster   49–50
Gaviria, Cesar   145
Geis, Gilbert   24
General Agreement on Tariffs and Trade
    (GATT)   166–7
General Electric   173, 191, 195
General Motors   70, 191
Genovese, Vito   74
George, Susan   120
Getnick, Neil   24
Ghorbanifar, Manuchar   182
Giancana, Sam   75
Gilpin, Robert   132
Gingrich, Newt   97
Giscard d'Estaing, Valéry   175
Giuliani, Rudolph   80, 81
Glasbeek, Harry   211
Glass-Steagall Banking Act 1933   65,
    99–100
GlaxoSmithKline   27
Global Crossing   99, 102
global governance   215–16
globalization   12–15, 166–7, 185–7,
    199–201
Godfather, The   8, 75
Golden State Transportation
    Company   203, 204
Goldstock, Ronald   3
Gomez, Luis Arce   145
Good, James W.   48
Gotti, John   3, 7, 13, 81, 86
Gould, Jay   4
Gramm, Phil   97
Gravano, Sammy 'The Bull'   3, 86
Great Depression   21, 40, 54–6,
    57, 120
Great Society   70, 129
Greenpeace   190–1
Greenspan, Alan   91
Greider, William   185
Guatemala   113, 124–5
Guevara, Ernesto 'Che'   125

Guiyu, China   194
Gulf Oil   123
Gurfein, Murray   58
Gurwin, Larry   179

Haig, Alexander   153
Harding, Warren   42–3, 47
Hargreaves, Clare   144, 145
Hayek, Friedrich von   91
healthcare system   23–8, 97
    accounting tricks   28
    fertility fraud   23–4
    insurance rackets   24–5
    mental patients   25–7, 37
    nursing homes   37
    unnecessary procedures   24, 26
HealthSouth   28
Hearst, William Randolph   48
hedge funds   36–7
Hekmatyar, Gulbuddin   142–3, 148
Helleiner, Eric   185, 187
Herrera-Buitrago, Helmer   146
Heritage Foundation   91, 135
heroin   11, 45, 107
Herrera, Vidal   38–9
Hezbi-i Islami   142, 143
Hines, Jimmy   63
Hobsbawm, Eric   198
Hobson, Richmond P.   45, 46
Hoffa, Jimmy   74
Hofstadter, Richard   153
Hollywood blacklist   69–70
Holt, Rush Dew   50
Honduras   113, 125
Hoover, Herbert   7, 48, 52, 54, 56,
    57, 60
Hoover, J. Edgar   63, 64, 69,
    74–5, 84
Hostetter, G.L.   19
House Committee on Un-American
    Activities   69
Houston Natural Gas   100
Huntington, Collis P.   4
Hussein, Saddam   179, 182

Ianni, Francis   108–9
IBM   28
illegal drugs
    control measures   43–6, 213–14
    from Afghanistan   142–3

and racist assumptions 44, 45, 213
statistics 107–8, 152, 159
and street gangs 111
trafficking/traffickers 8, 9, 13, 72,
152, 183, 208, 213
see also war on drugs
Immigration and Naturalization Service
(INS) 112–13, 202
Immigration Reform and Control Act
(ICRA) 1986 202–3
imprisonment 10, 108–10, 112
India
Bhopal disaster 50, 191–3
Dabhol project 195–7
pesticides 190
Indonesia 126, 169–71
industry
accidents 33, 41, 49
dangerous substances 30–1, 71
food products 32–3, 72
meat industry 32–4, 93–4
Ingersoll, John E. 138–9
Insull, Samuel 59
insurance companies
and asbestos 30
bid-rigging 25
fraud 188–9
Internal Revenue Service (IRS) 103,
105, 185
International Bank for Reconstruction
and Development 119
International Consortium of
Journalists 200
International Law of the Sea 194
International Monetary Fund (IMF) 13,
15, 119–21, 131, 135, 166–7
and kleptocracies 171, 172, 177
loan conditionality 164
structural adjustment
programmes 14, 164–5, 196
International Narcotics Control Strategy
Report 149
International Telephone and Telegraph
(ITT) 132–3, 134
Internet 28, 29–30
InterNorth 100
Interpol 152
Iowa Beef Packers (IBP) 32
Iran 123–4

Iran–Contra affair 182–3
Ivins, Molly 99

Jacobs, Michael 213, 215
Jacobson, Dr Cecil 23–4
Jassan, Elias 156
Jesilow, Paul 24
Johns-Manville corporation 30, 71
Johnson, Lyndon B. 70, 75, 129
Johnston, David Cay 105
Jones, Jesse H. 118
Josephson, Matthew 40
J.P. Morgan 65
Judt, Tony 122

Kaljunkar, Adiath 196
Kaptur, Marcy 99
Karzai, Hamid 143
Katznelson, Ira 70
Kay, John 176
Keenan, Vernon 37
Kefauver Committee 72–3
Kennan, George 122, 123
Kennedy, David 65
Kennedy, John F. 70
Kennedy, Joseph 66
Kennedy, Robert 84
Kerry, John 179
Kerry Report 180, 181–2
Khashoggi, Adnan 182–3
Khun Sa 141–2, 148
kidnapping 53–4, 64
Kirk, Robin 147
Kissinger, Henry 137
kleptocrats 13–14, 179
see also Marcos; Mobutu; Suharto
Kmett, Guy Henry 203
Kofman, Mila 25
Koko, Nigeria 193
Komisar, Lucy 186
Koslowski, Rey 215
Kuomintang (KMT) 141
Kyle, David 205

laissez-faire 42, 46, 57, 65, 91, 92,
120, 165, 166
LAPD (Los Angeles Police
Department) 10
Lapierre, Dominique 191
'late trading' 36

Lay, Ken 96, 100
Lent, Adam 213
Levi, Michael 212–13
Levine, Emanuel H. 55
Levy, Clifford 26
'lick and stick' technique 27
Lieberman, Joe 98
Lindbergh, Charles 53–4, 64
Lippmann, Walter 20, 58
Loiaza, Henry 146
Londono, José Santacruz 146
Lowenstein, Roger 98, 101
Luce, Henry 118, 121
Luciano, Charles 'Lucky' 6, 63, 73–4
Lumumba, Patrice 125, 175
Lytle, Mark 124

McClone, John 132
McCloy, John 169
McCormick family 48
McCoy, Alfred 142–3
McElvaine, Robert 56
McGovern, George 80, 107
Mafia 2–3, 39, 80–3, 143–4
    conspiracy theory 8, 22, 71–7, 78,
        153–4, 157
    waste disposal rackets 81–2
    and white-collar crimes 82–3
Maharashtra 195–7
Manufacturers Hanover 133
maquiladoras 191
Marathon Oil refinery 93
Marcos, Ferdinand 13, 172–4
Marcos, Imelda 173, 174
marijuana 44, 107
'market timing' 36
'marketing the spread' technique 27
Marsh and McLennan 25
Marsh, Ray Brent 37
Matusow, Allen 129, 130
Mazur, Robert 183
MCI 103
meat industry 32–3
    risks to consumers 34
    and water pollution 93–4
    workplace accidents 33–4
Medellin 144, 183
Medicaid and Medicare 24, 26, 27, 37
Merrill Dow 32
Merrill Lynch 101

methyl isocyanate (MIC) 191–2
Metropolitan Street Railway
    Company 40–1, 47
Mexican Mafia 109
Mexico 137–8, 164, 190, 191,
    198–9, 202
Mississippi 61
Mitchell, John N. 137
Mobil 123
Mobutu Sese Seko 13, 175–7
Mokhiber, Russell 211
monocrotophos 190
Moorer, Thomas H. 136
Morgan Guaranty 133
Morgan, J.P. 40
Morgenthau, Henry 118–19
Morgenthau, Robert M. 183–4, 185
Moro, Javier 191
morphine 45
Morris, Roger 175
Mossadegh, Mohammed 123
Motion Picture Alliance for the
    Preservation of American
    Ideals 69
Muller, Ronald 126
Mungal-Diaka 176
mutual funds 36–7
Myanmar oil pipeline 197
Myers, Gustavus 40

Nadelmann, Ethan 139–40, 150
Narcotic Control Trade Act 1974 140
National Bank of Georgia 180
National Commission on Law
    Observance and Enforcement 52
    see also Wickersham
        Commission 52, 140–1
National Firearms Act 1934 64
National Gypsum 31
National Labor Relations Act 1935 62
National Labor Relations Board
    (NLRB) 49, 62
National Recovery Administration
    (NRA) 62
National Rifle Association 64, 91
Naylor, R.T. 87, 173–4, 198, 212
Nazi Low Riders 109
'Ndrangeta 157
Nelson, George 'Baby Face' 53, 63

neo-liberalism 133, 135, 164–7
 see also free market
Nestlé 127
Nettleton, Stan 48
New Deal 7, 9, 15, 21, 57, 61–7, 68,
 104, 117, 120
New Kanawha Power Company 49–50
newspaper industry, circulation
 disputes 48–9
Newton, Scott 167
Nicaragua 125, 182–3
Nicorette Gum 32
Nixon, Richard 8, 22, 77–80, 107,
 129–32
 and Bretton Woods system 121,
 130–2, 163, 213
 and ITT 132–3
 war on drugs 9, 10–11, 79–80, 108,
 136–40
 and Watergate 8, 92
 welfare spending cuts 90–1
Noriega, Manuel 179
North, Oliver 182
La Nuestra Familia 109

O'Brien, Justin 104
Occupational Safety and Health
 Administration (OSHA) 33, 90
offshore banking 185–6, 212
Oklahoma 61
Oldenburg, J. William 96
'omerta' 73
O'Neill, Paul 186
Operation Ajax 123
Operation Intercept 137–8
Operation Phoenix 125–6
Operation Success 124–5
opium 44, 45, 142–3
Organization of Petroleum Exporting
 Countries (OPEC) 163
organized crime
 and capitalism 4–6, 58–60
 definitions 19, 21–2, 76
 foreign conspiracy explanation 8,
 22, 67, 71–7, 83–4, 153–4
Organized Crime Control Act
 1970 22, 77
Orgen, Jacob 'Little Augie' 6

Pahlavi, Reza, Shah of Iran 123–4

Pakistan Inter-Services Intelligence
 (ISI) 142
Palomares, Ruben 10
Paoli, Letizia 143
Parenti, Christian 110
Parmalat 13–14
Partington, John 85
Partnoy, Frank 36, 97, 100, 102
Passas, Nikos 182–3, 184, 212
Patino, Victor 146
Patriarca, Raymond 84, 85
Paz, Mario 88
Pearce, Frank 192, 211
people trafficking 14, 202–6, 213,
 214–15
Pertamina 170–1
pesticides 190–1
Pfizer 27
Philip Morris 32
Philippines 126, 172–4
Pinochet, Augusto 133
PKI (Communist Party of
 Indonesia) 169, 170
Polanyi, Karl 120, 216
police corruption 10, 45, 51
political action committees (PACs) 91
Pontell, Henry 24
Ponzi scheme 181, 189
Popoff, Frank 193
Porges, Robert 204
Port Moresby, Papua New
 Guinea 208–9
Potter, Gary 83
power industry 47–8, 49–50, 59, 64–5,
 100–2
 see also Enron
price-fixing 34–6
 legalized 62
prison gangs 109–10
Private Securities Litigation Reform Act
 (PSLRA) 1995 97–8
privatization 8, 164, 165–6
Proctor and Gamble 31
Prohibition 5, 21, 43, 51–3,
 140–1, 214
 repeal 7, 53, 60–1
Public Utility Holding Company Act
 (PUHCA) 1935 65

Pure Food and Drug Agency   91
Puzo, Mario   8, 75

Quest   99
Quinones, Rodrigo   147

Racketeer Influenced and Corrupt
    Organizations (RICO) statute
    1970   156–7
racketeering   50–1, 54, 58, 62–3
Rand, Ayn   69
Ranelagh, John   125–6
Rashbaum, William K.   82
Raybestos-Manhattan   31
Reagan, Ronald   8, 92–3, 94, 96–7,
    108, 135, 182
Reedy, Thomas   29–30
Reid, Ed   22
Rely Tampons   31
*Report on the International Opium
    Commission*   44
Rhinehart-Dennis Construction
    Company   49–50
Ricker, Robert A.   111–12
Riina, Totò   13
Rio de Janeiro   208
Rockefeller, John D.   4, 40
Rockefeller, John D. Jr   5
Rodriguez Gacha, Jose Gonzalo   183
Rodriguez Orejuela, Gilberto   146
Rodriguez Orejuela, Miguel   146
Rogers, William   137
Roosevelt, Franklin D.   7, 15, 21, 57,
    58–62, 65–6, 117–19, 213, 217
Rosoff, Stephen   32, 37
Ross, Edward A.   19–20
Rosselli, John   75
Rothstein, Arnold   6–7, 53
Roy, Arundhati   196
Royal Dutch Shell   123
Ruggiero, Vincenzo   206
Rural Electrification Administration   90
Russia
    and arms trade   198
    and privatization   154–5, 165
Russian Mafia   2, 153, 157
Russo, Gus   72
Ryan, Thomas F.   40–1

Safire, William   131

St Valentine's Day Massacre,
    Chicago   52
Salerno, Anthony 'Fat Tony'   75, 80–2
Salinas, Raul   188
Salvati, Joseph   84
Sands Casino   85
Sarangi, Satinath   191
Sarbanes-Oxley Act 2002   104
Satyarthi, Kailash   209
savings   36–7, 95–7
Schlosser, Eric   32–3, 34
Schulman, Bruce   8
Schultz, Dutch   53, 63
Scott, Donald   87–8
Seagram corporation   61
Seaport Manor, Brooklyn   26
Sears Roebuck   70
Securities Act 1933   65, 66
Securities Exchange Act 1934   65, 66
Securities and Exchange Commission
    (SEC)   66, 91, 97
Serious and Organized Crime Agency
    (SOCA)   12
Service Corporation International
    (SCI)   38
Shapiro, Jacob   63
Shapiro Packing   34
'shock therapy'   165
Sicilian Mafia   2, 142–4, 153, 157
Siciliano, Joe   72
Siegel, Benjamin 'Bugsy'   6
Sikka, Prem   186–7
silicosis   49–50
Sinatra, Frank   85
Skilling, Jeffrey   100
slaughterhouses   32–3
slums   207–10
Smith, Adam   35–6
Smithfield Foods   93–4
Snider, Laureen   211
Social Darwinism   41–2, 91
Société Générale de Belgique   175–6
South Asian Coalition on Child
    Servitude (SACCS)   209
Spencer, Herbert   42
Spitale, Salvy   54
Spitzer, Eliot   25, 36, 211
Standard Oil   5, 49, 123–4
Stearns, Robert   25

Sterling, Claire 153–4, 155
Stern, Robert 210
Stiglitz, Joseph 98–9, 165–6
stock market crash 1929 55
stock options 98–9, 103–4
'stock watering' 40, 47–8
Stone, Donald C. 21
Strange, Susan 12
street children 209
street gangs 110–13, 208–9
strike-breaking 48, 49
Structural Adjustment Programmes
    (SAPs) 14, 164–5, 196, 207, 210
Suarez, Roberto 144–5, 148
Suharto, Mohammed 13, 170–1
Sukarno, Achmed 169, 170
Summers, Anthony 74
Summers, Lawrence 194
Sumner, William Graham 42
Sutherland, Edwin 70–1
Sutowo, Ibnu 171

Tait, Anthony 86
Taub, Sherman 26
tax evasion 105–6, 185–7
Taxpayers Against Fraud Education
    Fund 27
Teale, Alan 188–9
Teamsters 63, 75, 81
Teapot Dome, Wyoming 47
Telecommunications Act 1996 99
telecommunications industry 99, 102–3
    billing fraud 82–3
Tenet Healthcare Corporation 24
Texas Syndicate 109
Third World
    and economic liberalism 120–1
    exploitation of 126–8, 179
    health and safety protection 190–1
Thornburgh, Richard 102–3, 135
Thoumi, Francisco E. 147
Tillman, Robert 188, 189
tobacco industry 31–2
Tombs, Steve 192, 211
Total 197
toxic shock syndrome 31
trade unions 43, 62, 63, 68–9, 212
    violence against 48, 49, 62
Trade Waste Commission (TWC) 81–2
transfer pricing 126–7, 186–7

Transparency International 172
Tri-Crematory 37
Triads 2, 153, 157
Truell, Peter 179
Truman, Harry 70, 122
Turkey, opium-growing ban 138
Turner, Stansfield 183
Tyson 35

Union Carbide 31, 49, 50, 191–3
United Fruit Company 124–5
United Nations 121, 149, 216
    5th Congress on the Prevention of
        Crime 133–4
    Centre for Transnational Corporations
        (UNCTC) 134–5
    Commission on Narcotic
        Drugs 138–9
    Convention against Illicit Traffic in
        Narcotics and Psychotropic
        Substances 152
    Convention against Transnational
        Organized Crime (UNTOC)
        1–2, 135, 157–8
    Fund for Drug Abuse Control 139
    Human Settlements Programme (UN-
        Habitat) 207, 208
    International Drug Control
        Programme (UNDCP) 159
    Single Convention 138–9
    World Ministerial Conference on
        Organized Transnational
        Crime 155–7
United Sacred Crown 157
United States
    and arms trade 198–9
    drug control policies 10–11
    and illegal immigration 112–13,
        137–8, 202–3
    moral authoritarianism 20–1, 43–6,
        51, 60, 83
    post-war foreign policy 122–6
    pro-business ideology 19–20
Universal Service Fund (USF)
    (E-Rate) 28–9
Unocal 197

Valachi, Joseph 74
Vanderbilt, Cornelius 41
Vanguarde Asset Group 25

Vaughn, Edward   86–7
Vernon Savings   95
Veterans Benefits Administration
    26, 47
Vickers, Raymond B.   55
Vietnam War   122, 125–6, 129, 142
Volcker, Paul   163
Volstead Act (National Prohibition Act)
    1920   51, 152

Wagner, Robert   60, 159
Wal-Mart   206
Wallace, Henry   118, 121
Wanniski, Jude   91
war on drugs   9, 10–11, 53, 79, 88,
    108, 136–53, 158–9
    eradication campaigns   149, 151, 213
War on Want   127
waste disposal   81–2, 93
    toxic waste   193–5
water, contamination   93–4
Watergate scandal   8, 92
Wathelet, Melchior   156
Watkins, Kevin   213
welfare cuts   90–1, 106
Wells, Celia   197
Westinghouse   70, 173, 191
Westmoreland, William   136
Whalen, Christopher   184
Whitacre, Mark   35
White, Harry Dexter   118–19
Whitney, William C.   40–1
Wickersham Commission   52, 140–1

Widdicombe, Rupert   113
Wiley, Steven   111
Willebrandt, Mabel   52
Willed Body Program, UCLA   38
Williams energy company   102
Williams, Ian   135
Witness Protection Program   2,
    85, 86
Wolf, Martin   187
Woolsey, R. James   154, 155
World Bank   13, 15, 119–21, 135, 151,
    166–7, 196
    and kleptocracies   172, 177
    structural adjustment
        programmes   14, 164–5, 196
World Health Organization
    (WHO)   209
World Trade Organization
    (WTO)   166–7
WorldCom   9, 99, 102–3, 104–5, 113
Wright, Dr Hamilton   44, 46
Wright, Jim   95
'write-ups'   47

Yakusa   153, 157
Yeltsin, Boris   154

Zaire   175–7
Zardari, Asif Ali   188
Zayed bin Sultan al-Nahyan,
    Sheikh   182
Zocor (simvastatin)   27
Zwillman, Abner 'Longy'   61
Zyskind, Beryl   26